The Historian and History

The HISTORIAN *and* HISTORY

PAGE SMITH

Provost, University of California at Santa Cruz

"Does the pilgrimage of mankind, triumphant and heart-rending by turns, through the duration of its history, have a value, a fecundity, a meaning?"

Henri Marrou,
De la connaissance historique

VINTAGE BOOKS

A Division of Random House

New York

To Eugen Rosenstock-Huessy

Introduction

❀ ❀ ❀

This book, like Gaul, is divided into three parts. Chapters 1 through 6 trace the development of the concept of history which characterizes Western civilization. Here I have followed the rather well-trodden path of R. G. Collingwood, Benedetto Croce, and others. The material will perhaps be familiar to many but it seemed to me important to give the general reader some notion, however sketchy, of the way in which our understanding of the nature of historic time has grown throughout the centuries. Obviously, no attempt has been made at comprehensiveness. Many historians worthy of inclusion have been omitted; those included have been, by and large, the ones whose work best illustrates the evolution of the idea of history.

The second part, chapters 7 through 10, is concerned with some of the modern thought—philosophical, theological, and professional—about the nature of history.

The third part, roughly chapters 11 through 14, contains a more specific critique of contemporary American academic history. If the book has any claim to originality, it lies primarily in these chapters, where, as a historian, I am dealing with the problems of my profession with which I am most familiar and to which I have given most thought.

The final chapter, chapter 15, is an effort to state for the general reader, as well as for the specialist, some of the ways in which the study of history and, perhaps even more, *an awareness of the historic dimension of human experience* may be of help to those who seek to chart a course through the turbulent waters of our time.

I wish to express my appreciation to my former student Joseph Botond-Blazek, for his interest and encouragement, and to my colleague Neal Oxenhandler, for his discerning and helpful criticisms. In a sense the most important contributors to this book are anonymous. They are the students who, over the years, have been in my section of the course *History and Historians* at the University of California at Los Angeles. As I struggled to illuminate for them some of the profounder meanings of history, my own ideas took on, I trust, a greater coherence and I discovered, as every teacher does, that I often learned as I taught. My students are thus contributors through their participation in many classroom discussions.

My indebtedness to the man to whom this book is dedicated is too extensive to catalogue. My only hope is that the pupil may be worthy of the master.

From Eugen Rosenstock-Huessy, who first directed my attention to the "autobiography of man," to the young men and women who have been my students is a span of three generations. Man lives, as I have certainly lived, in this span, not in the hellish isolation of his own generation. We are all both heirs and ancestors; beneficiaries and testators. That is what I would like this book to testify to, for that, after all, is the principal meaning of history.

SANTA MONICA, CALIFORNIA
January 1964

Contents

✤ ✤ ✤

The Historian and History

I

The Beginning of
History: the Hebrews
and the Greeks

Briefly stated, history is a record of what has taken place in the past. But even such a simple declarative sentence involves us at once in a maze of complexity. How is the record to be retrieved? Can it indeed ever be retrieved? Certainly not in the fullness of the original. Can it then ever properly be said to be retrieved? Or retrievable? Is a sense of history common to mankind? Or is it an especially developed area of awareness?

Whatever the answers to such questions may be, the problem of the nature and meaning of history has been one of the most persistent riddles with which man has concerned himself once he advanced beyond the level of the primitive. The study and writing of history may thus be said to be one of the principal means by which man has extended his understanding of himself and his strange destiny. Boris Pasternak has written: "Man does not die in a ditch like a dog; he lives in history." In the Christian view, history is the progressive revelation of God's purpose for the world He created and to which He gave His Son as the most complete revelation of Himself. Whether one accepts or rejects Christianity, it provides a useful metaphor. Whether God reveals Himself to man in history or whether man discovers new potentialities in himself through the unfolding of history, there is implicit in both concepts the notion that understanding grows as one traces the slow progress of man from the dawn of consciousness to the present day. There are here perhaps two points worth emphasizing: (1) our sense of history, conscious or unconscious, is one of the distinguishing elements of what we call, perhaps rather too loosely, Western civilization; (2) the non-Western cultures, with the conspicuous exception of the ancient Hebrews, have been generally deficient in historical consciousness.

As soon as men had the power to keep records, written on papyrus or carved on stone, stamped in wet clay or incised on temple walls, we had history of a kind, but it was history of the crudest sort, simple chronology without the power to open new paths into the future. Indeed, primitive or "traditional" societies have been distinguished by their desire to annul history, to escape from what Mircea Eliade has called "the terror of history." Such societies have, classically, employed two techniques, one belonging to an earlier stage of development, the other to a later. The use of "archetypes" and "repetition" serve to destroy any sense of genuine history as a sequence of unique events in time and to create in its place a kind of eternal present.[1] Every impor-

---

[1] I have taken the notion of "archetypes" and "repetition" as used here from Mircea Eliade's *The Myth of the Eternal Return*, published by Harper in its Torchbook Series (New York, 1959) under the title *Cosmos and History*.

tant historical figure in a primitive or traditional society is transformed into an archetype, a typical hero, and is divested of anything that would make him singular and thus historic. To primitive man, an act or a person is only real to the extent that it can be shown to imitate or repeat an archetype. In Eliade's words, the refusal of archaic man "to accept himself as an historical being, his refusal to grant value to memory and hence to the unusual events (i.e., events without an archetypal model)" shows his determination "to devaluate time." The myth of creation is also re-enacted periodically, generally yearly, in such societies, so that again history cannot intrude with its terrifying questions and anxieties.

In building cities, the men of early civilizations tried to model them after the constellations of the stars. In settling new lands, they emphasized that they were simply engaged in "the repetition of a primordial act: the transformation of chaos into cosmos by the divine act of Creation."[2]

It was in a world made up of such "historyless" civilizations that the Jews discovered history. The children of Israel, fighting to preserve their identity in a world full of violence and disorder, made a careful record of their transactions with their stern God—how he had lifted them up; how he had preserved them from the hand of their enemies; how, when they became heedless or unfaithful, he had chastened them and cast them down in wretchedness and humiliation; and how, above all, he gave them a promise of future greatness. The record that they made of their negotiations with Jehovah, their redemptions, their backslidings, their triumphs, and their defeats marked the dawn of the historical consciousness of Western man.

With the Hebrews, history transcended chronology for the first time; the relations of the people with their God constituted a drama of extraordinary richness. Alongside

---

[2] Eliade: *Cosmos and History*, p. 10.

the tedious chronologies of the warrior kings of Syria or Egypt, the account of the tribulations and the triumphs of a people chosen by God to be his special instruments make an enthralling story. The Hebrew chroniclers had discovered one of the most essential elements of history—that it is enacted by real people, with all their faults and blemishes. And this was so because they wrote not to instruct or entertain but out of the most urgent need to explain to themselves who and what they were and what the nature was of their particular commission from God so that successive generations would be able to identify themselves despite bondage and dispersion, despite subjugation and such persecutions as would have erased from the minds of a less gifted and tenacious people the memory of their origin and their promised destiny. They were as pitiless to their heroes as to their villains, to themselves as to their adversaries, because they were writing under the eye of God and had nothing to gain and much to lose by dissembling. Since we are captivated by a drama even if we cannot understand all its implications, the dramatization of history or of time was a unique and important achievement of the Hebrews. Beyond that, their chroniclers told a story that involved not simply mighty emperors and their generals but a whole people, all equally caught up in the story—a half-mad prophet clothed in the skins of wild animals as well as a great king or captain. Thus the Hebrews invented, so to speak, two familiar aspects of history as we think of it today. First, a fullness of characterization (both of individuals and events): the good with the bad, the favorable with the unfavorable; and then the account of a people as a mystical entity, a sacred community involved in a series of extraordinary dramatic events. To follow God's way was to be rewarded; to be obdurate and unfaithful was to be punished. The individual was thus both fulfilled and tightly bound within the community.

Finally, the Hebrews endowed their history with a meaning, a purpose, and a direction. The meaning derived from their "chosenness," from their peculiar status as those specially marked out by God. The purpose—to do God's will—followed. The direction came, at least in later years, from their messaniac expectation. Regardless of how the Jews may have interpreted the book we call Second Isaiah, they looked forward to the day when they would be restored to their ancient kingdom. Time, which was for so many ancient peoples cyclical, recurrent, unmeaning, and full of menace, came for the Hebrews to be the area in which was played out the most meaningful of all possible dramas—the contest between God's plan for man and man's willfulness. Time was filled by God; and man, or at least the men who were of the seed of Abraham, were freed from blind recurrence.

"All very well," replies the modern man, "but does this make the historical books of the Old Testament history?" Certainly the faithful men who recorded the epic events and prophetic voices had no notion of themselves as historians in any sense that the modern professor of history would find acceptable. Yet the professor is far closer to the Old Testament chroniclers than he is inclined to admit. The point is not whether we can measure the writers of the Old Testament by the canons of modern historical scholarship, but whether they created the pre-conditions of the modern historical consciousness. The Jewish people have survived through some three thousand years by discovering the power of history as the word of God.

Most academic courses that undertake to trace the development of historical scholarship begin with the Greeks. Arnold Toynbee has assembled impressive evidence that the Greek historians, almost without exception, adhered to a cyclical view of time. From Herodotus to Polybius, we get a concept of the historical process that, by modern standards, is pessimistic in the extreme. Herodotus, for example, quotes Artabanus, the uncle of Xerxes, as saying to his nephew: "The blows of misfortune and the ravages of disease make even the shortest life feel long; and so death comes as blessed release for man from an evil existence, while God is proved an envious God in his dealings with Man by the taste of sweetness in life with which he tantalizes him."[3]

Herodotus tells the story of Polycrates of Samos and Amasis, the king of Egypt. Polycrates, trying to escape the web of fate, cast a treasured ring into the sea. A few days later a fisherman brought him a "fine large fish," in whose belly was found the ring. When Polycrates wrote to Amasis of the incident, Amasis realized anew "that it is impossible for one human being to extricate another from the destiny awaiting him and that no good end could be awaiting Polycrates whose success was so unbroken that he recovered even what he had thrown away." Amasis, in consequence, withdrew from his entente with Polycrates in order to "save his own feelings from being harrowed, as they would be for a friend and ally, when Polycrates was overtaken by . . . a crushing disaster."[4]

Thucydides, who is usually referred to as the first "scientific" or "modern" historian, made a great point of the duty of the historian to be objective and dispassionate in the treatment of historical events. Yet Thucydides, like every other historian who has ever written, was guided or governed by certain presuppositions about the process of time, and these were not essentially different in their ultimate dimension from those of the civilization of which he was a part. Far less didactic than Herodotus, he had the same

---

[3] *Greek Historical Thought, From Homer to Heraclius*, introduction and translation by Arnold J. Toynbee (New York: Mentor Books, 1955), p. 100

[4] Herodotus, Book III, chapters 122–5, quoted in Toynbee: *Greek Historical Thought*, p. 119.

view of fate and the same gloomy notion of necessity as
the controlling element in human events. David Grene
argues convincingly that Thucydides believed that man's
basic and indeed inescapable motivation was "the aspiration toward power." The "perpetual aggressiveness" of both
individuals and states may be taken as his underlying
theme.[5]

Thucydides did not write his history, as the Old Testament chroniclers had, out of a conviction that man could
somehow effect his own destiny in partnership with God or
through his response to God's imperatives. If the world was
full of blind chance or directed by the malevolence of the
gods, what man did was of little avail. The historian's narrative might at best fortify future generations to endure
with stoicism what they could not, in any event, materially
change. It thus followed that if the events of history were
dictated by necessity it was futile to apportion praise or
blame except in terms of the individual leader's conformity
to the precepts of virtue. This is seen in Thucydides's praise
of Nicias; though Nicias brought about the ruin of the
Athenian army in the Sicilian campaign, Thucydides judged
him to be "the least worthy of all the Greeks of my time to
come to such a depth of misfortune, since he had lived all
his life in accordance with what is popularly called virtue."

It is well to keep in mind, moreover, that Thucydides
was a contemporary historian. Writing of the events of his
own lifetime, he shows little sympathy or interest in the
history of the past, except to debunk it. The resistance of
the Trojans to Agamemnon's besieging forces is not due
to the bravery of the Trojans but to the ineptness of the
Greeks, and Agamemnon's authority comes not from his
accomplishments as an inspiring leader but from his superior wealth.

Certainly Thucydides had very little notion of a sympa-

---

[5] *Man in His Pride* (University of Chicago Press; 1950), pp. 55, 59.

thetic reconstruction of the past. His appeal to later readers
rested largely on his superb narrative style and his determination to tell "the clear truth of what happened." But, as
Grene has put it, "the wisdom acquired by reading Thucydides is not to be directed to the elimination of the causes
of future catastrophes. He is not saying that by understanding the truth of what happened in the last quarter of the
fifth century you will know how to prevent men from re-
creating the same havoc and ruin."[6]

Just as Thucydides lacked any real feeling for the past,
he had no notion of the potentialities of the future as a
common human enterprise. What gave Thucydides his
remarkable power was, in essence, the Greek accomplishment of abstraction, the gift for taking the observed facts
of the natural world or of human society and deriving from
them abstract principles. Thales of Miletus shows clearly
this capacity of the Greeks for abstract thought. His pro-
nouncement "all is water" was not based on anything that
we today would call scientific research, nor was it postulated
as the basis for further investigation but simply as a philosophical principle. Indeed, Thales's principle was in accord
neither with the empirical facts nor with existing religious
attitudes. It was the consequence, rather, of observing the
flooding of the Nile, on which the Egyptian social order
rested; of seeing in Greece itself the effects of snow, ice,
and hail, which, if they made life more severe, were essential
to the farmer; of studying the salt water of the ocean, which
provided a highway to the rest of the world and was the
direct cause of the commercial prosperity of Miletus. In the
words of Eugen Rosenstock-Huessy, "Thales . . . abstracted
from the manner of living and the forms of life about him,
that element which seemed to affect everyone. All orders of
life, although seemingly so incredibly various, were given
unity by Thales' magnificent abstraction. . . . The world's

---

[6] Ibid., p. 65.

first theoretician, he created the first system, a system which refers the extraordinary multiformity of life back to one fundamental principle." As a consequence of the capacity to compare, through the power of abstraction, equally valid ways of living and of organizing people in political communities, Thucydides and his fellow Greeks achieved a degree of detachment about their own loyalties; moreover, neighboring city states passing, as it were, through their own cycles of development provided a convenient laboratory. In addition, a number of the Greek historians were exiled by sudden shifts of the political climate in their native cities, and their exile enabled them to view the history of their own states with a certain objectivity.

We find much the same spirit in Polybius, writing two hundred years after Thucydides. "The knowledge of past events is the sovereign corrective of human nature . . . ," he declares. "It is actually the note on which almost all historians have begun and ended their work, when they have eulogized the lessons of history as the truest education and training for political life, and the study of others' vicissitudes as the most effective, or indeed the only, school in which the right spirit for enduring the changes of fortune can be acquired."[7]

What so charms modern scholars is Polybius's conviction that "the progress of knowledge and technique has reached such a point that every phenomenon presented by the development of events lends itself to something approaching scientific treatment in expert hands."[8] But Polybius shared his predecessors' pessimism about the future, just as he shared their capacity for abstraction, and however "modern" his credo may sound, his notion of history was very far removed from that of the modern man.

[7] *World History*, Teubner text, ed. W. Butter-Wobst, Book I, chapters 1–4, quoted by Toynbee: *Greek Historians*, p. 43.
[8] *World History*, preface to Volume LX, Teubner text, Book IX, chapters 1–2.

Since philosophers generally formulate the world view which historians and poets exemplify in their writings, it might be well to turn to Plato for a systematic exposition of the Greek attitude toward the nature of time. The young Socrates and a stranger are discussing the nature of the universe and the stranger says to the youth: "Here is the story. This universe is sometimes conducted on its path and guided in its orbit by God, while at other times, when the cycles of its appointed time have arrived at their term, it is released from control by God and proceeds to revolve in the opposite direction by itself. . . . The tendency toward this reverse motion is inevitably innate in the universe." Thus at periodic intervals "when the entire earthborn race" was exhausted, "the Helmsman of the Universe" abandoned control of the world and allowed it to run "in the reverse direction by Destiny and innate Desire."[9]

We might say that the Greek effort to relate history to vast cycles of time is a more sophisticated form of the myth of repetition or eternal return. The same attempt to impose some meaning on time by a theory of recurrence can be seen quite clearly in Hinduism and Buddhism. Indeed, as Eliade points out, the myth has persisted among the simpler agricultural peoples of Christian nations and reappeared time and again in various heresies, especially in the millennial sects of Protestantism, and more recently and spectacularly, as we shall see, in modern times.

Greek history, like Greek thought in general, was concerned with the world as it is, not as it might be. The price paid for the power of abstraction and of scholarly detachment, for the creation of disciplines each of which provided a new perspective on the natural world, was the loss of any sense of purpose or direction in history, a loss of the prophetic and redemptive dimensions in history which were so central for the Old Testament chroniclers. Greek history

---

[9] Plato: *Collected Works*, ed. J. Burnet, Vol. I, Politicus, p. 269.

was written for other historians and for statesmen and generals. To the Greek intellectuals, "the struggle for life in which the common herd is involved seems like the milling of blind cattle."

The Greeks compared but they did not change. As Jacob Burkhardt pointed out, Greek thought did not close a single temple or destroy a single superstition. The academic world, which is the modern temple to the Greek spirit, is likewise much more preoccupied with what is than with what might be, with cataloguing and describing rather than exploring the creative potentialities of the future. Paradoxically, it might be said that the Greek attitude represented a kind of hostility to history at the same time that it advanced history enormously as a practical discipline. It is not surprising, therefore, that academic historians should look back to the Greeks as their spiritual godfathers while failing to recognize how thoroughly un-Greek they are in their basic attitudes toward history as a process. There was no future in Greek historical thought because the Greeks, in their concern with ideal types, placed themselves quite consciously outside the flow of time. "By doing so they managed," in Rosenstock-Huessy's words, "to purge themselves of most of the prejudices that we are involved in through our membership in a living, speaking group to which we give our loyalty. We . . . pay the price of prejudice to be involved . . . in activity that has meaning for us but which destroys our objectivity."

The point is worth emphasizing; we have been so uncritical in our admiration of things Greek that it is difficult for us to sort out what Greek historical thought was in fact from what we have wished it to be. For a profession which has been inclined to be snide about contemporary history, it is well to recall that most Greek history was, pre-eminently, contemporary history and that it was, moreover, highly parochial. It had no real sympathy with the accomplishments of past generations, even of fellow Greeks, and no systematic method of attempting to retrieve accurate information about the past. It was concerned only superficially with other contemporary cultures where they impinged upon its own. Humanistic it may have been, but concerned with humanity it was not, except as the mass of human beings provided a kind of background against which to display the genius of particular leaders. Unlike the history of the Hebrews, the history of the Greeks had no power to insure their survival. In fact, it assumed that because of the malice of the gods or the accidents of chance, survival was in any case impossible.

Yet so ingrained is the picture of the Greeks as having produced the first "modern" historians that students required to write papers on Thucydides or Polybius almost invariably express astonishment at their modernity, hail them in conventional terms as the originators of our present-day notions of historical process, and doggedly read into them a view of history as progress that was in fact completely alien to their way of thought.

Magnificent as the Greek historians are, they are only to be properly understood as Greeks, not as modern academics in togas or tunics. It is perhaps worth noting that if modern historians have been inclined to credit the Greeks with the invention of history, Josephus, the Jewish historian, declared more accurately that "recording the events is an Oriental (i.e. Jewish) rather than an Hellenic tradition."[1]

---

[1] *Collected Works*, Vol. V, Teubner text, ed. S. A. Naber, Book I, chapters 1–16.

2

Christianity and History

❀ ❀ ❀

Christianity transformed the pagan view of time, that is to say, of the historical process. Christ had given a millennial promise—the end of the world was imminent and those who were converted should have everlasting life. The early Church lived in the light of the millennial expectation. The primitive Christian community awaited the second coming, which should take place some said at one time, some said at another. For a time it was argued that there was Scriptural authority for believing it would come after the conversion of the Jews. In any event, Judgment Day, whenever it came, would mark the end of history. The devout Christian thus looked forward to the end of the world. Moreover, since he saw Christ as the fulfillment of the Old Testament prophecy of a Messiah, the Christian took over, part and parcel, the Hebraic view of time. God had created the world in the manner described in Genesis. The subsequent books described God's dialogue with man in dramatic form and gave the Jews, as God's chosen people, a glimpse of His plans for them. The story of the original covenant with Adam and Adam's seed was an indispensable prelude to God's most complete revelation of Himself through Christ, the Word made flesh, Christ whose life was the most unique and important episode in history.

The earliest Christian apologists realized at once the significance of this intrusion of God directly into human history. They set about to make abundantly clear to the Hellenistic world the dramatic differences between its view of time and history and that held by the disciples of Jesus Christ. In so doing, they took the essence of the Jewish view and raised it to a universal principle. Whoever would follow Christ's teachings might have hope of everlasting life without regard to race or nationality. The Christians were well aware of the attraction of their teaching that life had purpose and meaning and that death was not its end. Justin Martyr, addressing himself to the Emperor Hadrian, to Lucius, and "the whole Roman people," declared that God "in the beginning . . . made the race of men endowed with intelligence, able to choose the truth and do right." The consequence was that men were not blind instruments of fate or the pawns of capricious gods, "for they were made with the powers of reason and observation."[1]

Such writers were prompt to denounce the cyclical theory of the Greeks. Origen, writing early in the third century, struck out specifically against the notion that "in another Athens another Socrates will be born who will marry another Xanthippe." He declared that according to the Greek view "Adam and Eve will do once more exactly what they

---

[1] *Early Christian Fathers* (Philadelphia: Westminster Press, 1953), ed. Cyril C. Richardson, "First Apology of Justin, the Martyr," I, p. 259.

have already done; the same deluge will be repeated; the same Moses will bring the same six hundred thousand people out of Egypt; Judas will again betray the Lord; and Paul a second time will hold the coats of those who stone Stephen."

Eusebius, the first important Christian historian, wrote Christian history which stressed the continuity of the Judaic tradition and the Christian and which attempted to place all history within the framework of Christian dogma. He concentrated on the trials and sufferings and martyrdoms of the early Christian community; at the same time, he saw in Christianity the base for a new solidarity of mankind. He seemed to anticipate that there would be a reign of peace for mankind as a result of the conversion of Constantine and the Emperor's acceptance of Christianity as the official religion of the state; he saw history as the unfolding of God's purpose in the world.

It remained for Saint Augustine, as a by-product of his great theological treatise *The City of God*, to spell out most clearly the Christian doctrine of history. The pagan philosophers, Augustine pointed out, tried to solve the riddle of creation by "a theory of periodic cycles of time according to which there always has been and will be a continual renewal and repetition in the order of nature, because the coming and passing ages revolve as on a wheel. . . . And from this game of merry-go-round they could find no exemption for the immortal soul—not even for the soul of a philosopher." This doctrine Augustine rejected emphatically: "For once Christ died for our sins; and rising from the dead, He dieth no more. Death hath no dominion over Him." No wonder, Augustine adds, that the pagan philosophers "keep wandering around and around in these circles and can find neither the entrance nor the exit—neither the origin nor the end of our mortal human race." God, though "eternal and without beginning . . . caused time to have a beginning and, in time, created a man, who had not been made before."[2] It was this positive and specific act of creation that Augustine insisted upon—"the infinite quarry of creation," in his great phrase.

The pervasiveness of the Greek notion of recurrence is indicated by the fact that Augustine, the Bishop of Hippo, spends virtually all of Book XII refuting this particular heresy. He was equally specific in rejecting the pagan idea of fortune or chance. "Everything," he wrote, "must be referred to divine providence"—which, to be sure, would in many instances be quite inscrutable. The fact that finite human beings could not understand what, to their limited understanding, seemed a chance episode was no reason to assume that it represented the intervention of an arbitrary and erratic force. What to the pagan had appeared irrational was to the Christian "merely paradoxical." This helps to explain why the Christian historian gave little attention to causality. The Hellenistic historians were concerned with analysis and explanation, and when the tools of logic proved inadequate to explain certain events, they simply consigned these to the category of blind chance or the capriciousness of the gods. The Christian theologian, by accepting as part of the divine order what was apparently chance, robbed the world of much of its terror without at all diminishing the individual believer's sense of awe and reverence.

In Augustine's view, classical materialism and idealism were equally the enemies of the truth, "the former of which envisages the cosmos as one big machine, the latter as one big soul." He had, moreover, no patience with an ideology which allowed its adherents to put together a kind of do-it-yourself philosophy made up of the lumber of pagan thinkers. And indeed it might be said that this impulse generally marks the disintegration of society, since any common fate is unimaginable where everyone is free to pick and choose the particular combination of ideas which will give him

[2] Book XII, chapter 14.

the greatest personal comfort and assurance. Augustine, and the Christian historians who preceded and followed him, referred human history to one transcendent principle and thereby freed men from the need to give their ultimate allegiance to class or family, or state, all of whom must, in the final analysis, limit and distort the individual. Since God is, in Augustine's view, the fountainhead of all true creativity, the power derived from Him to transcend the limitations of tribe or caste or race or social group is also the power to transform the world.

Augustine understood that to anticipate a future is to have faith that the values which are physically and metaphysically real have a meaning and expression in history. History, instead of being a succession of sterile cycles, is seen as a schoolhouse in which God is the teacher, and the values expressed in the core of Christian doctrine can be observed "to be progressively embodied in the consciousness of the race." History thus came to have a far greater depth in time and a far greater range than the classical historian could have imagined. "Its prophetic voice is recovered, for its true significance is discerned to lie neither in the past nor the present, but in the future, 'life of the world to come,'" the common life of all mankind.

Implicit in the insistence of Christianity on the immortality of the soul, and especially in the belief in the resurrection of the body, which protected that doctrine from being reduced to a vague identification of the individual with some world spirit, was our modern notion of history. In the words of Charles Cochrane, "by giving significance to individual experience, it gave significance also to the experience of the race . . . The divergence between Christianity and Classicism was in no respect more conspicuously or emphatically displayed than with regard to history. . . ."[3]

---

[3] Charles Norris Cochrane: *Christianity and Classical Culture: A Study of Thought and Action from Augustus to Augustine* (New York: Oxford University Press; 1944), p. 456.

For the Christian, time was neither a "thing" in the naturalistic manner of the Greeks, nor was it an illusion. It was real and irreversible, the progressive revelation of the mind of God. In the words of Saint Ambrose, "time, space, matter and form are alike not gods but gifts, not causes but opportunities."

It was also Augustine's insight to conceive of epoch-making events, moments of history distinguished by a special character and significance, of which, of course, the life of Christ was the archetype. Against mechanistic or idealistic conceptions of history, Augustine opposed the notion of history as the working out of God's purpose. In one sense, man is the creator throughout history, since everything that happens in time happens directly or indirectly by his will; yet, in the deeper sense, God is the mover of history, since it is only through "the working of God's providence that the operation of man's will at any given moment leads to *this* result and not to a different one." Augustine may be said to have discovered, in Reinhold Niebuhr's words, "the significance of memory as part of the image of God."[4]

The modern reader coming to Saint Augustine is apt to be so untrained in theology and so unfamiliar with the intricacies of Hellenistic disputation that he has little inclination to try to extract from *The City of God* those elements which either changed or codified the existing change in world view that distinguished pagan from Judeo-Christian culture. Having perhaps already read Thucydides or Polybius with a thrill of recognition, he finds the greatest thinker of the early church insipid or impenetrable. Strangely, Augustine seems to him to be eons of time away while the Greeks seem his spiritual contemporaries. Yet this is an illusion. Modern man indisputably lives in a

---

[4] *Faith and History: A Comparison of Christian and Modern Views of History* (New York: Charles A. Scribner's; 1949), p. 18.

world far more clearly shaped by Augustine than by Plato. And this is as true of history as it is of a dozen other dimensions of his life. Indeed, it is more true of history because the Judeo-Christian view of the meaning of time and its potentialities underlies all other aspects of Western civilization,—which are, in fact, inconceivable without this primary transformation.

At the same time it should be said that the Judeo-Christian concept of time was slow to reveal its full implications. Christian optimism was limited, for the most part, to the hereafter and the City of Man was generally seen as irredeemably fallen. Moreover, it was certainly the case that classical scholarship had created the category of history as a field of study and prescribed the ground rules for the historian. Christian thought took a turn away from a concern with history toward the exploration of the world of faith and the conquest of disorderly space (the Cistercians, Benedictines, etc.), and when history once more began to preoccupy men, in the twelfth and thirteenth centuries, cyclical and astral theories were advanced and elaborated.

Throughout the Middle Ages, those Christian recorders of events who rose above the level of mere chroniclers insisted that truth was their guide. Although Otto of Freising, writing in the twelfth century, thought of himself as writing "not so much histories as pitiful tragedies made up of mortal woes,"[5] he appealed to "the careful student of history" and set out to follow the path of historical accuracy. He saw himself, no less than Thucydides or Polybius had seen themselves, as a "studious and painstaking investigator" bent on making "a record of past happenings free from all obscurity."[6] Otto of Freising's organizing principle was, of course, far different from that of the Greek histo-

---

[5] *Medieval Reader* (New York: Viking Press; 1949), ed. James Bruce Ross and Mary Martin McLaughlin, p. 563.

[6] Ibid., p. 565.

rians. Writing, as he felt, in the twilight of human history, he referred all events to "the glorious City of God."

William of Tyre, a contemporary of Otto of Freising, likewise wrote eloquently of the pitfalls that threaten the historian. If he passes in silence over certain events, for fear of arousing popular resentment, "he is not without fault." Historians who deliberately flatter the prejudices of their readers "are so detestable that they ought not to be regarded as belonging to the ranks of historians."[7] The first obligation of the historian was to God, the second to His truth.

The preoccupation of medieval historians with the City of God and their general despair over the low estate of the City of Man robbed their histories of much of their interest for later generations even while they instructed the faithful. Yet, as R. G. Collingwood has pointed out, the universalism of Christianity was symbolized in the seventh century by the chronology invented by Isidore of Seville and adopted by the Venerable Bede a century later. This chronology, which is our own and which illustrates dramatically the conquest of time by Christianity, places Christ in the center of world history and relates all previous and subsequent history to his birth.

---

[7] Ibid., p. 568.

3

The Renaissance and Machiavelli

❀ ❀ ❀

Historians are still contending over the character and meaning of the Renaissance. It is perhaps worth recalling, without embarking on the turbulent waters of that controversy, what Johan Huizinga has pointed out so effectively—namely, that the notion of rebirth and regeneration was a Christian notion far more than a classical one. "This sacramental, eschatological, and ethical concept of a spiritual renewal" was given fresh vigor and relevance when "late in the twelfth century Joachim of Floris transferred it to an expectation of a really impending transformation of the Christian world." Both the literary and Biblical humanists "were permeated by a nostalgia for the old primeval purity and an aspiration to renew themselves from within," Huizinga writes. "Whether their longings were directed toward primitive Christianity, the noble, well-governed Rome of the Catos and Scipios, or pure Latinity, perfect poetry, rediscovered art, it was always a longing to go backward in time: renovatio, restitutio, restauratio."[1]

Indeed, it could be argued that the impulse to go back, the capacity to fall in love with an earlier age, pagan or early Christian, which was so characteristic of the Renaissance, was in itself a consequence of the Christian world view to which antiquity offers no parallel. The Greeks could make what one might call horizontal comparisons, that is, comparisons among roughly coexisting societies and forms of government, especially those demonstrated by the city states, but they had no capacity for vertical comparisons, except in the form of certain abstract propositions about the recurrence of forms. Since the Christian historian, simple as were his concepts and crude as were his methods, felt compelled to construct a continuous and coherent narrative of human history around Christian doctrine, he inevitably acquired a depth perspective which, however dogmatic, eventually proved capable of extraordinary elaboration and refinement.

Whatever the nature of the Renaissance, one thing seems clear enough. In the fifteenth and sixteenth centuries there was a great revival of classical learning and men turned away from a God-centered universe toward a man-centered one. Pico della Mirandola gave classic expression to this spirit when he exclaimed that he "understood why man is the most fortunate of creatures and therefore worthy of all admiration," and why he had been granted such a position in the universal order, "so that not only the beasts but even the stars and the other worldly intelligences envy him. Incredible and marvelous! And why not, if it is for that

---

[1] *Men and Ideas* (New York: Meridan Books; 1959), translated by James S. Holmes and Hans van Marle, "The Problem of the Renaissance," pp. 274, 277.

that he is considered to be a great miracle and a wonderful creature?" The reason for man's superb nature, Mirandola argued, was that God, having created the world, "wanted some one to reflect upon the reason behind such a great creation, who might love its beauty and marvel over its grandeur." To other orders of creation, God had given specific places and tasks, but man he left free. "You, unhampered," He told man, "may determine your own limits according to your own will. . . . I have set you in the center of the world. . . . I have made you neither heavenly or terrestrial, neither mortal or immortal, in order that, like a free and sovereign artificer, you can fashion your own form out of your own substance." Mirandola's words express as well as words can the exuberance of fifteenth-century Italy, its concentration on man's potentialities rather than on God's imperatives, its exultation of the worldly over the other-worldly.[2]

Here we are most directly concerned with Niccolò Machiavelli, though it is necessary to point out that he was more of a political scientist than a historian and was, in the latter category, only one of a number of Italian historians of the fifteenth and sixteenth centuries and not perhaps the most distinguished. Machiavelli, after centuries of scrutiny, remains an enigmatic figure. We sense a contradiction between the ruthless opportunist of *The Prince* and the Florentine patriot of the *Discourses* who held up republican government as the ideal political form and seemed to prefer the wisdom of the people to that of their rulers. Two factors made it possible for Machiavelli to write his famous works. One was the greatly diminished power of the Church; the other was the chaotic state of Italy in the fourteenth century. The Church, weakened by the Babylonish captivity, the Conciliar Movement, and the corruption of the Papacy itself, could no longer assert its authority

---

[2] *Oration on the Dignity of Man*, translated by Elizabeth Livermore Forbes (Lexington, Kentucky: Anvil Press; 1953), p. 5.

over secular states or over the lives of the faithful as it once had. The time was thus propitious for a scholar with a new loyalty to antiquity to separate church and state and regard the state as an essentially secular organization of power that responded to its own laws and imperatives quite independent of ecclesiastical authority. Machiavelli was not by any means the first man to observe the innermost workings of that aspect of power whose understanding and control direct the course of secular political events. But he was the first since Polybius and Livy to focus attention on the nature and the significance of this phenomenon. His interest was the more forcefully directed to this subject by the condition of Italy and, above all, of his native Florence, which, like the city states of the Periclean age, was engaged in chronic and exhausting warfare.

Machiavelli's principal concern in the *Discourses* was to mine Livy for precepts which could guide the statesmen of his own day in acquiring and holding power. He was, in a sense, like a man in the grip of a compelling nightmare who hopes that by analyzing the nightmare he may escape it. Once church and state had been separated, the secular world indeed appeared as a nightmare in which only the skillful and cunning could survive. In trying to exorcise the demons of anarchy and disorder, Machiavelli hit upon a method of historical analogy. Comparing the Rome of Titus Livius with the state of Florence, he deduced principles and precepts of political action. And as a consequence of Machiavelli's spectacular success, this use of the past became the model for subsequent historians; analysis by analogy dominated historical thinking until the end of the eighteenth century.

Machiavelli's ruthless wresting of political history from its traditional ethical framework revitalized the study of history: it allowed the historian to view events unencumbered with the necessity to rationalize them with Christian dogma. As John Adams put it, Machiavelli was "the great restorer of the true politics."[3]

We have come to think of Machiavelli as an unrelenting realist but, as Herbert Butterfield and others have pointed out, he observed conventions as strict as any he abandoned. One of these was the revival of a modified form of the Greek conception of time as essentially cyclical and events as recurrent. After describing in the *Discourses* the rise and fall of the Roman republic, Machiavelli adds: "Such is the circle which all republics are destined to run through."[4] And again he declares: "Whoever considers the past and the present will readily observe that all cities and all peoples are and ever have been animated by the same desires and the same passions; so that it is easy, by diligent study of the past, to foresee what is likely to happen in the future in any republic." Yet Machiavelli assumes at the same time that the wise and well-informed prince *can*, if he applies himself diligently to the lessons of the past, alter the course of events, that is to say, of history—whereas the ancient historians are far more fatalistic. Thucydides and Polybius stress the degree to which the blind workings of fate control humans and see the role of historians as that of forearming their readers to endure the vicissitudes of fortune with equanimity.

We find in Francesco Guicciardini, Machiavelli's fellow Florentinian, the same conception. "Past events," he wrote, "throw light on the future, because the world has always been the same as it now is, and all that is now, or shall be hereafter, has been in time past. Things accordingly repeat themselves, but under changed names and colors, so that it is not everyone who can recognize them, but only he who is discerning and who notes them diligently."[5]

---

[3] *Defence of the Constitutions of the United States* (London, 1788), III, p. 210.

[4] Book I, chapter 3.

[5] *Ricordi*, translated by Nivian Hill Thomson (New York: S. F. Vanni; 1949), p. 71.

Free will or determinism, the paradox was not readily resolved. While formally accepting the classical notion of recurrent time, Machiavelli and Guicciardini, and those who for the next several generations followed their lead, persisted in the notion that history was a storehouse of examples and analogies that could instruct the wise and enable them to direct or at least modify the future.

Of course, although secular historians from the time of Machiavelli on wrote in terms of what might be called the "mechanics of history," with a sharp eye for the manipulations which lay beneath the surface of events, they still wrote within the context of Western Christianity. Moreover, the first rude violence of Machiavelli, intoxicated by what must have been, even to him, his strange power to dissect the body politic with a skill as cool and impersonal as that with which Leonardo dissected cadavers (the two activities are certainly not unrelated; the human body, like the state, had to be, in a sense, secularized before the restless curiosity of a Leonardo or a Vesalius could dare to penetrate its sheltering skin), was not to be repeated. Even his friend Guicciardini reproached him for his cynicism.

In fact, one of the notions of Machiavelli which found the readiest acceptance was that of the corruptibility of men (Chapter XLII of Book I of the *Discourses* is entitled "How Easily Men May be Corrupted"). Such a doctrine was entirely compatible with the Judeo-Christian image of man, tainted with original sin and in his own natural person "desperately wicked and deceitful above all things." That, and the corollary that followed from it—all political arrangements were precarious in the extreme—need not have been a stumbling block to the most rigorous orthodoxy.

4

The Reformation and the Enlightenment

Close on the Renaissance came Luther, Calvin, Zwingli, and the developments that we have chosen to comprehend under the name of the Reformation. Those elements of classical Humanism which had recently penetrated Christianity through the Roman Church were spewed out by the great Reformers, with the qualification, of course, that since it is impossible to repeal history some traces of the new learning survived even within the citadels of Protestantism. In fact, as we have suggested, Protestantism with its emphasis on original sin and human depravity had a special affinity for the disenchanted view of human motivation Machiavelli held up to the world. Machiavelli's world was simply a fallen world, the City of Man in which, as Luther expressed it, the Devil reigned. In addition, Protestantism employed the

same method of analogy in attacking the Papacy that
Machiavelli had used in criticizing fifteenth and early sixteenth century Italy. As Machiavelli referred everything
back to the ultimate measure of Republican Rome, Luther
and Calvin referred everything back to the primitive Christian Church. Here was the model of the perfect Christian
commonwealth.

On the other hand, the prophets of the Reformation
placed Christ once more at the center of history; they re-
vived the millennial expectation and insisted that God's
providence ruled the world of man and that man, unassisted
by God's grace, was radically deficient in goodness. Like the
chroniclers of the Old Testament, the historians of Protestantism saw every event, from a thunderstorm to the overthrow of a dynasty, as evidence of God's direct intervention
in the affairs of man. They employed history as analogy
primarily to vindicate the policy of the reformed Churches.
But they once more saw history in Augustinian terms, as
the progressive revelation of God's will, and they brought
all areas of the life of the faithful once again under the
scheme of Christian dogma. Every incident in the history of
the reformed community must be carefully scrutinized for
its meaning and preserved for the guidance of the faithful.
The thrust was clearly prophetic; this life must be mastered
as a preliminary to the life of the world to come.

The Age of Reason, carrying forward the secular, humanistic attitudes of the Renaissance, turned more sharply away
from Machiavelli's chilling realism than had the Reformers
and drew a picture of the powers of human reason, progressively developed in harmony with the laws of nature
and in the process of freeing itself from ignorance and superstition, that would have been recognized neither by Machiavelli nor by Calvin. The Enlightenment, with its social
Utopianism, its dazzling prospect of a heavenly city on
earth presided over by philosophers and spreading its benefi-

cence throughout the generality of mankind, was profoundly deficient in historical understanding. Yet it represented, in a sense, a variation of the Christian doctrine, inasmuch as it looked ahead to a new Garden of Eden and suffused its age with a dauntless optimism about the future of the race, not in some celestial region, but in the world itself.

The steps in the development of the idea of progress in the eighteenth century are familiar enough. The way was paved by Descartes's exaltation of reason and his insistence on the invariability of the laws of nature. Voltaire, in *The Age of Louis XIV* and *Essay on Manners and Customs*, enunciated the new creed as it applied to the writing of history.

Because the philosophers of the Enlightenment believed that modern man stood at the highest point in history, they favored recent history over the history of the more distant past. Moreover, recent history could be far more readily verified. The materials for composing it lay near at hand. The further one made one's way into the past, the more one encountered myths and legends which obscured the truth. In the definition of history contained in the *Philosophical Dictionary*, Voltaire offers the following characteristic observation: "History is the recital of facts given as true, in contradiction to the fable, which is the recital of facts given as false." Indeed, the whole "history of opinions"—what we today would call intellectual history—seemed an especially arid waste to the Frenchman. He was, in a sense, the first modern social and cultural historian who emphasized the growth of technology as perhaps the most important area of historical investigation. History was most useful and instructive when it "joins to the knowledge of the invention and the progress of the arts the description of their mechanism."

For Voltaire, only the "incontestable records" were worth the historian's attention, and these were few in number and largely chronological. Under this rubric, the Chinese were supreme. "What puts the Chinese above all the peoples of the earth," Voltaire wrote, "is that neither their laws, nor their customs, nor the language spoken among them by their lettered mandarins has changed for about four thousand years." It was the history of the human mind in the age of Louis XIV, "the most enlightened century that ever was," that attracted Voltaire. The four "blessed ages" were those in which "the arts were perfected"—Periclean Athens, the Rome of Caesar, the Italy of the Medici, and the France of Louis XIV. We can hear an echo of Machiavelli in Voltaire's contention that the chief advantage to be derived from the study of history lies "in the comparison which a statesman or a citizen can draw between foreign laws and customs and those of his own country." Such comparisons would spur modern man to emulation in the arts, in agriculture, and in trade. In addition, and perhaps most important of all, the "great errors" of the past were highly instructive. People could not be reminded too often of the crimes and disasters which made up the greater part of human history—"the usurpations of the Popes . . . the madness of theological quarrels . . . and the horrors that resulted." Such scandals could, Voltaire insisted, be forestalled, if the modern reader would take to heart the lessons that they taught.[1]

All creatures fulfilled "that law which nature has prescribed to their species. The bird builds its nest, as the stars perform their course, by a principle which can never alter." It was man's nature alone which had been perverted, but with the discovery, in the eighteenth century, of his true nature as a rational being, it might be assumed that he at last had arrived "at that degree of perfection which nature had preserved for man alone."[2]

---

[1] Fritz Stern: *Varieties of History* (New York: Meridian Books; 1956), pp. 35–45.
[2] *The Philosophy of History* (London, 1866), p. 38.

God had implanted in man "a principle of reason that is universal, as he has given feathers to birds and skins to bears"; and this principle was "so immutable" that it survived despite "those tyrants who would drown it in blood," despite "those impostors who would annihilate it by superstition."[3] To Voltaire, "the ancient religion of India, and that of the literary men in China," were the only ones that were not "barbarous." Indeed, most of the past of his own country was, in Voltaire's opinion, "obscure and disgusting."[4]

Voltaire's contemporary, Marie Jean Antoine Nicholas de Caritat, Marquis de Condorcet, to give him his full title, carried the master's teaching further than anyone of his generation. In Condorcet, the notion of progress is most clearly and explicitly stated. He wrote his *Sketch of an Historical Picture of the Progress of the Human Mind* while under the sentence of death passed by the revolutionary tribunal which was the creature of Robespierre and the Terror. Awaiting execution, he nonetheless anticipated a day when the sun would shine "on an earth of none but freemen, with no master save reason; for tyrants and slaves, priests and their stupid or hypocritical tools, will all have disappeared."

Condorcet saw ten distinct periods of civilization, nine in the past and the tenth ahead. The formation of primitive societies, the development of pastoral life, and the appearance of agricultural communities marked the first three stages, followed by the Greeks' invention of alphabetic writing. The fourth stage is marked by Aristotle's contributions to learning. Rome and the Middle Ages were simply a prelude to the seventh age, which saw the revival of classical learning, and to the eighth age, which was marked by the invention of printing. The scientific revolution ushered in by Descartes distinguished the beginning of

---

[3] Ibid., p. 43.
[4] Ibid., p. 101.

the ninth age, which reached its fulfillment in the French Revolution.

In Condorcet's view, history demonstrated the fact of progress, and the study of history, by suggesting the direction such progress must take, made it possible for men, by the use of their reason, to accelerate progress. Progress was, in any event and whatever its speed, inevitable and irreversible. The discovery of the true principles of science and their application to human needs guaranteed the progressive enlightenment of man and the constant improvement of social conditions. As men through reason came to understand better the laws of nature and to adjust themselves to these laws, they would improve in virtue as well as wisdom, wars would cease, and the goal of equality among men, between men and women, and among the various races of the earth would be achieved.

Condorcet and Voltaire, in common with most of their fellow illuminati, had little understanding of or sympathy with the forms and orders through which societies express their common experience. Political and social institutions remained unfathomable for them. All custom and tradition, whether expressed liturgically or ceremonially, was for them simply a constraint upon the freedom of mind, an inhibition to natural reason. Although Condorcet stressed the idea of progress in history, many of his contemporaries, of whom Voltaire may be taken as the exemplar, saw history as a kind of wasteland, a dark landscape in which man had been degraded and enslaved.

But if the foundations of traditional European society were eroded by the radical skepticism of the philosophes, the unexpected consequence was to make modern man more dependent on history than he had ever been before. A man's relation to the society of which he is a part must be represented to him in some form; it must be explained and rationalized. This, in most earlier societies, had been the function of myth and legend and later of tradition and custom. Church and state, as represented in institutions and confirmed and dramatized by ritual and ceremonial, defined the role and the purpose and even indicated the ultimate destiny of its constituent members. The relentless assault of the Enlightenment theorists upon those institutions and traditions left men in bewildering nakedness. The enlightened reason discovered a ruthlessness which enabled it to strip from the body politic every bit of raiment. Such an attitude was profoundly anti-historical.

But since history itself is not logic but paradox, the emphasis of the philosophes on the arts, on science, on technology, on what we might call today social and cultural history, represented a notable broadening in the range of historical study. To this significant contribution they added two others: an insistence on the importance of history, even if history was, to modify Lord Bolingbroke's aphorism, philosophy teaching by bad examples; and a determination to make past history relevant to the present and a guide to the future, even at the cost of doing violence to the very facts they so revered.

We are thus brought to the point of saying, in effect, that the profoundly anti- or, at the least, a-historical attitude of the French philosophers produced very considerable benefits for history as a humanistic study. Since the eighteenth century, although historians came to take a very different attitude toward the past than, let us say, Voltaire had, they continued to accept, for the most part, the assumptions of the philosophes, perhaps most notably the idea of progress. And in the nineteenth century this idea was reinforced by a number of new concepts, such as Darwinian evolution and Marxian materialism.

5

History
and the
Age of Revolution

The so-called "Age of Democratic Revolution" which produced the American and the French Revolutions acted as a spur to the study and writing of history. Political and social upheaval stimulated a search for models and analogies. Americans, especially, were anxious to prove that in cutting the ties that bound them to the mother country they were striking a blow for the principles of Magna Charta and reviving the classic political virtues of republican Rome.

Scholarly procedures in the study and writing of history had of course been familiar to any number of sixteenth- or seventeenth-century historians. What had been missing was the impulse to recover source materials for an earlier period and the techniques required to authenticate authorities and reconcile those in conflict, to penetrate the meaning of myths and legends instead of simply brushing them aside.

The modern passion for documentation revealed itself first at the time of the American Revolution and subsequently in France. There is much truth in Lord Acton's assertion that the revolutionary upheavals at the end of the eighteenth century, of which the French Revolution was the most traumatic, made historical study "infinitely more effectual as a factor of civilization than ever before." A change took place in "the world of minds . . . deeper and more serious than the revival of ancient learning. . . . Those who lived through it with intelligence," Acton wrote, "had a larger experience, and more intense, than other men have ever had."[1]

When Abbé Mably told John Adams that he was planning a history of the American Revolution, Adams asked him—it may be imagined, with some asperity—where he had obtained the materials. And he was plainly dissatisfied with the Abbé's vague reference to "the public papers" and "inquiry of individuals." Adams admonished him on the spot and later wrote a long letter detailing the sources which the Abbé must master before he presumed to write about the American Revolution. Starting with "the first establishment of the colonies in 1600," he must "read all the charters granted to the colonies, and the commissions and instructions given to governors, all the codes of laws of the several colonies . . . (which cannot be found but in manuscript and by travelling in person from New Hampshire to Georgia); the records of the board of trade and plantations in Great Britain, from its institution to its dissolution; as also the files in the offices of some of the Secretaries of State." In addition there were various secondary works, ranging from the histories of John Winthrop and Thomas Winslow

---

[1] Quoted by Herbert Butterfield: *Man on His Past: the Study of the History of Historical Scholarship* (Cambridge University Press, 1955), p. 67.

to that of Thomas Hutchinson. Mably must consult the writings and wherever possible the personal correspondence of all the revolutionary leaders, the "records, pamphlets, and gazettes of the thirteen states . . . as well as the journals of Congress." *The Remembrancer*, the *Annual Register*, and the periodical papers published in England during the crisis should all be read and the important continental newspapers scrutinized as well as those archives which were accessible. "The whole of a long life . . . will be necessary to assemble from all nations, and from all parts of the world in which they are deposited, the documents proper to form a complete history of the American Revolution, because it is indeed the history of mankind during that epoch," Adams concluded.[2]

If the Abbé had any plan to write a history, he at once disavowed it; he would be dead, he protested, before he had a chance to assemble half the necessary materials. Adams's letter is worth quoting at some length, for it demonstrates, one would suppose, as thorough an appreciation of the importance of sources as it is possible to have. Indeed, Adams came to feel that a history of the Revolution which approximated the truth would never be written. Partisan feelings, such as those which divided Republicans and Federalists, would engender partisan histories and obscure the facts.

After the Revolution, the Massachusetts Historical Society was founded, one of the first institutions in the modern world supported by private funds and dedicated to the collection and preservation of historical materials. It is not mere chance that the United States, a nation with the briefest history of all modern powers, has led the world in the development of archival techniques and the establishment of repositories from the local to the national level. We have been, par excellence, the example of a nation without

---

[2] John Adams: *Works*, edited by Charles Francis Adams (Boston: Little, Brown; 1856), V, pp. 492–6.

formal traditions or pre-history which needed to develop a history in order to define itself. Such activity was pragmatic in nature. Lacking the support of a theoretical system, it was based, for the most part, on the conviction that an extraordinary revolution was taking place in human affairs, the records of which should be scrupulously preserved. It remained for others to supply the philosophical superstructure which offered a rationale for the historical enterprise.

The most influential contribution to the idea of history in the early nineteenth century was that of Hegel. The Reformation view of history as the arena in which God, through man, worked out his grand design existed alongside the secular views of the Enlightenment philosophers. Hegel, in a practical demonstration of his dialectic, merged the two currents. The German philosopher presented to a responsive audience a notion of history as the progressive development of reason through God's providence. Man's spirit, made up of nature and the divine Idea, was fulfilled in history. Spirit was inherently free; therefore history was to be understood as the progress of freedom. The human mind was a reflection of the divine; the laws of logic have their archetype in the mind of the Creator. In the words of one of Hegel's modern critics, "God for Hegel not only *has* but *is* History." History was not the appearance but the reality of God.[3] The task of understanding God through history belonged to the historian and the philosopher rather than to the theologian. To Hegel, man became free through the development of his self-consciousness: "World history is the progress of Freedom, because it is the progress of the self-consciousness of Spirit."[4]

It is important to note that Hegel rejected the notion that "rulers, statesmen, and peoples" learn from the experi-

---

[3] *Reason in History*, edited by Robert S. Hartman (Liberal Arts Press, 1953), pp. xix–xxi.
[4] Ibid., p. xxv.

ences of history. "Every age," he wrote, "has conditions of its own and is an individual situation; decisions must be made only within, and in accordance with the age itself . . . a vague memory has no power against the vitality and freedom of the present."[5]

Every historian, however much he might pose as "merely surrendering himself to the data, . . . brings his categories with him and sees the data through them." Thus, Hegel insisted, the philosopher had the special responsibility of making clear to the historian the true nature of his undertaking. If the historian, guided by the philosopher, would but look rationally at the world, the world would look rationally back. Only the study of world history could show "that it has proceeded rationally, that it represents the rationally necessary course of the World Spirit, the Spirit whose nature is indeed always one and the same, but whose one nature unfolds in the course of the world."[6]

That a divine Providence "presides over the events of the world" was entirely compatible with Hegel's system. Providence was wisdom "endowed with infinite power which realizes its own aim, that is, the absolute, rational, final purpose of the world-freedom." Reason was not only the way to God. It was God: "This Reason, in its most concrete representation, is God. . . . The actual working of His government, the carrying out of His plan is the history of the world. Philosophy strives to comprehend this plan, for only that which has been carried out according to it has reality. . . ."[7] Man can know God, indeed has the *obligation* to know him, for "God wishes no narrow souls and empty heads for his children." What before had been grasped imperfectly by faith must now be the subject of "intellectual comprehension." The knowledge of the freedom of man

---

[5] Ibid., p. 8.
[6] Ibid., p. 12.
[7] Ibid., p. 47.

"first arose in religion"; its application to the secular world was a task which could be carried out "by a long and severe effort of civilization."[8]

Hegel's treatment of necessity and free will clearly owed a debt to Christian theology. Since the individual was an instrument of the divine purpose, he might not realize that in pursuing what seemed to be his own interests he was actually helping to complete the designs of Providence. From this there followed the important corollary "that human actions in history produce additional results, beyond their immediate purpose and attainment, beyond their immediate knowledge and desire. They gratify their own interests; but something more is thereby accomplished, which is latent in the action though not present in their consciousness." Augustine had taken much the same line, pointing out that the individual could not hope entirely to understand or control the consequences of his actions. Where Hegel differed most sharply from the Bishop of Hippo was in his conviction that "the historical men, the world-historical individuals" (the elect, in Augustinian terms) could grasp "just such a higher universal, make it their own purpose, and realize this purpose in accordance with the higher law of the spirit."[9]

The historical men, moreover, in Hegel's system, were freed from the ethical and moral imperatives which governed ordinary society. Because they were the special instruments of the universal spirit, they often had to "trample down many an innocent flower, crush to pieces many things in [their] path."

Two other elements in Hegel's system of thought are worthy of notice. One was his realization that people acted for reasons that were often very different from what they professed. "Though passions are not wanting," he wrote,

---

[8] Ibid., pp. 15–17, 24.
[9] Ibid., pp. 35, 39.

"history exhibits partly and predominately a struggle of justifiable ideas and partly a struggle of passions and subjective interests under the mask of such higher pretensions."[1] This insight was to be most effectively developed by Karl Marx.

Equally important was Hegel's view that the universal Idea manifests itself in the state. "Thus the state is the definite object of world history proper . . . For law is the objectivity of Spirit; it is will in its true form. Only that will that obeys the law is free, for it obeys itself and being in itself, is free." At that point freedom and necessity disappear, since the individual in accepting the law achieves true freedom.[2]

In its simplest formulation—that history was the progressive revelation of Freedom, a freedom achieved through Reason, which was somehow both God and History— Hegel's philosophy was especially attractive to American historians. The American Revolution was, for many of them, the latest and the most important example of the realization of freedom through Reason.

Although the United States did not concern Hegel—it lacked the external pressures which would force it to define itself as a state and thereby achieve the requisite degree of self-consciousness—he was gracious enough to describe it as "the land of the future, where, in the ages that lie before us, the burden of the World's History shall reveal itself. . . . It is a land of desire for all those who are weary of the historical lumber-room of old Europe." It was for America "to abandon the ground on which hitherto the History of the World has developed itself."[3] It was thus hardly an accident that an American historian, George Bancroft, emerged as one of Hegel's most enthusiastic disciples. Ban-

---

[1] Ibid., pp. 43, 46.
[2] Ibid., p. 53.
[3] *Philosophy of History*, translated by J. Sibree (New York, 1902), p. 143.

croft was charmed with Hegel's doctrine that Divine Wisdom was discoverable through the study of history. History, Bancroft wrote, traced "the vestiges of moral law through the practice of nations in every age" and confirmed "by induction the intuitions of reason." The historian had the task of revealing these principles to his readers, for only through the increasing self-consciousness of a people could progress be achieved. Such a view led Bancroft to see the American Revolution as a simple struggle between good and evil in which England's cause, morally wrong, had been doomed from the moment when the Mother Country "made war on human freedom." The outcome was one "which no human policy or force could hold back, proceeding as majestically as the laws of being." Since time was irreversible and progress inevitable, the Revolution sounded the death knell of the "ages of servitude and inequality," and rang in "those of equality and brotherhood." America's feet were, thereby, set on a "never-ending career of reform and progress."[4]

Bancroft's countrymen demonstrated how congenial such ideas were to them by making him the most widely read and most influential historian of the first half of the nineteenth century. His only rival, ironically, was the Englishman Thomas Babington Macaulay, who wrote, in the same spirit of liberal optimism, about the England of James I.

Hegel's famous dialectic of thesis, antithesis, and synthesis made relatively little impression on practicing historians, who seemed determined to write history as though certain men and parties constituted all that was good, and any events that were not comprehended under such a rubric had no real relevance. In this sense they remained children of the Enlightenment. But the Enlightenment formula was too rickety, too lacking in an adequate metaphysic to

---

[4] George Bancroft: *History of the United States* (Boston: Little, Brown & Co., 1876), V, pp. 69–70.

be satisfactory. Romanticism and the Neo-Idealism of Kant threatened it and its forthright skepticism made it unacceptable to the majority of historians, who were, generally speaking, more or less orthodox theists. Hegel gave the liberal Christians enough God to satisfy them and the rationalists enough Reason to meet their requirements, the more so since it is not likely that many of them understood what the philosopher meant by "Reason."

The Hegelian system, then, as it reached the working historian, was almost ideal. It mentioned God and Spirit favorably. It was unflaggingly optimistic. It made history essential to an understanding of God, and, finally, it rested on metaphysical premises so abstruse as to be virtually inaccessible to a layman. Moreover, since it contained more than a modicum of Romanticism, it repaired one of the principal deficiencies of Enlightenment thought—its basic contempt for the past. The nineteenth century put a premium on order and stability and on tracing the rise and the proper function of political and, to a lesser extent, social institutions. In both these endeavors it received support from the man who became, in effect, the official philosopher of the German state.

Hegel's disciple, Karl Marx, was the first political and social theorist to place the fact of revolution at the center of his thinking. Marx's words echoed like thunder when he wrote "not criticism, but revolution is the driving force of history."[5] This was the most astonishing fact of modern history—the American Revolution had hinted at it and the French Revolution had confirmed it. These revolutionary upheavals had two results: They called into question all the foundations of traditional and customary society, the presuppositions which, though they had been frequently debated, had nonetheless remained the solid underpinnings of

---

[5] Marx and Engels: *The German Ideology*, edited and translated by R. Pascal, Part I (New York: International Publishers; 1939), pp. 13–24.

Christendom for a thousand years. And they turned men to a study of the past in an effort to understand how such things could have happened. The difference between the history of Voltaire and that of Ranke, let us say, was a revolution. Moreover, the American and French Revolutions showed, for the first time, how revolution could be made the agency for transforming man's political life (the American Revolution) and his social life (the French Revolution). The endless revolutions of the Italian city states were little different from the palace revolts that have distinguished the political life of Latin America. Machiavelli's *Discourses* and his *Prince* were the manuals of such revolutions, which weary us with their succession of generally meaningless upheavals by which one band of condottieri are replaced by another. It is small wonder that Machiavelli was tempted by the cyclical view of history.

But Marx, with the discernment of genius, grasped that revolution was the key to modern history, and from this he concluded that "all struggles within the State, the struggle between democracy, aristocracy and monarchy, the struggle for the franchise, etc., etc., are merely the illusory forms in which the real struggles of the different classes are fought out among one another." Of this, Marx added, "the German theoreticians have not the faintest inkling."[6]

Despite Marx's insights, his theories were to remain a kind of subterranean current in the study and writing of history. What he asserted was too novel, too shattering to penetrate the rather conventional consciousness of historians. The historians of the nineteenth century were wooed by less strident voices. For the most part, Marx was absorbed, where he was absorbed at all, by a kind of osmosis. And, in America at least, materialistic and deterministic thought, rising from the same stream Marx drank from, flowed along concurrently with Marxist thought

---

[6] Ibid., p. 24.

until the depression years of the nineteen-thirties, when Marxism burst from its subterranean channel and became for a few years the dominant school of historical interpretation.

However much the Age of Revolution may have been a spur to the study of history, modern historical-mindedness is primarily a by-product of what we have come to call, rather loosely, the Romantic Movement. By the phrase we mean a willingness to accept the past on its own terms, to enter sympathetically into the spirit of another and often remote period, as far at least as it is possible to do so. Romanticism, in sharp contrast to the Enlightenment, loved that which was remote, colorful, dramatic, and indeed different from the drab present. Whereas the philosophes had judged the past only in the light of the present, the Romantics were inclined to flee from the present into the picturesqueness of the past and of exotic lands. Yet even as Romanticism influenced attitudes toward history, bringing to historical study a more catholic spirit, it was firmly contained within the framework of eighteenth-century utopian social expectations—the notion of progress in history. We can see this most clearly in three American historians who were, at least in part, the products of Romanticism. William Prescott, Francis Parkman, and John Lothrop Motley all chose subjects comparatively remote from mid-nineteenth-century America, subjects full of dramatic highlights: Prescott, the conquest of Mexico and Peru; Parkman, the drama of French colonial exploration and settlement in the New World; and Motley, the rise of the Dutch Republic in the seventeenth century. All of them conducted laborious research into original documents and wrote their histories with such a scrupulous regard for the facts that, at least in the case of Parkman and Prescott, their works have been little modified by a subsequent century of scholarship.

At the same time, each historian saw the particular episode to which he devoted his efforts as marking a step in the progress of mankind. Just as, to Prescott, the Incas of Peru were a great advance over the primitive peoples of the jungle whom they had drawn into their empire, so the Spanish invaders who supplanted them represented a far higher step in the process of civilization. "We cannot regret," Prescott wrote of the Aztecs, "the fall of an empire which did so little to promote the happiness of its subjects, or the real interests of humanity. . . . Its fate may serve as a striking proof that a government which does not rest upon the sympathies of its subjects cannot long abide; that human institutions when not connected with human prosperity and progress must fall,—if not before the increasing light of civilization, by the hand of violence. . . . And who shall lament their fall?"

The story of the conquest of Mexico, Prescott noted in a characteristic effusion, "has the air of a fable, rather than of history! a legend of romance,—a tale of the genii!"[7] Indeed, he could well have been speaking for Parkman and Motley when he wrote that the story of the Spanish in Mexico should "teach us charity . . . [and] make us the more distrustful of applying the standard of the present to measure the actions of the past." And again he expressed the Romantic credo when he wrote: "To judge [an] action fairly, we must transport ourselves to the age when it happened."[8]

Similarly, Parkman viewed the classic struggle between France and England for dominion on the continent of North America as a contest between an autocratic church and state on the one hand and a free church and a free people on the other, with the outcome predestined. France,

---

[7] *The Conquest of Mexico* (Philadelphia: Lippincott; 1873), Book VI, chapter viii.

[8] Ibid., Book IV, chapter iii; Book III, chapter vii.

colorful and romantic as was its New World history, must give way, in the inevitable march of history, to a freer and more enlightened nation, the agent of Divine Providence.

Motley, equally, employed the story of the casting off of the yoke of Spain by the Netherlands to point a moral. Those nations which represented the past must give way to those which represented the progress of man toward the fulfillment of the Idea in history, the goal of universal freedom.

Accompanying the rise of Romanticism was a growing concern with history as a "scientific" study. The idea that history should be a science was not new; but the word *science*, as it was used until well into the nineteenth century, meant something like "the thoughtful and systematic investigation of natural or human phenomenon." As the natural sciences increased in importance and prestige, *scientific* came more and more to refer to the particular methodology that the scientist was supposed to employ— the collection of data and the "induction" from the data (which was, in a sense, supposed to speak for itself) of certain generalizations. When Fustel de Coulanges in his inaugural lecture delivered at Strasbourg in 1862 spoke of history as a science, "surely one of the most sublime that could be suggested for the study of man . . . man, who to be wholly known, requires several sciences for himself," he was using *science* in the older sense. George Bancroft likewise spoke of history as a "social science" in much the same spirit. But Henry Thomas Buckle expressed the new hopes of the scientific historians when he headed the first chapter of his *History of Civilization in England:* "Statement of the resources for investigating history, and proofs of the regularity of human actions. These actions are governed by mental and physical laws: therefore both sets of laws must be studied, and there can be no history without the natural sciences." And J. B. Bury at the end of the century declared that "erudition has now been supplemented by scientific method."[9]

The most influential figure in the development of the notion of history as a scientific study was Leopold von Ranke. Indeed, one of the best indices of the general frame of mind of most historians of the latter half of the nineteenth century may be found in their attitude toward Ranke. His unfortunate phrase—*wie es eigentlich gewesen* —was actually very far from what Ranke in fact considered to be the essential task of the historian, but it was seized on with remarkable avidity by successive generations of historians, who took it to mean much more than Ranke had ever intended. He uttered these famous words as a judgment on the frequently over-romanticized history of the late eighteenth century, when the authors' concern was often with the construction of glittering hypotheses based on only a slight acquaintance with the original sources, but he was taken to mean that the historian discharged his obligation best by remaining aloof from his subject, by eschewing generalization and interpretation and simply relating "what had happened." In fact, Ranke was deeply concerned with the generalizations which might be drawn from a careful marshaling of the facts. The crowning work of his life was *Weltgeschichte*. Here Ranke, in his eighties and blind and deaf, undertook to tell the universal story of man, to compose a work which would draw together man's diverse past, and in so doing, form a unity out of which a common future could be created. But it was in his contributions to method rather than to the concept of history that his influence was most widely felt. As G. P. Gooch writes, perhaps too fulsomely: "When he laid down his pen, every scholar with a reputation to make or to lose had learned to content himself with nothing less than the papers

---

[9] Inaugural Lecture as Regina Professor of Modern History, at Cambridge, 1902, in Fritz Stern: *Varieties of History*, pp. 179, 121–2, 211.

and correspondence of the actors themselves and those in immediate contact with the events they describe."[1]

Even if we accept Gooch's encomium, it might be well to point out that Ranke's precept tempted many historians to avoid, or to wish to seem to avoid, giving any personal judgment on the facts they were presenting and to rely solely on the sheer accumulation of data, which was quite out of harmony with the temper of the master's work. This faith in facts was rather akin to a belief in magic. The implications were that if one encompassed all the facts, searched all relevant documents, delved into all the available sources, one would emerge, *mirabile dictu*, with the truth.

Inspired by Ranke's aphorism, historians came to think of themselves as scientists whose duty it was simply to state "the facts." It was the illusion that he was doing this that enabled one American historian to proclaim that he had viewed the American Revolution with "scientific detachment," that in his study he had used the "ruthless methods of modern scholarship" rather than the sentimental and romantic presuppositions of earlier historians. Statements such as this, made by leading scholars, encouraged the notion that history was, in fact, a science. Concomitant with this position was the belief in the value of highly specialized research topics. "Monographs," dealing intensively with narrowly prescribed subjects, were analogous to the detailed experiments of the physical scientists, and like them could be expected to yield, if not laws of scientific validity, at least more and more accurate generalizations. Historians hesitated to claim that they would eventually discover "the Truth" about an event or a congery of events constituting an important historical episode, but this assumption underlay much of their work. Specialized studies were compared to bricks, which, when enough had accumulated, could be used by a historian gifted in generalization

---

[1] *History and Historians in the Nineteenth Century* (New York: Peter Smith; 1949), p. 102.

to erect a building that would be complete or "definitive," a word used frequently, if with increasing wistfulness, by historians of the new dispensation.

The reader should bear in mind that the new concern with "method" developed within the framework of the optimistic, Utopian, progressive view of time first enunciated by the philosophes and in a sense ratified by Hegel. The two most important theoretical formulations of the nineteenth century were used to reinforce this world view. The Darwinian idea of natural selection, when applied to human society, was taken to confirm the progressive character of history. Similarly, in the twentieth century Marxism with its dialectical materialism, its emphasis on economic conflicts as the motivating force in history, and its Utopian expectations of the classless society was at least a potential reinforcement for the progressive view and often a welcome alternative for those who could not accept the comparatively naïve formulations of the philosophes and their successors or the complex abstractions of Hegel.

In sharp contrast to the historians of the Enlightenment who distrusted past history and felt that modern history was far more reliable as well as more instructive, the nineteenth-century historians, intoxicated by the refinement of techniques of historical and archaeological investigation, by the impressive development of canons of critical scholarship, and by the ingenious and indefatigable exploitation of source materials, considered that it was in fact contemporary history which was unreliable because the writer was emotionally involved in the events and, as a consequence, hopelessly biased in his judgments. The cautious scholar put great emphasis on the perspective which distance in time was presumed to afford him. There could be no more significant index to the complacent self-assurance of the "scientific" historian than this particular axiom. Distance in time from the events described was the historian's equivalent of the much envied detachment of the scientist in his laboratory. The historian might find it impossible to be objective about his own generation but, it was assumed, he could view dispassionately the tumults and crises of more remote times. Another important development of the late eighteenth and more particularly the nineteenth century occurred when German scholars, particularly those working at Göttingen, academicized historical scholarship. By this act they took it from the hands of the amateurs, the statesmen, the philosophers, the learned dilettantes, from Turgot and Burke, Hume and Voltaire, Gibbon and Montesquieu, and planted it solidly in the universities; the rest of Europe, and eventually England and America, followed suit.

There were both advantages and disadvantages in this development but, by and large, the losses have outweighed the gains. Historical studies burgeoned in the academic atmosphere and became part of the formal structure of the university curriculum. (It might be noted here that the attitude toward history in the academies of the various universities has remained essentially that which predominated in the general field of history at the time it found a place in the academic life of a particular nation.) In America, at least, this meant that history was divided into segments corresponding to modern states and to such chronological divisions as ancient and medieval history. What was considered to be the pertinent information was communicated to the student, for the most part, in lectures and was tested in papers and examinations. On the graduate level, students were trained in modern methodology, in the use of sources, in the critical handling of authorities, the techniques required for the writing of historical monographs—detailed studies of sharply limited subjects. Much of this training was conducted in the form of seminars, a form borrowed from the German university.

Underlying this type of training on the undergraduate and graduate level was the assumption that has been referred to earlier—that history was a "social science" in which the labors of the monographers, like the experiments of the scientist in his laboratory, would inevitably lead to a better understanding of the truths of history. As a consequence of placing history within the university curriculum, there developed a growing uniformity in the preparation of historians: certain canons of historical scholarship were established which eventually prevailed among virtually all institutions of higher learning and more especially, of course, in graduate schools.

The system, after its early years, was not conducive to fresh and original thinking about the more general problems of historical interpretation. It was, indeed, only endurable as long as its basic assumption remained unchallenged—that history was, in some degree, a science capable of constant refinement. And this view, in turn, rested to a considerable extent upon the concept of human history as a progressive development in time. The ubiquitous textbook, which by the early decades of the twentieth century had come to dominate the teaching of history, can be taken as a symbol of the conviction on the part of historians that academic history could be reduced to simple declarative sentences and embalmed in the handsomely illustrated but blandly innocuous works that are, in one form or another, the constant companion of every American student from elementary school through college. A by-product of the notion that history was scientific was contempt for all the bad old history that had been written before the new dispensation. Many students learned only one thing clearly: that no history written before Ranke was worthy of attention. And Ranke himself was honored more for his fatal *wie es eigentlich gewesen* than for his *History of the Reformation*, which no one had time to read, and which was, in any event, out of date.

The history to which the student was thus introduced in

school and college (for the school sedulously aped its parent institution) was curiously rigid and inflexible and less and less related to anything the student could recognize as his own experience in the real world. History was taught not as the basis for effective action (as in earlier and less sophisticated days) but more and more as an end in itself.

We should not leave Ranke without a word about the man himself. The great German historian was very far from being what many of his disciples wished to make him—a painstaking recorder of "the facts" of history. Ranke's concern was with the history of mankind. To him, man's progress through time was a kind of symphony in which one nation or "group of nations" after the other was featured as soloist. "Critical inquiry and intelligent generalization" were "mutually indispensable."[2]

Ranke can thus be taken as a representative of the new secular spirit in history placed within the all-encompassing framework of Christian cosmology. It might almost be said that if St. Augustine had been able to imagine a historian who would fulfill the image he had adumbrated he would have imagined Ranke. Christianity was for Ranke the ultimate truth and although he did not profess to discern the end toward which history moved, he was confident that "history was the record of divine manifestations imperfectly understood." History was Ranke's path to God: "Every action testifies to Him, every moment, and above all the connection of history," he wrote to his brother Heinrich.[3] And this was the man who was to become the patron saint of the monographers.

When one stops to consider Parkman or Prescott in America, or their masters, such as Ranke and Niebuhr in Germany and compares them with their predecessors of,

---

[2] *Universal History*, edited by G. W. Prothero (London, 1884), pp. xi–xiv, 2.

[3] Quoted by Gooch, pp. 77, 100.

say, a century before, one can hardly hesitate to second Herbert Butterfield's observation that the "historical-mindedness" of the nineteenth century added "almost a new dimension to our thinking."[4]

It might only be remarked that the dimension was, in a sense, already there; that it had been there since the ancient Hebrews discovered that a people might be defined and preserved through time by the creation of a common history; that it had existed as a real if unfulfilled dimension since Saint Augustine had demolished the sterile time cycles of antiquity.

The Reformation had destroyed the shell of Christian unity which still gave a kind of order and direction to individual and social life. In the centuries that followed, the rise of modern nation states and the spread of sectarian warfare within Western Christendom presented European theorists with such a bewildering diversity of explanations about the nature of man and his social and political institutions that those responsible for its intellectual life were forced to search history for the rationale of their own divergent theories, theological and secular. Tradition had lost its authority; history must then be pressed into service. From such a multiplicity of efforts, which produced histories that made competing claims and gave widely varying interpretations of the same events, came the power to criticize, analyze, and compare. In this sense, modern historical scholarship can be seen as a massive effort to reconstruct a disintegrating world. Men were forced to think in historical terms. A new nation, if it did not have a history, must invent or borrow one. We can currently observe this process in many former colonies newly come to independence.

An additional irony is that historical consciousness is as plainly a product of Western civilization as are the political and moral principles in the name of which the underde-

[4] *Man on His Past*, p. 17.

veloped nations claim their independence and their place among the nations of the earth. It is tempting to compare this process (which is seen in the new nations simply as a more exaggerated form of the national histories of European states in the early nineteenth century) with the therapy of the psychoanalyst, who, it may be suspected, is most successful when he invents, with the aid of his patient, a personal history which, however fictitious, reassures the patient and reinforces his ability to operate in the real world.

Enough has been said and written about history as a process of myth-making. No further comment is needed. What is perhaps less clearly recognized is that the myths often enable the peoples who accepted them to continue to exist as a nation.

The nineteenth century developed a historical awareness in such an extraordinary fashion because it needed the cohesion of history to counteract the centrifugal forces of the modern world—the rise of industrialism, with the accompanying urbanization of society; the growth of skepticism; the development of extreme self-consciousness in groups and classes within nations, and national self-consciousness itself. Added to these were the after-effects of the scientific revolution, which was both the consequence of a new world view and the cause of so many dramatic changes in the relationship of man to nature, to that which he has called God, and to his fellows.

Thus we are bound to see history as it appeared in the nineteenth century as a kind of rescue operation, an urgent response to a crisis in modern society, rather than as the slow accumulation of data and the refinement of methodology.

In the twentieth century the story has been somewhat different. While academic history, the victim of nineteenth-century orthodoxies, remained locked in the cold slumber of formalism, two of the greatest dramas of modern times—

World Wars I and II—were enacted on the stage of world history. World War I, which set loose vast new forces of revolutionary political and technological change, disturbed its dreams hardly at all, but it led a number of people outside the academies to undertake an anxious examination of the past. Apparently history contained riddles beyond the imaginings of the great historians and the historical theorists of the nineteenth century.

6

Nietzsche, Burckhardt, and Dilthey

We must pause here to consider three nineteenth-century figures whose influence on the historical thought of their time was negligible but whose theories bore fruit in the generations after their death. It was Friedrich Nietzsche's passionate conviction that history which did not provide a spur to action was worse than useless. He saw academic history as the negation of life and its practitioners as "jaded idlers in the garden of knowledge." The Western world, and especially Germany, was, in Nietzsche's view, "suffering from a malignant historical fever."

History, for Nietzsche, contained both a promise and a threat; life needed "the service of history," but it was also true that "an excess of history hurts it." History was necessary to man in three ways: "in relation to his action and struggle, his conservatism and reverence, his suffering and his desire for deliverance."[1] (And it might be said that these were precisely the ways in which religion had served man until the Age of Reason.) Whoever had learned to find these great themes in history "must hate to see curious tourists and laborious beetle-hunters climbing up the great pyramids of antiquity," Nietzsche wrote. "He does not wish to meet the idler who is rushing through the picture galleries of the past for a new distraction of sensation, where he himself is looking for example and encouragement." Through history the tradition-oriented man "looks back to the origins of his existence with love and trust; through it he gives thanks for life." At the same time history threatened the future; consequently, "man must have the strength to break up the past, and apply it, too, in order to live."[2]

A good measure of Nietzsche's purest contempt is reserved for historians who profess "objectivity." The only true objectivity, for him, is the positive objectivity of the great artist. The historian will do well enough if he achieves a degree of justice. "Cold detachment" is trivial and lacking in moral feeling. "The unrestrained historical sense" with its proud skepticism, he noted, "uproots the future because it destroys illusions and robs existing things of the only atmosphere in which they can live." The historian who fancies himself as cool and precise as the physician or the engineer is a kind of murderer. His proper task, as a critical historian, is no more than "to leave the ground free for the hopeful living future to build its house. . . . For man is creative only through love and in the shadow of love's illusions. . . . The history that merely destroys," he wrote, "without any impulse to construct, will in the long run make its instruments tired of life. . . ."[3]

[1] *The Use and Abuse of History*, translated by Adrian Collins, introduction by Julius Kraft (New York: Liberal Arts Press; 1949), pp. 11, 12.
[2] Ibid., pp. 20, 25.
[3] Ibid., pp. 49, 50.

Nietzsche perceived that history had, in effect, sucked the life out of Christianity, and nowhere was this more apparent than in the Biblical criticism of the nineteenth century. What Nietzsche saw so clearly was a truth that academic history has tried consistently, and on the whole successfully, to ignore—that the vanity and presumption of historians in professing to speak the substantial truth about man, based on their "scientific" researches, was preparing the way for a day of judgment in which all of Western civilization would be involved. The gains assumed to follow from stripping man of the theological vestments that had so long concealed his nakedness were not unambiguous. There was much that theology said about man and much that it did for him that history, with all its grand pretensions, could not say or do. The problem would have been simple enough if, with the destruction of traditional society, historians had indeed been what they claimed to be—the objective interpreters of the past. Had they, by some alchemy, been able to stand outside time, they could, presumably, have identified the hideous deformities which were to be the shame of the twentieth century and thus made possible the creation of a future free of them. But they could not, and their pose of objectivity in most instances simply made them more vulnerable to the grosser prejudices of their time and their nation.

The conservative historians did far better in forecasting the future than their liberal rivals. They were in love with something relatively concrete—the past—and this love gave them an insight into the dangers of liberal Utopianism. Perhaps the most distinguished of these conservative historians was Jacob Burckhardt (1818–1897). The Swiss historian began by rejecting the idea of progress so dear to the nineteenth century and the first three decades of the twentieth. "Neither man's spirit nor his intellect has demonstrably improved in the period known to history," he wrote. For him Voltaire, with his cavalier attitude toward the great traditions of the past, was an "impudently ignorant mocker."

One of Burckhardt's most effective practical contributions to historical writing was his emphasis on the "style" of a particular period. Instead of making a routine inventory of the institutions, political developments, diplomacy, and so on, of each nation in successive eras, Burckhardt sought the "peculiar equilibrium" which gave a certain epoch its "hierarchy of values": the relationship of church and state, the quality of the cultural life, the curious "mix" that constitutes the distinctive character of a nation or an era.

Burckhardt was certain that if the historian could rise above the limits of partisan national history, above the personal and the temporal, the study of history might help to solve a part "of the great and grievous riddle of life."[4]

State, Religion, and Culture, in shifting equilibrium, were the elements that revealed the essential character of an epoch. Sometimes the State determined Culture and sometimes it was Culture which shaped the State. Religion might, equally, shape the State or the Culture. (Islam was Burckhardt's example of a State shaped by Religion, as Egypt was the most conspicuous example of a Culture moulded by the State, and Greece of the State determined by Culture.) Religion had been determined by Culture in late Latin and Byzantine Christianity and by the State in Russia, among other nations.

It was above all the crises of his own time, more particularly the invasion of France by Germany in 1870, that gave a sense of urgency to Burckhardt's reflections on history. The war threatened to accelerate the dominion of the State over the lives of modern men, and the State would, increasingly, undertake to define the boundaries between itself and Society, assuming more and more a moral tone inconsistent with its proper role.

Much as Burckhardt distrusted revolution, he praised crises because they gave birth to passion, which "is the

---

[4] *Force and Freedom: Reflections on History*, edited by James Hasting Nichols (New York: Pantheon Books; 1943), p. 88.

mother of great things. . . . Unsuspected forces awake in individuals and even heaven takes on a different hue." Since "all spiritual growth takes places by leaps and bounds, both in the individual and . . . in the community, the crisis is to be regarded as a new nexus of growth." Crises cleared the ground of "a host of institutions from which life has long since departed, and which, given their historical privilege, could not have been swept away in any other fashion." Crises also abolished the "cumulative dread of 'disturbance' " and cleared the way for "strong personalities." They brought into jaded and indifferent lives a new power to "know again what they love and what they hate, what is trivial and what is fundamental in life."[5]

As Burckhardt saw it from the perspective of the late nineteenth century, "all business [was] swelling into big business," and the businessman wished the State to be no more than the guarantor "of his interests and of his type of intelligence, henceforth assumed to be the main purpose of the world." The businessman wished to obtain possession of the State by constitutional "adjustments," but at the same time he showed a profound distrust for constitutional liberty, which he feared would be used by forces inimical to his interests. To Burckhardt, the events of 1870–1871 resulted in an "extraordinary intensification of money-making." He saw the best minds going into business, while art and science were in danger of becoming mere adjuncts of urban capitalism. Ulysses S. Grant, President of the United States, spoke for the new age when he proposed "one State and one language as the necessary goal of a purely money-making world."[6]

The Utopian optimism of the eighteenth-century Enlightenment had taken as its soul mate the entrepreneurship of the nineteenth, which made a religion out of making

[5] Ibid., pp. 289, 290.
[6] Ibid., p. 299.

money and dared to anticipate a future of ever increasing profits. Burckhardt was less sanguine. He rejected all systems and all notions of progress; he saw history as an intense, ultimately unfathomable, human drama in which great men often played a central role. Of the modern age, about which his feelings were so ambiguous, he wrote: "Time and the man enter into a great, mysterious covenant."

Burckhardt curtly rejected Hegel's system and spoke with scorn of Buckle's naïve astonishment at discovering that there was no evidence of moral progress in history: "If, even in bygone times, men gave their lives for each other, we have not progressed since."

Yet, contemplating the problem of Fortune and Misfortune in history, Burckhardt passed from the "question of good and evil fortune to that of the survival of the human spirit," and here he displayed the very optimism he was usually so suspicious of. The life of the individual "becomes self-conscious *in* and *through* history," he wrote, and this was the great and perpetually absorbing subject of all true historical study. The history of the "immediate future" might well, if man could penetrate it, reveal "one of the greatest chapters in the history of the human mind." A series of new crises seemed to be at hand. "The established political forms of the greatest civilized peoples" were "tottering or changing." With the spread of education and communication, "the realization and impatience of suffering" was "visibly and rapidly growing." Out of the chaos and disorder of a decaying world, it might well be that the "spirit of man [would] build its new dwelling."[7]

Wilhelm Dilthey (1833–1911), the German philosopher, who had been trained in the critical-historical school of Ranke, directed his fire primarily at the champions of scientific history. Dilthey insisted that historical study had noth-

---

[7] Ibid., pp. 307, 369–70.

ing to gain by borrowing methods from the natural sciences. The notion of the structural system was derived, Dilthey pointed out, not from external observations but from an inner sense of order. Therefore, to apply scientific notions to the study of man would be simply to transpose from nature a system outside the one which is given to us. "Consciousness cannot go behind itself."[8] True history was that which was discerned by the "living, artistic process of understanding," rather than by pseudoscientific methods. "What man is," Dilthey stated, "he learns not by rummaging about in himself, nor yet by psychological experiments, but by means of history." Dilthey might be numbered among the anti-Hegelians, for he was opposed to all efforts to go behind the facts of history to a single grand principle by which everything might be explained. If history had a meaning, it was a human meaning which was to be found in the concrete experiences of the race, not in the airy speculations of philosophers.

"We go forward with history," he wrote, "with an event in a far land or with something that is going on in the soul of a human being close to us. It reaches its fulfillment where the event has passed through the consciousness of the poet, the artist, or the historian, and now lies before us fixed and enduring in his work." It was in reliving a historical milieu or episode that a man enlarged his understanding and opened "a wide realm of possibilities which are not to hand in the determination of his actual life."[9]

Dilthey was convinced that the "genuinely historical" was that which engaged not merely the powers of mind but those "of the heart, of sympathy, of enthusiasm." Surrender of the self makes the "true born historian" into a mirror

---

[8] *Gesammelte Schriften*, V, 194, quoted in H. A. Hodges: *Wilhelm Dilthey, an Introduction* (London: Routledge and Kegan Paul; 1944), p. 45.
[9] *An Introduction*, pp. 122, 123.

which reflects the whole historical world. The German philosopher insisted, above all, on the irreconcilability of the multitude of historical facts and any concept which professed to comprehend that extraordinary richness. "No concept," he wrote, "exhausts the contents of these individual selves. Rather, the variety directly given in them can only be lived, understood, and described. . . . The method of the human studies involves the perpetual reciprocity of lived experience and concept. In the reliving of individual and collective structural systems the concepts of the human studies find their fulfillment, while conversely the immediate reliving itself is raised to systematic knowledge by the universal forms of thought."[1]

Nietzsche, Burckhardt, and Dilthey represented discordant voices in the nineteenth-century chorus of liberalism. Nietzsche demanded a special palate; Burckhardt's fame rested on his remarkable study of the Renaissance. Dilthey was virtually ignored outside Germany. To this day, only fragments of his work have been translated into English. The three men clearly stood outside the mainstream of nineteenth-century historical and philosophical thought.

---

[1] William Dilthey: *The Essence of Philosophy*, translated into English by Stephen A. and William T. Emery (Chapel Hill: University of North Carolina Press; 1954), p. 3.

7

The Theologians of Crisis

❀ ❀ ❀

Like social and political thought in the nineteenth and early twentieth centuries, Protestant theology was committed to a view of the universe that was optimistic, melioristic, progressive, rationalistic, and Utopian. The so-called "Social Gospel" emphasized the churches' responsibility for reform of intolerable social and economic conditions, and one of the foremost spokesmen of the Social Gospel, Walter Rauschenbusch, writing shortly after the turn of the century, spoke of the corruptions of modern life as being "so virulent that characters and reputations are collapsing all about us with sickening frequency."[1] The fault obviously lay in the system itself, which put a premium on the most

---

[1] *Christianity and the Social Crisis* (New York: Macmillan; 1907), p. 264.

ruthless forms of competition. "It pits men against one another in a gladiatorial game," Rauschenbusch wrote, "in
which there is no mercy and in which ninety per cent of
the combatants finally strew the arena. It makes Ishmaels
of our best men and teaches them that their hands must
be against every man, since every man's hand is against
them. . . . Men offer us goods on credit and dangle the small-
ness of the first instalment before our eyes as an incentive
to go into debt heedlessly. They try to break down the fore-
sight and self-restraint which are the slow product of moral
education, and reduce us to the moral habits of savages who
gorge today and fast tomorrow. Kleptomania multiplies. It
is the inevitable product of a society in which covetousness
is stimulated by all the ingenuity of highly paid specialists."[2]
Rauschenbusch went on to paint an alarming picture of the
breakdown of morality in the American business and professional world.

Too much of the country's time and energy and money
went into emulating the foolish extravagance of the wealthy,
to "keeping up the procession." The bonds of the community, the wholesomeness of family life, the springs of
religious faith all were corrupted by the system of competi-
tive capitalism. America and the Western Christian world
seemed to Rauschenbusch and his fellow Social Gospelers
to be standing at the crossroads, faced with decadence and
degeneration or reform and regeneration. "The Church,"
he wrote, "must either condemn the world and seek to
change it, or tolerate the world and conform to it." In the
latter case it must share the fate of a dying civilization. The
sin of mankind lay not so much in personal sin but in "the
very constitution of the present order." Repentance must be
repentance for "our social sins"; men must throw off the
spell which the existing system had "cast over our moral
judgment." Rauschenbusch challenged his readers to "see

---

[2] Ibid., p. 265.

through the fictions of capitalism." What was needed was individuals who set "justice above policy and profit" and possessed an "intellect emancipated from falsehood."[3]

In the coming "Messanic era," Christians with an awakened social consciousness would reform the economic system and its institutions until at last men lived in a society that conformed to the morality of Christ.

The Social Gospelers associated themselves with the secular reformers. Evil lay not so much in the individual as in the social system. If reason and justice were brought to bear on problems of social organization, a better, more moral, more equitable system must result. There was, among the Gospelers, very little sense of human limitation. By and large, they accepted a view of man that suggested almost limitless potentialities, and they were inclined to see the Christian religion less as a set of dogmas which promised, among other things, life eternal than as a moral yardstick against which human societies might be measured. However critical they were of the particular evils and abuses of the existing system, they were highly optimistic about the possibilities of reform, were decidedly world-centered, and had a serene confidence in human reason. They had little or nothing to say about history. In Rauschenbusch's influential book, history is not even mentioned in the extensive index. The attitude of the gospelers toward the past was hardly to be distinguished from that of secular liberals. Certainly the Social Gospelers gave no evidence of having a conception of history as a dramatic encounter between God and man, or of being conscious of any real dependence on Christ as Lord and Master of the Universe.

Because Rauschenbusch and his followers had no notion of historic man, they saw "only the individual acts of evil, dependent on the free decisions of the conscious personality." They believed that the great majority of individuals

---
[3] Ibid., pp. 350–1.

could "follow the demands of an integrated personal and social life by education, persuasion, and adequate institutions."[4]

Such was the general temper of the most active and progressive element in American Protestantism. On this *Zeitgeist* the crisis of World War I made remarkably little impression. In most intellectual quarters, optimism prevailed. "The Crusade of the Star-Spangled Banner" had, hopefully, made the world safe for democracy. The principle of the self-determination of nations had been established at American insistence. What was characterized, by a German philosopher who had fought in the war, as "the European Revolution" had small impact on the other side of the Atlantic. Americans first accepted the view that the war had been caused by the half-mad Kaiser Wilhelm; then they advanced to the somewhat more sophisticated (but no more accurate) position that it was the result of the machinations of an international cartel of weapons-makers. Both interpretations effectively concealed the fact that the war represented a profound crisis for the conscience of modern man: that the old order of nation states under joint European and American hegemony was obsolete; and that the liberal optimism which it had spawned was no longer adequate to describe the world and adumbrate the future of mankind.

In Europe a small group of theologians and Christian philosophers viewed the war as a crisis whose implications for the soul of modern man, and thus for Christian theology, could not be ignored. The crisis of the times demanded a "theology of crisis." And for these men the heart of this endeavor became the effort to recapture the essential elements of Christian faith. The various members of the group, who were shortly to diverge, shared the initial conviction that there is no salvation and no true knowledge of

---

[4] Paul Tillich: *The Protestant Era*, translated by James Luther Adams (University of Chicago Press, 1948), p. xx.

God "save in and through Jesus Christ." Man, as traditional Protestantism had insisted, was totally corrupt and could not raise himself except through the word of God, which came to man through Christ, "vertically from above." The disaster which had overtaken modern man, swollen with pride and full of self-will, was evidence that apart from God man could create only chaos.

As Paul Tillich has explained the origin of the movement, it was founded on the notion of *kairos*, the "fulness of time," which in its New Testament use describes the moment " in which the eternal breaks into the temporal, and the temporal is prepared to receive it." The great, unique historic moment at which this happened was the moment of the birth of Christ. This event cannot take place again in the same form, but there may be lesser manifestations of the eternal breaking through into the temporal, "creating centers of lesser importance on which the periodization of history is dependent." In other words, history is primarily the record of those dramatic occasions on which the "eternal breaks into the temporal" in the "fulness of time." If this is the case, then history is of critical importance for the theologian because he finds therein a continuing revelation of God. "The presence of such a dependent *kairos*," Tillich writes, "was felt by many people after the first World War." The *kairos* principle could not be accepted by Catholicism because of its profoundly conservative view of history; and it could not be accepted by the Christian sects because they looked eagerly toward the end of history. Only through Orthodox Protestantism, according to Tillich, was the "creative omnipresence of the divine in the course of history . . . concretely indicated." Protestantism, among other things, provided "a theonomous foundation for the creation of the new in history."[5] A corollary to the *kairos* was the idea of the demonic, "the mythical

---

[5] Ibid., pp. xviii–xx.

expression of a reality that was in the center of Luther's experience . . . namely the structural, and therefore inescapable, power of evil."

Good and evil were inextricably mixed in every human act. The potentiality for good was also the potentiality for evil. The theological reformers, who were soon identified as champions of Neo-Orthodoxy, attacked all naturalistic or mechanical interpretations of history. Indeed, they might be said to be the first theoreticians who spelled out the moral and philosophical implications of the then-fashionable schools of historical interpretation. Religion and philosophy must choose between history interpreted through nature and history interpreted through itself, that is, as possessing an "original reality" which cannot be derived from nature but which includes nature in itself. "And this choice," Tillich adds, "is the decision against or for Christianity." In other words, the individual's attitude toward history becomes a touchstone of the depth and sincerity of his Christian faith. The critique of Neo-Orthodoxy was extended to contemporary nationalism. Here "the gods of space revolt against the Lord of time. Nation, soil, blood, and race defy the idea of a world-historical development and a world-historical aim. . . . Christianity is essentially historical, while paganism is essentially nonhistorical."[6]

Tillich, in the late nineteen-thirties, summarized the Neo-Orthodox view of history as follows: "History is an independent and, finally, the outstanding category of interpreting reality. . . . Time is predominant against space. The movement of time is directed, has a definite beginning and end, and is moving toward an ultimate fulfillment. . . . Salvation is the salvation of a community from the evil powers *in* history *through* history. History is essentially 'history of salvation!'" It has a "turning-point or a center in which the meaning of history appears, overcoming the

------

[6] Ibid., pp. 17, 20.

self-destructive trend of the historical process and creating something *new*." God appears here "as the Lord of time controlling the universal history of mankind, acting in history and through history."[7]

These ideas are already familiar to us in somewhat different form in the writings of St. Augustine: the rejection of any cyclical interpretation of time; the notion of a beginning and an end and consequently of a direction in history; the idea of a single God and a single and universal history for all mankind; the insistence that history involves human as well as divine creativity (as Augustine put it, "it is possible for new things to happen which never happened before"). Thus Tillich was quite right when he spoke of having "reintroduced the problem of history into theological thought."

The consequence of naturalistic interpretations of history, the Neo-Orthodox thinker pointed out, was to limit the possibilities of historical development to non-human laws, which, even if not clearly understood by men, nevertheless controlled the circuits to the future. And, correspondingly, the consequence was to destroy any element of free will. The historians' lust for prediction was, in effect, a denial of human freedom. Only that which could be determined could be predicted. Tillich was enough of a German to respect the ideal of scientific objectivity, but he wished to see it wedded with "passionate self-interpretation and self-transformation" and, beyond that, "with a passionate understanding and transformation of the historical situation."[8] He wished to see historiography change history rather than describe or analyze it. In the same spirit in which the Social Gospelers had revolted against a religion concerned only with individual salvation in a world full of corruption and injustice, seeking to use religion to change the social system,

---

[7] Ibid., pp. 26–7.
[8] Ibid., pp. 74–5.

the Neo-Orthodox wished to use "historical realism" to change history.

The Russian philosopher Nikolay Berdyaev independently followed a line which, at least as it related to history, was similar to that of Tillich and the advance guard of Neo-Orthodoxy. Berdyaev pointed out that in periods when the human spirit had been "wholly and organically" contained in some "fully matured and settled epoch" the problem of the meaning of history did not arise. People found a meaning to life in the established customs and traditions of their society. Stability and security turned their attention away from the profounder questions of human existence.

Berdyaev discerned three stages of historical consciousness. The first was an unself-conscious "organic experience in some settled historical order"; the second was marked by "schism and disruption when the foundations of an established order are tottering." The second produces both a historical sense and a sense of separation between the individual and the historical process. Such a period may see the development of historical science, but it is likely also to see in most men the development of a sense of schism between themselves as subjects and as objects. The temptation is overwhelming to treat history as an object rather than as a creative process.

In the third stage, under the catastrophic social and political conditions attending "the collapse of a given historical order," the human spirit is sometimes able to combine the earlier power of total involvement in the historical process itself—a stage of pre-Adamic historical innocence in which the deeper currents of history are experienced but not rationalized—with the objective and scientific temper of the second spirit, thereby achieving a "depth and . . . penetration into the mysteries of history."[9] It was this last stage that Berdyaev hopefully anticipated.

---

[9] *Meaning of History* (London: Geoffrey Bles; 1936), pp. 2–5.

Man was, to Berdyaev, "in the highest degree an historical being." Between man and history there existed such "a deep, mysterious primordial and coherent relationship, such a concrete interdependence, that a divorce between them is impossible." To detach man from history and consider him abstractly, as the psychologists and sociologists seemed bent on doing, was as impossible as "to detach history from man and to examine it from without, that is, from a non-human point of view." In order to understand history, it was necessary "to situate oneself within historical destiny." History, Berdyaev asserted, in words that echoed Dilthey, "is not a given empirical fact or a naked factual material. . . . It can, however, be approached through the historical memory."[1] Like Tillich, Berdyaev saw "the closed circle of terrestrial reality . . . invaded by the energies of a higher plane." History, he insisted, was "not an endless development in time," nor was it subject to natural law. Rather, the destiny of man involved "a super-historical goal, a super-historical consummation of history in eternal time."[2] The moment had come when celestial history must be reintegrated with terrestial history.

In the works of the theologians who took up the banner of Neo-Orthodoxy, history continued to play a prominent role. The leading American exponent of Neo-Orthodoxy was Reinhold Niebuhr, who, in a series of books published from the mid-thirties on, developed with great skill and persuasiveness many of the ideas of the continental theologians. But Niebuhr did not by any means simply import European ideas. He made major contributions to the doctrines of Neo-Orthodoxy and, like Tillich, he placed great emphasis on the relationship of Christianity to history. In *Faith and History* Niebuhr gave a detailed critique of the secular views of history, pointing out that they erred in

---

[1] Ibid., pp. 15–17.
[2] Ibid., pp. 205–6.

offering either too extravagant or too mechanical an esti-
mate of human freedom. At the end of the book Niebuhr
stated the Christian credo: the history of man was comparable to his individual life; "he does not have the power
and wisdom to overcome the ambiguity of his existence. He
must and does increase his freedom, both as an individual
and in the total human enterprise; and his creativity is enhanced by the growth of his freedom. But this freedom
tempts him to deny his mortality. . . . Evils in history are
the consequence of this pretension. Confusion follows upon
man's effort to complete his life by his own power and solve
its enigma by his own wisdom." Yet, to understand "that
man cannot complete his own life, and can neither define
nor fulfill the final mystery and meaning of his historical
pilgrimage," was not, Niebuhr insisted, "to rob life of meaning or responsibility." History remains open to "all possibilities of good and evil to the end."[3]

In the *Irony of American History*, Niebuhr applied his
concept of history to the American past and present. The
United States, he argued, was a perfect case of the paradoxes and contradictions inherent in claiming wisdom,
goodness, and progress as part of the historical process or
as the unique achievement of a particular people. To Niebuhr, America was a "vivid symbol of the spiritual perplexi-
ties of modern man, because the degree of American power
tends to generate illusions to which a technocratic culture
is already too prone." By equating the mastery of nature
with the mastery of human destiny, such a culture invites
chastisement. The field of American foreign policy provided an ideal subject for Niebuhr's analysis. The American
notion that rectitude and good will were sufficient armor
in which to venture into the arena of international power
politics was typical of a nation that saw the world in simple

---

[3] *Faith and History: A Comparison of Christian and Modern Views of History* (New York: Charles Scribner's Sons; 1949), pp. 233–5.

tones of black and white. Our "moral and spiritual complacency" led us to insist self-righteously on a peace treaty at the end of World War I which did much to make World War II inevitable; it induced us to impose on the defeated Japanese and Germans after World War II a policy of perpetual defenselessness which we were promptly forced to rescind over the protests of many Japanese and Germans. It encouraged us to mistake the nature and the significance of Russian Communism. Such naïve errors might have been avoided, Niebuhr suggests, if Americans had understood better that the "ironic view of human evil in history [is] the normative one." Indeed, we would have a better insight into the course of history in general if we realized that unfavorable events (such as the triumph of Communism in China) are not necessarily the result of weakness or conspiracy. If the folk wisdom that the road to hell is paved with good intentions were projected onto the stage of world history, we would have a better comprehension of the true nature of the historical process. Not only is the future not, in any human sense, determined, Niebuhr insisted, but there is no prospect that man can control its course through the refinement of his reason.

In *The Self and the Dramas of History*, which appeared in 1955, Niebuhr related the "self" to the great historical eras. A study of history, he suggested, would enlarge the self's knowledge of its true nature and provide the best possible therapy for demoralized and anguished souls. In the same way, the national community would be able to make its best contributions to the development of a world culture "as it is purged of its illusions by the experiences of history."[4]

Paul Tillich disqualified Catholic theologians as serious contributors to a theology of history because the Roman

---

[4] *The Self and the Dramas of History* (New York: Charles Scribner's Sons; 1955), p. 216.

Church lacked a notion of *kairos*, but the Church refused to accept this summary exile. The distinguished Catholic philosopher Jacques Maritain advanced some highly perceptive ideas about a Christian philosophy of history. Maritain pointed out that "the entire *intellectual* disposition of the subject (the historian) plays an indispensable part in the attainment of historical truth; a situation which is at total variance with scientific objectivity, where all that pertains to the subjective dispositions of man . . . disappears or should disappear." The historian in consequence must have "a sound philosophy of man, an integrated culture, an accurate appreciation of the human being's various activities and their comparative importance, a correct scale of moral, political, religious, technical and artistic values." The value, or "the *truth*," of the historical work, Maritain declared, must be "in proportion to the human richness of the historian."[5]

To Maritain, the philosophy of history was part of moral philosophy. Human understanding advances from experience through philosophy of nature to metaphysics, then back through moral philosophy and finally through history to philosophy of history. "We cannot think of the philosophy of history as separated from philosophy in general," he wrote. "It deals with exemplifications of general truths established by philosophy, which it sees embodied in a most singular and contingent manner. . . . It is because the philosophy of history is the final return of philosophical knowledge to the individual and the contingent that it is absolutely impossible for it to have the same degree of certitude as metaphysics."[6]

History, to be sure, had a direction, determined to a degree "by the immense dynamic mass of the past pushing it

---

[5] *On the Philosophy of History*, edited by Joseph W. Evans (New York: Charles Scribner's Sons; 1957), pp. 6, 7, 8.
[6] Ibid., p. 19.

forward, but undetermined with regard to specific orientations and with regard to the spirit or the manner in which a change, necessary in other respects, will be carried into existence."

Like Tillich and Niebuhr, Maritain believed that "a genuine philosophy of history . . . does not claim to dismantle the cogs and gear-wheels of human history so as to see how it works and master it intellectually. History . . . is not a problem to be solved, but a mystery to be looked at: a mystery which is in some way supra-intelligible . . . and in some way infra-intelligible. . . . Analogically, the philosophy of history does not *explain* history."[7]

Maritain, who saw a number of laws in history, made a useful distinction between "necessary laws"—those which pose problems that are open to free solution—and "necessitating laws," those which are determined and thus deprive the human actors in history of any element of free will. As Maritain puts it: "It is not by trying in vain to make itself into a pseudo-science; it is by integrating itself with a true system of human, moral and cultural values, in other words, by orienting itself toward philosophy, or by philosophically maturing, that history reaches its full typical dimensions *qua* history, and is real history." Maritain considers it "normal for the historian to have a yearning for, and a leaning toward, the philosophy of history . . ."[8]

In England the English historian Herbert Butterfield wrote on *Christianity and History*, arguing that "it is the combination of the history with a religion or with something equivalent to a religion, which generates power and fills the story with significance." To Butterfield, as to the proponents of Neo-Orthodoxy, "our final interpretation of history is the most sovereign decision we can take. . . . It is our decision about religion, about our total attitude to

[7] Ibid., pp. 27, 31.
[8] Ibid., p. 169.

things, and about the way we will appropriate life. And it is inseparable from our decision about the role we are going to play ourselves in that very drama of history."[9]

Butterfield asserted that, as modern men, we create "tragedy after tragedy for ourselves by a lazy unexamined doctrine of man . . . which the study of history does not support. . . . It is essential not to have faith in human nature." Butterfield, as a practicing historian, went on to point out that since man has to have "a religion," a loyalty to some value or system of ideas or principles, call it what he will, a devotion to the Christian faith offered the wisest and most exalted perspective possible for the historian. "We can do worse," he declared at the end of his book, "than remember a principle which both gives us a firm Rock and leaves us the maximum elasticity for our minds: the principle: Hold to Christ, and for the rest be totally uncommitted."[1]

All the Christian theorists, lay or clerical, who took the new view of history were at pains to attack one of the dominant heresies of the nineteenth century (seen in its most rigid and cruel form in Marxism), the idea that there was to be fulfillment *in* history, that the religious, or social or political, millennium would come in time, rather than at the end of time or outside of time.

Karl Löwith wrote *Meaning in History* to prove that there was no meaning in the historical process itself and that such meaning as it had came from the outside, that is, from God. Maritain, the Catholic, spoke for the whole company of modern theologians concerned with history when he declared: "We will never have the Kingdom of God within temporal history." At the same time, with the exception of the followers of Karl Barth, most of them affirmed the

---

[9] *Christianity and History* (New York: Charles Scribner's Sons; 1950), p. 25.

[1] Ibid., pp. 46–7, 146.

importance of striving toward the Kingdom, that is, they affirmed the relevance of the Christian's faith to man's terrestrial condition.

Herbert Butterfield can be taken to ratify the new concensus on the relation of Christianity and history. If our modern sense of history is, as I have suggested earlier, a product of the Judeo-Christian view of time, the reintroduction of a classic Christian view of the historical process was an event of considerable moment. Christian theology, or what passed for it in the nineteenth century, had been so infiltrated by Enlightenment ideas and, as far as history itself was concerned, by Hegelian idealism, which professed to absorb traditional Christianity, that it required a considerable effort of the imagination and the will to throw off this accumulated residue of secular thought. Indeed, it is hard to think of a more significant episode in modern intellectual history. The effects were soon felt far beyond the area of Christian dogmatics. A new vocabulary appeared in the writings of the more alert and responsive critics; some of it even invaded historical sanctuaries. Such words as *ambiguity, complexity, paradox, mystery, irony, ambivalence*, and *dilemma* replaced the old liberal vocabulary. Arthur Schlesinger, Jr., who emerged after World War II as one of the most conspicuous liberal critics and historians, sprinkled his books and essays with the new vocabulary and acknowledged his debt to Reinhold Niebuhr, although he rejected orthodox Christianity, while the so-called "New Conservatives," a group of feckless young intellectuals, exploited the language and the insights of Neo-Orthodoxy in an effort to establish a conservative political credo.

8

The Philosophers and History

❀ ❀ ❀

The attitude of philosophers toward history was distinguished by no such self-conscious break with tradition as marked history's emergence in the field of theology. We have already seen in Wilhelm Dilthey the beginning of a revolt against the rigid formulas of Hegelianism. In Italy, Benedetto Croce took up Dilthey's ideas and offered a kind of modified Hegelianism that proved most seductive. The Italian philosopher insisted that history recorded the progress of the spirit, or, more specifically, of human liberty. All genuine history is contemporary history—because, "however remote in time events there recounted may seem to be, the history in reality refers to present needs and present situations wherein those events vibrate." Any notion of necessity, "causal or transcendent" is flatly rejected. Neither

material nor technological forces nor divine power determines the course of history, but man alone. "On a par with
causality, the transcendental God is a stranger to human
history, which would exist if God did not exist; for History
is its own mystic Dionysius, its own suffering Christ, re-
deemer of sins."[1]

Historical judgment, Croce argued, is not "a variety of
knowledge but . . . knowledge itself; it is the form which
completely fills and exhausts the field of knowing, leaving
no room for anything else." Philosophy was absorbed by
history at precisely the moment when it came under historical criticism. Since its "claim to autonomy was founded
on its metaphysical character," it lost its independent position and became simply the history of philosophy, a branch
of historiography, as soon as it was seen to have a historical
life. Whereas history had once been considered subordinate
to philosophy, it was now evident that history "not only is
superior to philosophy but annihilates it."

The philosophers' unacceptable pretension was to think
outside of particular occasions, or rather to have the illusion
that they did so, but "every serious history and every serious philosophy" must grow out of the particular circumstances of the historian's or philosopher's own time. Each
must be, like poetry, rooted in the passions and crises of
the day.[2]

Croce saw man as a product of the past, "immersed in
the past." Yet at the same time he was obliged to move
toward a future. The only way he could do this was to write
history. This was "the one way of way of getting rid of the
past," by making the past serve the present. Historical
thought, Croce wrote, "transforms [the past] into its own
material and transfigures it into its object. . . ."

---

[1] *History as the Story of Liberty* (New York: Meridian Books; 1955),
pp. 17, 18.
[2] Ibid., pp. 30, 33–4.

Liberty is "on the one hand the explanatory principle of the course of history, and on the other the moral idea of humanity." Whether the age was "propitious or unfavourable, liberty appeared as abiding purely and invincibly and even consciously only in a few spirits."[3]

When Croce declared that "history is in all of us and . . . its sources are in our own breasts," he made the critical point that history is not something "objective," something "out there," about which we speculate and about which we reach certain scientific conclusions. His writings on history gave new life to nineteenth-century Hegelianism and to its stepchild, historical relativism.

Ortega y Gasset, the Spanish philosopher, acknowledged Dilthey as his intellectual father. In classic Existential terms, Ortega announced that man had not a "nature" but a history. All that he was was comprehended in his history. History was his meaning and his destiny. Ortega sounded very much like Croce when he insisted that "if . . . there is a past, it must be as something present, something active in us now. And, in effect, if we analyze what we are now . . . we find . . . that this life of ours that is always . . . the life of the present, actual moment is *composed* of what, personally or collectively, we have been. . . . The past is man's moment of identity, his only element of the thing: nothing besides is inexorable and fatal. . . . Let us say . . . not that man *is*, but that he *lives*."[4]

Ortega shared with Croce a fundamental belief in spiritual progress and celebrated with him the "illimitableness of possibilities that characterizes one who has no nature" and "only one limit: the past." In this Ortega made a valiant effort to retrieve the principal idea of the Enlightenment —the limitless potentiality of man. He also sought to re-

---

[3] Ibid., pp. 42, 57, 59.
[4] Ortega y Gasset: *Toward a Philosophy of History* (New York: W. W. Norton; 1941), pp. 212-13.

establish reason as historical reason, a reason chastened by the impenetrable mystery of the past. The effect was to make history far more open-ended than the Neo-Orthodox theologians would concede it to be. To them, man had a nature as well as a history, and the essential drama of life was to be found in the unending conflict between that nature on the one hand and the divine imperatives, manifested in time, on the other. This being the case, man could, indeed, be once more what he had been before. He could make the same errors, suffer the same disasters. In this sense at least, history was clearly not irreversible. To say that "man is history" was as blasphemous as to say man was God; in fact, it was the same thing. To call man, as Ortega did, "a substantial emigrant on a pilgrimage of being," was to beg the question of where he was going and to assign to history a power it had never revealed.

According to Ortega, if the modern man, armed with historical reason, asks himself "why his life is thus and not otherwise," it will appear to him at once that aside from a few chance elements "the broad lines of its reality [are] perfectly comprehensible . . . because . . . the society—'collective man'—in which he lives is thus." History might therefore be seen as "a system, the system of human experiences linked in a single, inexorable chain." What man needed was a "new revelation" and this new revelation, Ortega was convinced, was history. Man, alienated from the past, and finding the successive revelations of religion and science no longer meaningful, was "brought up against himself as reality, as history," not God, not science, but historical reason was the proud arbiter of human destiny.[5]

Since few American scholars read any language but English with fluency, the ideas of Dilthey, Croce, and Ortega were slow in penetrating the American consciousness—although Croce and Ortega fared better than their master.

[5] Ibid., pp. 221, 230.

A further impediment to the spread in the United States of the doctrines of these three philosophers was undoubtedly the preference of American scholars for rather simple forms of empiricism, of which they found a ready supply in Great Britain. Moreover, a basic intellectual conservatism, evident throughout American history, has made us content to import most seminal European ideas a generation or more after they have circulated on the other side of the Atlantic.

Unquestionably, the persistence of the English philosophical tradition of empiricism and its domination well into the present century, as well as the rise of the school of F. H. Bradley, with its particular form of idealism, delayed the acceptance of Dilthey and his followers in England and, in consequence, in America. R. G. Collingwood, professor of philosophy at Oxford, is the man most responsible for introducing into the Anglo-American scholarly community the idea of history as the proper if not the primary preoccupation of philosophy. Collingwood wrote in *The Idea of History* that "history occupies in the world of today a position analogous to that occupied by physics in the time of Locke: it is recognized as a special and autonomous form of thought, lately established, whose possibilities have not yet been completely explored." The work which the so-called sciences of human nature professed to do could only be done, Collingwood maintained, by history. The task of the historian was to discover the thoughts which have motivated the events of the past. And there was, to Collingwood, only one way in which the historian could do this: "by re-thinking them in his own mind. . . . The history of thought, and therefore all history, is the reenactment of past thoughts in the historian's own mind." The characterization of *all* history as the history of thought will strike the practicing historian as an excessively idealistic as well as arbitrary concept, and the notion that the historian can ever re-enact past thought except in a very crude sense will seem equally Utopian.[6]

Collingwood echoes Croce in his statement that "by historical thinking, the mind whose self-knowledge is history not only discovers within itself those powers of which historical thought reveals the possession, but actually develops those powers from a latent to an actual state, brings them into effective existence."[7] (If we were to change "historical thinking" into "historical reasoning," the formula would hardly be distinguishable from that of Ortega y Gasset.) Man is only rational, Collingwood admits, "in a flickering and dubious manner," but what he does have, in place of rationality, is an awareness of himself as a historical creature. Here Collingwood, like Croce and Ortega y Gasset, is again distinguished from the theologians whom we have discussed because of his determination to substitute history for the older, absolute categories. And it must seem to the layman that in so doing he muddies the waters of historical thought far more than he clarifies them. Moreover, Collingwood suggests that the process by which the historian thinks himself back into the mind of an earlier age may be carried out independent of the prejudices of the historian's own day. Indeed, it can be argued that since there is no greater reality than the historian's own era, the problem of "objectivity" ceases to exist, at least in the traditional sense in which the question is usually debated. If the proper methods of inquiry are followed, what results is not "objectivity" certainly, but an accurate representation of the modes of thought of the past. Consequently, if we may here extrapolate from Croce and Ortega y Gasset, contemporary history supplies answers to the particular questions which are most urgent at that particular moment in time and which are therefore as true for that time as any truth can be for any

---

[6] *The Idea of History* (Oxford University Press; 1946), pp. 209, 215.
[7] Ibid., p. 226.

time. Meanwhile, this process of recapitulation deepens the historian's awareness and in turn that of his contemporaries—the politicians and statesmen who direct the course of events or actualize thought, as we might better put it— and increases freedom (Croce) and historical reason (Ortega y Gasset).

The instrument by which this recovery of the past is to take place is the historical imagination. The historical imagination, therefore, is a most appropriate subject for investigation by philosophers. This a priori imagination is characteristic of the novelist as well as the historian, each of whom "makes it his business to construct a picture which is partly a narrative of events, partly a description of situations, exhibition of motives, analysis of character. Each aims at making his picture a coherent whole, where every character and every situation is so bound up with the rest that this character in this situation cannot but act in this way, and we cannot imagine him acting otherwise."[8]

Historical thinking is the means by which philosophers and historians should attempt to provide the "innate idea of the past with detailed content," thus strengthening the hold of history over men's minds and, by increasing its power, increasing the power of men over their own society. Yet, on the subject of progress and improvement Collingwood is inconclusive. It is possible but not necessary.

This is not the place to undertake an extended critique of Croce, Ortega y Gasset, and Collingwood, but it might be well to emphasize the relevance of Paul Weiss's charge that these heirs of Dilthey deny, in effect, "that a history makes reference to an objective, past, historic world." Croce and his followers, Weiss argues, speak of "monuments, documents, and histories as though they were ideas to be used in some subsequent history." Such an approach to the past tends to flatten out the historic world by ignoring the

---

[8] Ibid., p. 245.

role of the crisis events which, in reality, shape history. Just as Freud would absorb all of history in nature, Croce would absorb all philosophy in history, a prescription which, it may be suspected, would serve history as poorly as it would serve philosophy. If Collingwood did nothing else, he provided an entry for the ideas of Dilthey and Croce into England and founded a school of philosophy at Oxford which continued to examine the nature of historical knowledge. W. H. Walsh, Fellow and Tutor of Merton College, wrote a modest *Introduction to Philosophy of History* which reviewed philosophical thinking about history with special emphasis on Collingwood, and two of Walsh's students, Patrick Gardiner (*The Nature of Historical Explanation*) and William Dray (*Laws and Explanation in History*) carried on further examinations of the historian's function. It was Gardiner's unexceptional if painstaking conclusion that "there are no absolute Real Causes waiting to be discovered by historians with sufficiently powerful magnifying glasses. . . . The search for the Grail of Real Causes ends —in bad metaphysics."[9] Gardiner makes a good case for his contention that the supposed distinction between materialistic and idealistic interpretations of history is illusory. They are simply different perspectives or different ways of explaining the same event: "explanations in terms of reasons given, plans or policies adopted, principles followed, are likewise distinct from causal explanations."[1] The effect is to undermine Collingwood's own theory that the historian is concerned only with past thoughts. The world, Gardiner states reasonably enough, is made up of matter and of mind working on each other. Neither materialism nor idealism therefore can presume to give us an adequate explanation of the historical process.

---

[9] *The Nature of Historical Explanation* (University of Oxford Press; 1955), pp. 109, 110.
[1] Ibid., p. 139.

One of the most vigorous movements in philosophy after World War I came to be comprehended under the name *Existentialism*. Categories are, admittedly, dangerous things. Once they have been created, it is difficult to avoid them and easy to become their victim. This is certainly true of Existentialism. While most of the theologians whom we have discussed might be called Christian Existentialists, the movement, in its non-Christian aspects, is associated primarily with a group of German philosophers who traced their intellectual lineage to Nietzsche. Edmund Husserl was the modern father of this school, which went from Martin Heidegger to Karl Jaspers. In France, Jean-Paul Sartre, who as a student in Germany had attended Husserl's lectures, became after World War II the most famous exponent of Existentialism. Among French philosophers, Gabriel Marcel and Emmanuel Mounier were the foremost champions of Christian Existentialism. The principal doctrines of Existentialism did not initially incline it to a particularly sympathetic attitude toward history. Existentialist philosophers rejected any kind of systemization which, in their view, robbed man of his humanity. Being, as Mounier has expressed it, "is an 'inexhaustible concretion' which cannot be defined, but can only be recognized, in the same way that a person is recognized, or, perhaps, it would be better to say 'greeted' rather than recognized."[2] To try to *know* a thing, to attempt to *understand* it completely, is to kill it. The Existentialists generally shared Nietzsche's anxiety about formal history which obscured the living present under a dead weight of pedantry. They opposed the history of individuals to the history of the world and, whatever their views of formal history (in Sartre, complete unimportance; in Jaspers, considerable attention), they were avowed enemies of any deterministic notion of history, even the notion of history as the progressive freedom of man-

---

[2] *Existential Philosophies* (New York: Macmillan; 1949), p. 13.

kind. History might reveal a particular conception of man, but "it must be a conception which acknowledges the superiority of man over history."[3]

Like the theology of crisis, modern Existentialism was born of the ruins of a complacent and secure nineteenth century. It tried to explain, or at least to call to the attention of philosophers, a world that was very much out of joint, a suffering, despairing world far different from that which the Idealists and Romantics of earlier generations professed to see. Among the leaders of Existentialism, Karl Jaspers has perhaps made the most concentrated study of history. His *Origin and Goal of History*, published in Germany in 1949 and in the United States four years later, is divided into three sections: World History, Present and Future, and The Meaning of History.

In place of the Son of God, who stood at the axis of world history as seen by Christian theology, Jaspers offers an "Axial Period," between 800 and 200 B.C., when "man as we know him today came into being." This was the "overwhelmingly fruitful" point in history which gave rise to "a common frame of historical self-consciousness for all peoples—for the West, for Asia, and for all men on earth —without regard to particular articles of faith." It marked the end of the mythical age and the beginning of the spiritualization of humanity. Philosophers and men of speculative thought appeared not only in Greece but in Persia and in Israel, in the persons of the prophets Confucius and Lao-tse in China, Zarathustra in Persia, Gautama Buddha in India, and King Numa in Rome. As a consequence, human existence became "the object of meditation, as *history*."[4]

Like his fellow Existentialists, Jaspers insisted on the unique in history: "The more decisive the uniquely single,

---

[3] Mounier: *Existential Philosophies*, p. 106.
[4] *The Origin and Goal of History* (New Haven: Yale University Press; 1953), pp. 1–5.

the less identical repetition there is, the more authentic is history." He looked to history to express the unity of mankind and predicted that it would "cease to be a mere field of knowledge, and become once again a question of the consciousness of life and existence; it will cease to be an affair of aesthetic culture, and become the earnestness of hearing and response."[5] Man found his home in history: "He who cannot give himself an account of three thousand years is left without landmarks in the dark, and can live only from day to day." In common with the theologians of crisis, Jaspers saw World War I as the turning point of modern history. "After the First World War," he wrote, "it was no longer the sunset glow merely of Europe [which Kierkegaard and Nietzsche had discerned more than half a century before] but of all the cultures of the earth. An end of mankind, a recasting from which no people and no man was exempt—whether it was to annihilation, or to rebirth —could be felt. It was still not the end itself; but the knowledge of its possible imminence became prevalent."[6]

It was, according to Jaspers, the particular destiny of the West to develop modern science and technology. The consequence threatened to be "the metamorphosis of [Western man's] whole existence into a technically perfect piece of machinery and of the planet into a single great factory." In the process, Jaspers wrote, modern man "has been and is being deprived of all roots. He is becoming a dweller on earth with no home. He is losing the continuity of tradition. The spirit is being reduced to the learning of facts and training for utilitarian functions."[7] One consequence of the technological revolution has been to make history a technological subject and thus to destroy its power over man. Another by-product has been the destruction of genuine

---

[5] Ibid., pp. 243, 266.
[6] Ibid., pp. 271, 232.
[7] Ibid., p. 98.

communities and the creation of masses that can be swayed by ideologies. As for the demand of the more radical social scientists to know or to manage the future, Jaspers declares that the unknown character of the future is "the most compelling element in our lives. . . . To know the future would be the death of our souls."[8] Like Croce, Jaspers saw freedom as an essential goal of history. Freedom, or liberty, is present when we live in a healthy tension between antitheses and choose, out of the infinite variety and mutability of historical situations, the one which will become our path to the future. ("To be human means to be free; to become specifically human is the meaning of history. History is man's advance toward liberty through the cultivation of faith.")[9] The true task of man is to live in the area of historical possibilities, to see the open world. Again in Jasper's words: "The echo from history, which lends wings to our intercourse with our ancestors as far back as the origin of the human race, is their quest for freedom, the fashion in which they realized freedom, the forms in which they discovered and desired it. We recognize ourselves in what men were capable of, and what they say to us out of their historical reality."[1]

Jasper's words recall Dilthey and serve to redefine a vein in European philosophical thought which spans three quarters of a century. Man known through the concrete reality of historical being, rather than the abstract man of the sociologists and the psychologists—this man is the primary concern of the philosopher.

It should not be thought that the historians who hankered after science were without support in the ranks of the philosophers. The logical positivists, whose stronghold after World War I was Vienna, rallied to the defense of history

---

[8] Ibid., p. 151.
[9] Ibid., pp. 155, 187.
[1] Ibid., p. 220.

as a science. Once the claim had been advanced by Croce
and Collingwood that history pre-empted philosophy and
was not subject to scientific techniques of investigation and
analysis, the positivists had to engage the enemy or retire
from the field. They showed characteristic ingenuity in
their counter-attack. Champions of logic, they strained it
to its limits to prove that historiography was susceptible of
scientific treatment.

When the historian functioned properly, they maintained, he was unconsciously "subsuming what is to be
explained under a general law," sometimes referred to as
"regularity analysis." The Austrian philosopher Karl Popper, who emerged as the leader of the positivists, expressed
his central doctrine in these words: "To give a *causal explanation* of a certain event means to derive deductively a
statement (it will be called a *prognosis*) which describes
that event, using as premises of the deduction some *universal laws* together with certain singular or specific sentences
which we may call *initial conditions*." The initial conditions
are generally taken as "the *cause* of the event in question
and the prognosis (or rather, the event described by the
prognosis) as the effect."[2] Popper's concern is to make
history more scientific "by insisting on rigorous logical
standards for what may count as explanation." His book
The Poverty of Historicism was directed against a nineteenth-century version of history which stressed the immuta-
bility of historical laws, a view which had been rejected by
Croce and Collingwood, and earlier by Dilthey. Popper's
strictures are thus directed against Comte and John Stuart
Mill; he does not even mention Croce, Ortega y Gasset,
and Collingwood, the three principal modern figures associated with the more recent versions of historical idealism.

Professor C. G. Hempel in an article entitled "The Func-

[2] *The Open Society and Its Enemies* (London: G. Routledge & Sons;
1952), II, p. 262.

tion of General Laws in History"[3] has carried Popper's arguments somewhat further. The historian, trying to justify his apparently hopelessly makeshift procedures, uses an "explanation sketch." The sketch "consists of a more or less vague indication of the laws and initial conditions considered as relevant, and it needs 'filling out' in order to turn into a full-fledged explanation. This filling out requires further empirical research, for which the sketch suggests the direction." In other words, what is required is greater precision on the part of the historian, or perhaps a historian assisted by a logical positivist to point out his sloppiness and his logical deficiencies. The conclusion (and this is Popper's too) is that there are no such things as historical explanations. The explanations that historians give, "to the extent that they are acceptable explanations, must be scientific ones." However, as Dray indicates, this point is won at the cost of stretching the notion of universal laws—of what the author calls "covering law models"—so far that they cease to have much meaning, at least for the practicing historian. And while the philosopher may find some comfort in drawing history by such means into the realm of science, the stunt has little relevance for the working historian, however dazzling the mental processes by which it has been accomplished.

To the layman, sampling the literature of the various philosophical controversies over history, it rather seems as though the principal subject of philosophical discourse for some years has been the question of how (and why) the historian was doing his job. There is, surely, something comic in the spectacle of this heated debate being carried on by philosophers while professional historians proceed with their familiar monographic exercises, quite oblivious of

---

[3] Reprinted in *Readings in Philosophical Analysis*, edited by Herbert Feigl and Wilfred Sellars (New York: Appleton-Century-Crofts; 1949), pp. 459–71.

the storm that has blown up about them in philosophic circles.

While the Idealists, the Existentialists, and the Positivists contended over the nature of history, a philosopher-historian who could not be placed with confidence in any camp undertook to write history which might shed light on the course of man's progress by reference to the great events of Western history. Eugen Rosenstock-Huessy was one of those Europeans who at the end of World War I decided that the war had made the familiar categories of thought obsolete. He undertook, in a series of books and articles, to illuminate the relation between history and experience and to explicate the progress of man through history toward a common future. And whereas many men at this time wrote *about* the new concept of history, Rosenstock-Huessy undertook to write history under this imperative. In *Die Hochzeit des Krieges and Revolution*, published by the Patmos Press in 1920, he put forth his thesis that with World War I war and revolution had become one and that henceforth the most basic assumptions of the prewar West must be rethought in the light of this universal cataclysm. In the years that followed, Huessy continued to explore the relation of history to the life of the individual. *Die Europäischen Revolutionen*, which appeared in 1931, developed his ideas more fully, and in 1938, after he had come to America as a refugee from Nazi Germany, he published *Out of Revolution: Autobiography of Western Man*. This book, full of extraordinary insights, was virtually ignored by the historical guild, still largely under the sway of Marxian or other deterministic concepts of history.

"Our passions give life to the world. Our collective passions constitute the history of mankind," Huessy declared in his preface to *Out of Revolution*. Any political effort had to single out "the peculiar human passion which, at that moment in history, will create unanimity and coherence among men. . . . When a nation or individual declines the experiences that present themselves to passionate hearts only, they are automatically turned out from the realm of history. The heart of man either falls in love with somebody or something, or it falls ill. It can never go unoccupied. And the great question for mankind is what is to be loved or hated next, whenever an old love or fear has lost its hold."

Man's social customs were, to Huessy, "the fruit of [the] sufferings which reshape our ways of life. The Body Politic as well as the cellular body is the reward of the sacrifices which our heart has paid for its privileges to love." Huessy had chosen as his topic "the creation of mankind," and the inspiration for it had come directly out of his own experience in the war. Europe had tried to forget World War I, he wrote, but this was impossible. "A great new event is more than an additional paragraph to be inserted in the next edition of a book. It rewrites history, it simplifies history, it changes the past because it initiates a new future. . . . Men who did not long for a new history of mankind after the World War showed thereby that they were withered leaves of the tree of humanity. Their souls had been killed in the World War."[4]

The revolutions of mankind, Huessy wrote, "create new time-spans for our life on earth. They give man's soul a new relation between present, past, and future; and by doing so they give us time to start our life on earth all over again, with a new rhythm and a new faith." This is the framework for Huessy's history of Europe and it may safely be said to be the first historical work written under the new dispensation. As such, it is of profound significance for contemporary history, but its very uniqueness has left it high and dry on the sand banks of academe. Nobody knew what to make of it because nobody had seen anything like

---

[4] *Out of Revolution: Autobiography of Western Man* (New York: William Morrow; 1938), pp. 3–6.

it before. The difference between the formulations of Neo-Orthodoxy regarding history and the kind of history that Rosenstock-Huessy set out to write was the difference between idea and action. The theorists of Christian Existentialism or Orthodoxy could, after all, be pillaged by the traditional historian for whatever insights seemed applicable. They contained no explicit threat to the canons of modern historiography. They could be, and were for the most part, disregarded. But anyone who undertook actually to write history, rather than write about how it should be written (or what it meant), posed a far more direct challenge to the professional historian with his own elaborate system of orthodoxy. *Out of Revolution* demanded to be accepted or rejected. It was rejected, or, worse, ignored.

In terms of historiography it might thus be said that despite the theorizing of a considerable number of individuals about the nature and meaning of history, only one historian-philosopher undertook to write history in the spirit of the new dispensation. Rosenstock-Huessy called himself a social philosopher, and, as though to underline the fact that the common life of man, past, present, and future, is the province of the historian, he entitled his universal history *Sociology*.[5]

---

[5] Published in Germany in two volumes (*Soziologie I: Die Ubermacht der Raume*, Stuttgart, 1956; *Soziologie II: Die Vollzahl der Zeiten*, Stuttgart, 1958).

9

Spengler, Toynbee, and Voegelin

The theology of crisis and philosophical Existentjalism were products of the trauma of World War I, but one remarkable history preceded that event. Oswald Spengler's *The Decline of the West* clearly owed a debt to the nineteenth-century conception that human history was comparable to a biological process. For Spengler, history was like the cycle of organic life—initial growth, maturity, decay, and death. The process, as Spengler saw it, was recurrent and immutable; it remained only to trace it through the history of the great civilizations of the world. The West was in its last stage of irreversible decline and would soon take its place in the graveyard of great civilizations, and another would rise to take its place.

The Decline of the West was completed before the outbreak of World War I and first published in 1918. Spengler's principal debt was to Nietzsche. He spoke of a new morphology of world history which he wished to plant in the "metaphysically-exhausted soil of the West." Spengler set out to explore the relationship between "differential calculus and the dynastic principle of politics in the age of Louis XIV, between the Classical city-state and the Euclidean geometry, between the space-perspective of Western oil-painting and the conquest of space by railroad, telephone and long-range weapon, between contrapuntal music and credit economics"—convinced that they must reveal "deep uniformities."[1] So viewed, the humdrum facts of political history took on "a symbolic and even a metaphysical character" which would be made "*uniformly* understandable and appreciable."

Spengler was also one of the first to insist that philosophy *must* concern itself with history: "All genuine historical work is philosophy, unless it is mere ant-industry." The philosopher "overlooks the fact that every thought lives in a historical world and is therefore involved in the common destiny of mortality"—in history.

Spengler, at least, opposed an organic, living world to a mechanical one. "Sympathy, observation, comparison, immediate and inward certainty, intellectual flair"—these were the means by which his master, Goethe, "had approached the secrets of the phenomenal world in motion." "*Now these are the means of historical* research," Spengler added, "precisely these and no others."[2]

Once Spengler's organic analogy has been dismissed, or seen for what it truly is—a poetic metaphor—his book can be the better appreciated for the astonishing fertility of his mind. His explication of the relationship between the art

---

[1] *Decline of the West*, 2 vols., translated by Charles Francis Atkinson (New York: Alfred A. Knopf; 1932), I, p. 7.

[2] Ibid., I, p. 25.

and architecture of a culture and the other forms of its social and political life abounds in remarkable insights. Indeed, it could be said that only today, almost fifty years after the appearance of *The Decline of the West*, are professional historians beginning to develop Spengler's approach to the total culture of a society as an index to its essential character.

By selecting certain key themes—space, time, death—and examining the way in which various cultures treated such themes in symbol and myth, Spengler opened a wealth of new historical perspectives. Such sentences as "Indian man forgot everything, but Egyptian man forgot nothing," cryptic as they seem at first reading, under Spengler's touch become remarkably suggestive. Speaking of the discovery of the mechanical clock, Spengler refers to the clock as "the dread symbol of the flow of time." For him, the chimes "of countless clock towers that echo day and night over Western Europe [are] perhaps the most wonderful expression of which a historical world-feeling is capable."[3]

Spengler argued that the efforts of modern man to give some kind of orderly progressive account of the development of mankind was a specious exercise. Genuine cultures lived and died like plants, each with its "peculiar blossom or fruit, its special type of growth and decline." And those cultures grew, and grew, "with the same superb aimlessness as the flowers of the field. . . ." "I see," he declared, "world history as a picture of endless formations and transformations, of the marvelous waxing and waning of organic forms. The professional historian, on the contrary, sees it as a sort of tapeworm industriously adding on to itself one epoch after another."[4]

Spengler's didactic and prophetic tone is unmistakable. In one sense *The Decline of the West* can be taken as an

---

[3] Ibid., I, p. 14.
[4] Ibid., I, p. 22.

extended moral tract. Spengler's criticism of the decadence of contemporary art has not lost its relevance or its power to chill us: "We go through all the exhibitions, the concerts, the theatres, and find only industrious cobblers and noisy fools, who delight to produce something for the market, something that will 'catch on' with a public for whom art and music and drama have long ceased to be spiritual necessities."[5] As much as anything else, *The Decline* was an attack on the primacy of reason and in this it showed most clearly its Nietzschean ancestry: "*Understanding detached from sensation is called thought. . . .* But thought itself persistently credits itself with much too high a rank in the ensemble of life, and through its ignorance of, or indifference to, the fact that there are other modes of ascertainment besides itself, forfeits its opportunity of surveying the whole without prejudice." "Cold abstract thought," Spengler wrote, had been confident in every culture that it was "the way of approach to 'last things.' "[6]

Spengler wished to dethrone abstract, critical thought. For him "the will-to-system is a will to kill something living . . . to stiffen it, to bind it in the train of logic." As a radical relativist, Spengler felt that there was no history-in-itself, that such a history was inconceivable. The hawk and the farmer must see a flock of pigeons through different eyes. Here he associates himself quite clearly with the school of historical relativists, even while his over-all system is derived from a naturalistic model.[7]

Spengler's pessimistic analysis of the decline of Western civilization may be taken to close a bracket opened by Hegel. At the beginning was Hegel's optimistic and Utopian conception of historical development, and at the end was Spengler's diagnosis of a doomed society. Spengler was

[5] Ibid., I, p. 293.
[6] Ibid., II, p. 10.
[7] Ibid., II, p. 12.

neither a philosopher nor a historian; he was a school teacher with an extraordinary insight into history.

There are three facets to Spengler's thesis and they are not necessarily related. Two of these, if not entirely discredited, have lost their force. First, his analogy between the life of historic civilizations and the life cycles in the biological world was hardly more than a metaphor in which to dress his doom-haunted vision. Whatever persuasiveness it possessed was the result of the nineteenth-century disposition to a naturalistic view of human society, past and present. Darwinism, the germ-theory, environmentalism, various genetic or racist interpretations had great vogue. Spengler's analogy, in the intellectual climate of his day, was thus not nearly as preposterous as it seems to us today. It was inevitable, too, that the darkest pessimism should follow the exaggerated optimism that characterized the Enlightenment and its long twilight. Christianity had hardly begun to emerge from its unhappy involvement with middle-class capitalism on the one hand and secular reform on the other. That classical pre-Christian notions of the time process should reappear was hardly surprising. Like Spengler, the Greeks had made an analogy between the cycles of the natural world and those of human history. The fact that these aspects of Spengler's work seem archaic today, in addition to Spengler's glorification of the Nazis and the book's taint of anti-intellectualism, has, unfortunately, prevented students and scholars from reading this work. Nevertheless, it remains a book of remarkable eloquence and insight.

The other great enterprise of our time in the realm of world history is Arnold Toynbee's massive *A Study of History*. Despite an apparent similarity of theme, *A Study of History* is as different from *The Decline of the West* as two books on the same general subject could be. Toynbee, who had received the classic Classical education of late

Victorian England, was, like the theologians of crisis, shocked into motion by the First World War. Steeped in his Classical training and admittedly influenced by the cyclical theories of the ancients, Toynbee set out to trace the rise and fall of civilizations through genesis, growth, breakdown, and disintegration. Like Spengler, Toynbee began with the conviction that Western civilization had already entered the phase of disintegration. But as he progressed in the writing of his world history "as an analytico-classificatory comparative study of human affairs" in a professedly empirical spirit, the larger problems of "meta-history" intruded themselves. After Volume VI, religion played a larger and larger role—causing some of his critics to denounce the latter part of the *Study* as a "theodicy," or a history of religion rather than a history of civilizations. At the same time the historical determinism with which Toynbee had started out was progressively modified until he became in the end an eloquent spokesman for man's freedom to shape his own destiny. Indeed, Toynbee describes himself as a "creationist," as opposed to those who believed in any form of determinism. By his own admission, he reversed himself: he had initially tried to contain religion within his conceptional framework of "civilization"; now he explained civilization in terms of religions.

Toynbee's work has not fared well at the hands of professional historians, but he has, at the very least, contributed a set of extremely useful "laws" or characteristics of major civilizations: challenge-and-response, withdrawal-and-return, internal proletariat, creative minority, the fossilization of societies, the character of universal states and universal churches. Moreover, he has forced historians of the monographic age to consider the problems of world history and thus has provoked a debate within the profession, and beyond, about some of the most crucial problems of historical interpretation. Historians, for the most part, had ignored the theologians of crisis and the philosophers, both Existential and Positivist, who concerned themselves with history, but Toynbee confronted them with a historical enterprise that they could not very well overlook, even though they might denigrate it. (It is interesting to note that one of the most frequent criticisms of the *Study* was that, in attempting to write a universal history, Toynbee was essaying "the impossible and for that reason . . . miscarries." This statement seems to imply that knowledge has become so specialized that meaningful general statements about mankind can no longer be made.)

Among the most valuable sections in the *Study* are Volume XI, subtitled "The Inspirations of Historians"—a fascinating and discursive reflection about the influences which shaped Toynbee's thinking and the ways in which he reached his various insights—and Volume XII, "Reconsiderations," in which Toynbee reviews his whole great venture, modifies some of his earlier judgments, and revises others completely in the light of criticism and subsequent scholarship.

In Volume XII Toynbee is able to indulge in an exercise denied most authors—that of reviewing his reviewers. The result, at least for me, is a heightened picture of a generous, urbane, and perceptive man. The criticisms, reviewed by Toynbee and treated, it must be said, with far more regard than most of them deserve, make an absorbing compendium of the present state of historical thought.

Most of the critics focus their attention on whether Toynbee was "right" in his over-all system and in his various hypotheses. And since the majority of the reviewers were specialists in a particular, often quite narrow field of history, they were especially severe in their criticisms of Toynbee's treatment of their own area of expertise. One critic suggested that *A Study of History* was "an anachronism, a book essentially backward-looking, that seeks to rationalize the failures of religion into the terms of an indomitable and unquenchable faith," and hinted that the author was one of those "who are not at home, and who, therefore, are not happy, in the atomic relativisitic universe revealed by science."[8] The anthropoligist Philip Bagby declared that Toynbee had "done a great disservice to the comparative study of civilizations" and brought discredit "on the whole enterprise by undertaking his investigations in so ill-conceived and unscientific a manner." To Bagby, the work was a step backward from Spengler toward "the pre-scientific moralizing philosophy of history."[9]

These criticisms are typical. Toynbee was attacked more bitterly as his history took on a more specifically moral point of view; as it came, more and more clearly, to suggest that man has in his own keeping at least a substantial part of his destiny and that a strong sense of the religious is essential if the future is to be genuinely human in its character. One senses, among many of the reviewers, an indignation born of a sense of betrayal. It was as though Toynbee had broken faith with a cardinal tenet of the profession by abandoning the empirical spirit in which he had begun his work for a tone that bordered on the polemical. Especially significant were the objections to Volume XI, *"The Inspirations of Historians."* A number of critics upbraided Toynbee for interjecting a personal note into his work. They accused him of egotism and vainglory in recounting the steps by which he had become a historian; they declared that such autobiographical elements had no place in a scholarly treatise. A recapitulation and analysis of the reviews of *A Study of History* would, one suspects, give a rather accurate profile of the creed of historians in the middle decades of the twentieth century.

---

[8] Max Savelle: *The Pacific Historical Review* (February, 1956), p. 67, quoted by Toynbee: *Reconsiderations*, p. 607.

[9] *Culture and History*, p. 181.

Another scholar, Eric Voėgelin, professor of political science at the University of Munich, has since 1956 published three volumes of a projected six-volume work under the general title *Order and History*. (The titles of these are *Israel and Revelation, The World of the Polis, Plato and Aristotle.* The volumes that remain to be published are *Empire and Christianity, The Protestant Centuries,* and *The Crisis of Western Civilization.*) Called by one enthusiastic reviewer "the most profoundly creative and searching reconstruction of political thought to appear since the time of Hegel,"[1] and hailed by Crane Brinton as ranking with the work of Toynbee, Spengler, and Collingwood, Voegelin's undertaking is far enough along to give some notion of his philosophy of history. The idea of "a leap in being"—that is, of man's experience of the Divine as world-transcendent —seems central to his system. "The personal soul as the sensorium of transcendence," Voegelin writes, "must develop parallel with the understanding of a transcendent God."[2]

Voegelin states his purpose in his preface. "Every society," he writes, "is burdened with the task . . . of creating an order that will endow the facts of its existence with meaning in terms of ends divine and human." Much of history can be read as an effort to find symbolic forms that will express this order. While there is no "simple pattern" of progress in history, there is an "intelligible structure," not within particular societies but rather in the interaction of societies throughout history. The historic orders Voegelin is tracing are those of the imperial organizations of the ancient Near East as expressed in the form of a cosmological myth; that of the Chosen People of Israel; that of the Greek polis and its myth (it was among the Greeks, he

[1] Ellis Sandoz: *Cross Currents,* XII (Winter, 1962), p. 41.
[2] *Order and History: Israel and Revelation* (Louisiana State University Press, 1958), I, p. 235.

points out, that philosophy emerged as a symbolic form of order); the "multi-civilizational empires" which followed the breakup of the Alexandrine empire and the rise of Christianity; and, finally, the appearance of national states and the development of what Voegelin calls "Gnosis" (apparently the cult of intellectual specialization which creates its own mysteries) as the symbolic form of order in the modern Western world.

Although Voegelin states that his study has been made possible by the decline of different forms of nationalism, of progressive, positivist, liberal, socialist, Marxian, and Freudian ideologies, by the growing disinclination to imitate the methods of the natural sciences, and by "the withering of Victorian agnosticism," as well as by "the more recent fashions of existentialism and theologism," he is clearly indebted to the Existentialists and the theologians of crisis. When he describes man not as a "self-contained spectator" but as "an actor, playing a part in the drama of being," he is using the rhetoric of the Existentialists. He calls his work "a philosophical inquiry concerning the order of human existence in society and history."[3] "The role of existence," he concludes, "must be played in uncertainty of its meaning, as an adventure of decision on the edge of freedom and necessity"; and he speaks in familiar terms of "the anxiety of existence." Man derives much of his sense of order from the feeling that he acts his proper role "in the greater play of the divine being that enters passing existence in order to redeem precarious being for eternity,"[4] and it is this sense of order and of "partnership in being" which Voegelin wishes, through this work, to help to restore to an anxious and disoriented world. Since "existence is partnership in the community of being," the greatest horror in life is "the danger of a fall from being" through improper "attune-

[3] Ibid., I, pp. xii–xiv.
[4] Ibid., I, p. 5.

ment." One of the most effective means of attunement comes from the experience of conversion, which indeed constitutes "a qualitative leap," a leap into partnership with God. The converted community gains great power by its conversion, but it pays the price of intolerance. However, since it must continue to operate in the order of mundane existence, it must develop a tolerance "inspired by the love of existence and a respect for the tortuous ways on which man moves historically closer to the true order of being."[5]

According to Voegelin, the "leap in being" has been characteristic of every civilization. The climactic leap was in the revelation of Jesus, which marked "the entrance of God into history through the sacrificial assumption of human form." "Multiple and parallel" leaps occurred in the India of Buddha and the China of Confucius and Lao-tse. Western civilization transcends the parochialism of all "other" civilizations, and insists on the common destiny of all mankind. It is in man's successive experiences of transcendence that his true history is to be found.[6]

Voegelin (although he has been a critic of the English "metahistorian") may thus be seen as a successor of Toynbee in his conviction that man's religious experience lies at the center of his historic life. His thinking is close to that of Jaspers and far removed from that of the positivists and historical relativists. The emphasis, at least so far, is very largely political and religious: more specifically, a study of politics as an effort to emulate divine order. The broader cultural aspects of civilization—art, architecture, music, poetry—which played such a dominant role in Spengler's work appear hardly at all and there is no indication that Voegelin intends to deal with them as essential elements in his system.

---

[5] Ibid., I, pp. 7–11.
[6] Ibid., I, pp. 11–13.

Spengler, Toynbee, and, prospectively, Voegelin have enormously enriched both the vocabulary and the scope of history. Although all three have been severely criticized by more conventional historians for various lapses and sins, their systems can be regarded, from the point of view of orthodoxy, as the logical outcome of several generations of highly specialized monographic studies. After all, the explicit as well as the implicit assumption of the monographers has been that the individual building blocks had to be laboriously fashioned before the general edifice could be raised. Voegelin has said specifically that he was able to undertake a work of such ambitious scope "because . . . the advance of the historical disciplines in the first half of this century has provided the basis of materials."[7] It thus is curious to hear the historical specialists state that universal histories are unfeasible because of the vast amount of material that must be mastered by a single historian. If the monographic work has been conscientious and accurate, it would seem to follow that the seed has been sowed for the universal historians to reap. The catch is that the universal history which has so far appeared is not the sort of history the champions of "scientific" method had envisioned. Mixed with philosophy and, more alarming still, with elements of theology, it is hardly analogous to the general propositions of physics or chemistry.

---

[7] Ibid., I, p. xii.

10

The Professionals:
History
and the "Social Sciences"

Below the level of philosophic discourse, historians pursued their more mundane ways. When the more reflective or philosophically inclined considered the broader problems of historical interpretation, their views were apt to be rather simple and mechanical. Devoted to what they conceived of as scientific method and secure in the expectation of progress, inevitable or to come as a result of the mastery of process by reason, they varied only in the particular mechanical system which undergirded their individual historical works. Some took economics as the causal principle; others, the germ theory by which modern constitutional government was said to be the heir of the council of the Germanic tribes, just as the mature oak is contained within the acorn. Others preferred an environmental theory which reached back to Herder and attempted to account for cultural differences on the basis of soil and climate, mountains, rivers, and oceans. Frederick Jackson Turner's enormously influential account of the effect of the frontier on American history is an excellent example of this school. In a subsequent essay, Turner put forth the classic naturalistic notion that the rural areas with the richest soil produced the most outstanding people, almost as though human beings were a species of turnip.

Armed with their scientific method, the new historians spoke complacently of their "scientific detachment" and of the "ruthless methods of modern scholarship." Claude Van Tyne, an American historian writing on the causes of the American Revolution, offered a convenient list of those elements of the new scientific history which he and his colleagues were confident would lead them eventually, over a path paved with monographs, to the truth.

On the other side of the Atlantic, the English historian J. B. Bury gave a classical formulation of the analogy between natural science and history. The genetic idea which had revolutionized natural science belonged "to the same order of thought as the conception of human history as a continuous, genetic, causal process—a conception which has revolutionized historical research and made it scientific. . . . The genetic principle, progressive development, general laws, the significance of time, the conception of society as an organic aggregate, the metaphysical theory of history as the self-evolution of spirit—all these ideas show that historical inquiry [has] been advancing independently on somewhat parallel lines to the sciences of nature."[1]

In the generation following Turner, Carl Becker and Charles Beard were the principal transmitters of European ideas of historical process to their American colleagues.

---

[1] *The Idea of Progress*, introduction by Charles Beard (New York: Dover Publications; 1955), pp. xvii–xviii.

Both men had a much greater interest in theory than was common in the profession. Becker read and was influenced by both Croce and Collingwood and Beard had much the same nurture; Beard perhaps owed his greatest debt to Dilthey. Becker, with his ironic and elegant style, had the subtler and more penetrating mind of the two. He accepted without reservation the relativity of historical knowledge and outraged many of his fellow historians with his essay, "Every Man His Own Historian," which to the champions of objectivity seemed a complete surrender to individual judgment. History was only important, Becker argued, when it threw light on the dilemmas of the present. The facts, by which the "scientific" historians put so much store, Becker scoffed at as simply neutral, without meaning until called to life by the historian. The historian, try as he might, could never "eliminate the personal equation."[2] Like the Existentialists, Becker wanted men to enter into the domain of history through their own personal experience rather than have history presented to them as something "objective." He even went so far as to question, in his wry way, whether there was indeed any "progress" in history—for an American historian a most eccentric view.

Becker's contemporary, Charles Beard, was much more typical of his time and, as a consequence, much more influential in the profession. First of all, Beard had a system and the man with a system, however inadequate it may ultimately turn out to be, has a vast advantage over a systemless rival, however brilliant. Moreover, Becker's very sophistication was a barrier to his acceptance by the majority of his colleagues. Beard, on the other hand, in classic pragmatic American spirit, took from various sources whatever appealed to him to use in constructing his own

---

[2] "What Are Historical Facts," *Western Political Quarterly* (September, 1955), pp. 327–40.

system. He saw the historian as an active fighter for a better social order—"Written History as an Act of Faith" was the title of his presidential address to the American Historical Association. In it Beard spoke of history as "a science, an art, an illustration of theology, a phase of philosophy, a branch of literature"—all combined.[3] He seemed clearly a relativist in his insistence that "any written history inevitably reflects the thought of the author in his time and cultural setting." He rejected the idea that history was a science comparable to physics or biology, but at the same time he attacked the extreme relativist position, declaring that the conception of reality was "itself relative." "As the actuality of history moves forward into the future," he declared, sounding more like a continental theorist than an American historian, "the conception of relativity will also pass, as previous conceptions and interpretations of events have passed." This rather inscrutable dictum offered little comfort to relativists or historians-cum-scientists. But Beard accompanied it with a challenge to the profession to keep up with "the disclosures of contemporary thought," however painful this might be to cherished illusions. The conscientious historian must examine and enlarge his own frame of reference by "acquiring knowledge of greater areas of thought and events, and give it consistency of structure by a deliberate conjecture respecting the nature or direction of the vast movements of ideas and interests called world history." The implication was plain enough, at least for some of his listeners: the historian must incorporate into his work the latest findings of his sister disciplines; he must opt for a particular kind of world and give his history the form that would help to bring this world into existence. For Beard, this was to be "a collectivist democracy." If the historian could not explain history, he could help to make it. He thus must

---

[3] *American Historical Review* (January, 1934), XXXIX, pp. 219–29.

consciously choose a particular interpretation—history as chaos, as recurrent cycles, history as "a line, straight or spiral," moving in a particular direction. And this choice was the historian's "act of faith."

Thus Beard came out for a progressive, basically optimistic view of history. He waved aside the issue of relativity, aligned himself with the most advanced scholars in the other social sciences, and urged his colleagues to associate themselves with the direction in which history, at least to him, seemed to be moving. There were, to be sure, paradoxes and inconsistencies in Beard's approach which apparently were not perceived by him, but the declaration pleased most American historians, with the exception of those too deeply committed to the idea of history as "science" to modify their views and those who thought that for the historian to espouse some particular social and political order meant, inevitably, a compromise with that spirit of balance and judiciousness, of fairness—in the word of Samuel Eliot Morison, *mesure*—which should at all times distinguish the historian from the partisan and special pleader. Furthermore, Beard could not dispose of the issue of relativity simply by urging the historian to become the open advocate of a particular future, unless, of course, that future was in some way determined, predestined, or foreordained. Even historians generally sympathetic to Beard's views continued to exalt objectivity.

Perhaps the most notable consequence of Beard's address was a study entitled *Use of Personal Documents in History, Anthropology and Sociology,* underwritten by the Social Science Research Council and published in 1945. Like the wider world, the scholarly world has its own jargon. In the forties, one of its favorite phrases was *interdisciplinary.* The truth was to be apprehended through a combination of the social sciences or, more recently and fashionably, the behavioral sciences, among which history was generally included although its relation to the other social sciences—psychology, sociology, cultural anthropology, economics, and political science—was anomalous at best. Louis Gottschalk, in *Use of Personal Documents*, described the social scientist as "more interested in prediction and control than the humanist and the humanist usually more interested in the unique example than the social scientist."[4] The humanist emphasized the past; the social scientist, the present and the future, according to Gottschalk.

Use of Personal Documents recommended, as might have been anticipated, that historians should be better informed about the work of sociologists and that sociologists should have some knowledge of history and the so-called historical method. This desideratum was to be achieved by "(1) a comprehensive course in *historical method* . . . with illustrative materials carefully chosen for their anthropological, social, political, economic, and statistical implications, and with a conspicuous place assigned to the problem of causation and the philosophy of history." This would be supplemented with "(2) a course or courses on the *origins of contemporary ideas and institutions* . . . which would start out with an indication (or perhaps a detailed analysis) of the present status of selected ideas and institutions for the purpose of laying down a starting line from which to work backward into time searching for earlier developments and origins. And (3) courses tracing *trends*, or *comparative studies* of recurrences and *analogies* of more or less comparable episodes and movements. . . ."[5]

Implicit in all this was the assumption that the real and important task of the social sciences is the development of laws or, more modestly, generalizations about human behavior upon which social and political decisions can be based. The notion is, essentially, that mankind can be man-

---

[4] *Use of Personal Documents*, p. 3.
[5] Ibid., p. 74.

aged if we know enough about man's behavior (hence behavioral sciences). Thus, we are urged to undertake a program to "train specialists in each of the social studies (as well as in other disciplines) to carry on historical investigation and instruction especially appropriate to that science," and to incorporate such specialists into history departments.

The Social Science Research Council, having taken a flyer in the interdisciplinary approach, followed up *Uses* nine years later with *Bulletin 54, Theory and Practice in Historical Study.* The most provocative chapter in *Bulletin 54* was by Howard K. Beale and was entitled "What Historians Have Said About the Causes of the Civil War." At the end of a fascinating review of the various interpretations of the causes of that conflict which have been put forward in the years since its outbreak, Professor Beale, with engaging candor, admitted that every idea he had thought "a contribution of recent historical scholarship, he [had] found in one of several nineteenth century historians. Indeed, every explanation of the War presented by historians with the benefit of hindsight . . . was comprehended and stated before the War occurred." He found, moreover, that, after some eighty years of historical research into the war, Northern and Southern historians by and large took very much the same positions that their predecessors had taken immediately following the war. In other words, that so-called historical perspective had not resulted in a clearer or a more or less universally accepted interpretation of the war and its causes. And the reason was plain enough—the same basic issues that engaged the loyalties of the North and the South in 1860 were still alive in 1945.

Another of Beale's conclusions was that "the causes of the Civil War [were] bafflingly complex. No simple explanation is possible. . . . The tendency has been from simple explanations to many-sided ones until recently the picture has become complicated indeed."[6] So, one might interpose, what is one to tell an inquiring student—that no simple and precise statement is possible about the greatest crisis of American history? Is this the fruit of eighty years of painstaking scientific inquiry dedicated to the proposition that through this study man is slowly but surely approaching a clearer understanding of what happened in the past and why? Certainly, no answers are better than easy or specious ones, but if Professor Beale's thesis is correct, academic historians are performing a poor service for their students and indeed for their country and their profession.

At the end of the essay, Beale plucks up courage in the face of his disheartening analysis and affirms his conviction that "the repeated efforts to discover the 'truth' about the causes of the Civil War," while singularly unsuccessful in terms of anything that might properly be called a "social science," have, nonetheless, been "fruitful" and "that both the methods and the quality of history have improved in the period analysed" (it might be added parenthetically, however, that the conclusions leave us in greater doubt and confusion than ever).

Beale plainly regrets that the "limitations inherent in a study of human activities prevent the historian's becoming an exact scientist in the sense in which the physicist or biologist is a scientist." In view of all the difficulties inherent in attaining genuine objectivity, or finding "answers of scientific exactitude" and sifting through the various hypotheses about the causes of the war, Beale asks a little plaintively whether there is really any justification for such detailed study. The answer, as we might anticipate, is "yes." A concentrated study of the Civil War may presumably confuse the student and it may not tell him the specific cause of the war (a cause such as chattel slavery), but it will tell him something about the causes of war in general,

---

[6] *Theory and Practice in Historical Study*, p. 88.

"indeed, about human motives and human actions in any time or place."[7]

Here then we have it. We may not ever be able to learn precisely what caused the Civil War (in which case we shall be worse off than the people who fought the war, for they at least thought they knew why they were fighting). But from a study of that conflict we can garner some general principles, some postulates about man's behavior under stress, and this knowledge may enable us somehow, in some not clearly specified way, to do—what? Prevent similar outbreaks of violence? Prevail on people not to become so attached to abstract issues such as abolition or union or freedom that war must be the consequence? Learn how to manipulate the masses in terms of ideologies? Here, where we might expect science to be specific, it is distressingly vague. We are asked to spend our lives in the devoted pursuit of a most elusive truth for an end that is most vaguely defined. And what are we given to feed on meanwhile? Faith. Faith that somehow, at last, our patient labors will have their reward, though it is not for us to know what that reward shall be or when it may be bestowed.

A subsequent volume entitled *The Social Sciences in Historical Study (Bulletin 64)*, written with an appealing innocence, advocated "objective relativism," which is defined as "freeing oneself as far as possible from one's scheme of reference."

The editor assured his readers that there was "vigorous animation in historiography" and urged historians to reject "occupational isolation" and amalgamate with other disciplines, even while freely admitting that amalgamation "often has failed to achieve the effectiveness that was hoped for." Historical scholarship, he insisted, "can be no better than its tools, instruments, or techniques. . . . The assessment of the instruments of scholarship is a vital part [of knowledge]." (Note the mechanical and scientific terms—

[7] *Theory and Practice in Historiography*, pp. 90–92.

tools, instruments.) These must be sharpened, refined, modified, or perhaps "retooled." The writing of history may be improved by "making investigation more penetrating, analysis more precise, and demonstration more rigorous."[8]

By "objective relativity," historians "will be able to accept certain propositions as tentatively established with a degree of probability sufficient to warrant their acceptance. The accumulation of knowledge, the ability to build with confidence upon foundations solidly established," will, hopefully, be the consequence of "greater communication between history and the other social sciences." But the contradiction is unresolved. On the one hand, it is admitted that the historian views the past through lenses colored by the ideals and attitudes of his time; on the other hand, we are nonetheless encouraged to believe that he will base his studies on propositions that seem more and more true, and, finally, we are assured that this will be the outcome of a closer alliance between history and the other social sciences. The editor also expressed the cautious hope that "in history, as in other sciences, the results of research may become increasingly cumulative."[9]

The committee which drew together and edited the various contributions to *The Social Sciences in Historical Study* expressed its conviction that "people from different disciplines should work together on shared tasks." Indeed, it stated, only if this is done can we look forward to "encouraging prospects both for the development of social sciences and for the progress of historical study." It quoted, apparently with approval, the statement of Paul Lazarsfeld that "it is certainly possible to make human judgment somewhat objective by systematizing the training and instruction of classifiers as much as possible."[1]

The study, launched with such optimistic predictions of

---

[8] *Social Sciences in Historical Study*, pp. 10, 18, 21.
[9] Ibid., pp. 23, 25.
[1] Ibid., pp. 32, 55.

the advantages to be derived from co-operation between history and "the other social sciences," soon ran on the rocks. Psychology had little to offer the historian. "The inadequacies of scientific psychology" made it "inevitable that common sense assumptions, guided by wisdom and humanistic lore, must play a large part" in the "diagnosis of facts" and in the "selection of explanatory principles."[2] Behavioristic psychology seemed to the committee dogmatic and rigid, and Gestalt psychology a belaboring of the obvious. It thus followed that the historian, despite constant injunctions to engage in interdisciplinary studies, would find sparse pickings in the area of psychology.

After reviewing contemporary sociology, one author came to a not-very-reassuring conclusion. "If the reader," he wrote, "is not quite sure that he understands the meaning of many of the terms and concepts mentioned in this chapter, he is in no worse situation than other social scientists." It appeared, indeed, that the principal advantage to be derived by the historian from a study of his often muddled and distressingly imprecise sister "sciences" was that it warned him "against accepting superficial social generalizations, and oversimplifying historical problems."[3]

The editors seemed ultimately satisfied to advocate "cumulative" history, which "requires the work of many, who build on the work of their predecessors and in turn furnish a body of analysis from which their successors proceed cumulatively to a more advanced stage of substantive knowledge and procedure." "Theory and practice in history as social science," they added reassuringly, "are still in an experimental, exploratory stage."[4]

Unfortunately, in the opinion of the editors of the *Social Sciences in Historical Study*, certain traditional-minded his-

---

[2] Ibid., p. 58.
[3] Ibid., pp. 83, 84.
[4] Ibid., pp. 141, 155.

torians still clung to the outmoded notion of history as a narrative, although "neither narrative nor popular drama is usually suited to the analysis of mass phenomena." These historians have preferred to retain "a misleading emphasis on colorful individuals and exciting events"; they have clung to "storytelling" rather than high-level abstract analysis.[5] The implication is plain enough: history must analyze the behavior of social groups, not mediate the past to the present generation. The historian must approach problems "in the spirit of scientific analysis"; such is the path of "historical realism." The American historian, for example, should cast aside such outmoded concepts as "Jeffersonian and Jacksonian Democracy, the Era of Good Feeling, the Square Deal, the New Freedom, etc." "Time must doom" these "ancient subdivisions." Even the Civil War will fade in significance when viewed in the light of "long-run social criteria."[6] History will become, presumably, as esoteric as sociology or the higher branches of linguistics. Proud man will be cut down at last to his proper size—the height of a statistic, the width of "a descriptive integration," a residue of historical data. The fact that nobody will be interested in reading such history is immaterial. Nobody is supposed to read it except the managers, those autonomous individuals freed by ruthless self-analysis from the unthinking prejudices and blind partialities of the masses.

Although the authors of *The Social Sciences in Historical Study* came, rather paradoxically, to the conclusion that in the area of psychology the historian "has little to learn . . . from what he may regard as the rediscovery of the obvious,"[7] something more remains to be said about the relation of psychology to history.

---

[5] Ibid., p. 160.
[6] Ibid., pp. 171, 170.
[7] Ibid., p. 61.

In the first place, what, for want of a better phrase, we might call "states-of-mind" are a vital ingredient of history. The historian must be concerned with such problems as "the extent to which the individual life-style of a person determines what he perceives," and the extent to which the general *Zeitgeist* of his society determines what he sees and how he responds to it. Psychologists have given considerable attention to the fact that, apparently, "there are certain forms in the external world that appear no matter how great the variation in individual and cultural factors."[8] In other words, some aspects of human experience are constant and some are profoundly affected by the cultural climate. The problem of the dominant psychology of an age, a society, or a subculture is one of the most difficult and elusive that the historian has to deal with. Take, for example, the Puritan attitude toward sexual relations. Superficially, the Freudian concept of repression seems made to order for application to the New England Puritans, but the historian who penetrates behind an intervening Victorianism will discover that the Puritans had an extremely practical, almost matter-of-fact approach to the problem of sex.

We are aware, of course, of the very different ways in which people of different cultures have viewed old age or youth (Philippe Ariès's *Centuries of Childhood* is a fascinating account of the emergence of childhood as a clearly demarcated period of life), money, property, death, etc. Rollo May, for instance, has argued that the Freudian system was most clearly applicable to a late Victorian middle-class European society and that if sexual repression and the

---

[8] Rudolf Arnheim: "The Gestalt Theory of Expression," *Psychological Review,* LVI, No. 3 (May, 1949), p. 160. One of the most sophisticated and closely reasoned analyses of the problem of recapturing the psychology of a past era is contained in Richard R. Niebuhr's *Resurrection and Historical Reason* (New York: Charles Scribner's Sons; 1957), especially pages 81–102.

death wish were the most critical problems of that age, status anxiety most clearly characterizes present-day American society.

There are many indications that competition, often thought of as characteristic of modern America, was more prevalent and far more corrosive in the late eighteenth century than it is today. Hints from the diaries of Pepys, James Boswell, and William Byrd, as well as the blunt and explicit church records of Puritan New England, suggest that sexual vitality in the seventeenth and eighteenth centuries may have been far in excess of what it is today. If true, this must have affected the psychology of the individual in profound ways. Similarly, the incidence of infant mortality plainly affected the attitude of people toward death, toward children, and, of course, toward each other. Ariès tells a story from the seventeenth century of a neighbor standing at the bedside of a woman, the mother of five "little brats," who had just given birth to another. The neighbor comforts the woman by assuring her that "before they are old enough to bother you, you will have lost half of them, perhaps all of them," and he quotes Montaigne's comment: "I have lost two or three children in their infancy, not without regret but without great sorrow."[9]

It may also be true, as evidenced in letters and diaries, that relationships between men and women, and more particularly between husbands and wives, were far closer, more intimate, and confidential in the late eighteenth century, for example, than in the mid-nineteenth century. This kind of "psychological" evidence is of vital importance to the historian, and he dare not ignore any help he may be able to get from the professional psychologist.

One branch of psychology has been featured lately as providing an over-all system which can illuminate both

---

[9] *Centuries of Childhood*, translated by Robert Baldick (New York: Alfred A. Knopf; 1962), pp. 38, 39.

biography and general history (much as Marxism did in the 1930's).[1] The proponents of psychoanalytic theory have offered Freudian or neo-Freudian intepretations of the past, and professional historians have been exhorted to follow suit. William Langer, in his presidential address to the American Historical Association, urged historians to embrace the insights of psychoanalysis. The minds of historians, he told his audience, were locked "in the molds of the past." They have failed to seek new horizons "as our cousins in the natural sciences are constantly doing." If progress was to be made, the historians must constantly employ "new ideas, new points of view, and new techniques." Depth psychology was what Langer recommended to his fellow historians. It was in the "coldly penetrating calculus" of psychoanalysis that the historians must find their "next assignment." Langer had "no doubt that modern psychology is bound to play an ever greater role in historical interpretation."[2]

Responding to such injunctions, a few bold spirits have raised the flag of psychoanalytic theory over historical works of considerable substance. It might be well, therefore, to take some note of the relevance of Freudian psychology for the practicing historian.

It must be admitted at once that the available evidence is inconclusive. There are perhaps half a dozen biographies and articles which purport to make use of psychoanalytic insights.[3] These vary in quality, depending primarily on the skill and insight of the authors. The worst are embarrassingly bad and reveal too clearly the dangers of applying a rather rigid and mechanical system to the problems of bi-

---

[1] See Donald Meyer's review of Erik Erikson's *Young Man Luther: A Study in Psychoanalysis and History* in *History and Theory*, I, No. 3 (1961), pp. 291–7. Also Bruce Mazlish's introduction to *Psychoanalysis and History* (New Jersey: Prentice-Hall; 1963).

[2] *American Historical Review*, LXIII (January, 1958), p. 303.

[3] Psychoanalytic history, as Donald Meyer has pointed out, is primarily "biography-centered history." *History and Theory*, I, No. 3 (1961), p. 292.

ography. The best represent a triumph of the professional historian over the amateur psychoanalyst. And the most successful biographies with a professed psychoanalytic orientation are quite restrained in the application of Freudian concepts.

Alexander and Juliette George in their biographical study of *Woodrow Wilson and Colonel House,* published in 1956, set out to explain Wilson's character and his behavior as President, more especially his defeat on the issue of the League of Nations, in psychoanalytic terms. They found that he had the usual father problem—a strong and authoritarian parent who repressed young Woodrow. That young Wilson's "resentment and rage" (the phrase is Bernard Brodie's, in a review of the Georges' book) at his father's treatment of him were "almost entirely repressed" (in the world of Freud, the love of a son for a strict and demanding father is not really love, of course, but repressed rage and hostility) is indicated by "the esteem and apparent affection in which he held his father throughout his life." The Georges observe what has been observed by many others—that Wilson in his adult life showed a strong impulse toward political domination (as indeed have most successful politicians), which represented "for him a compensatory value, a means of restoring the self-esteem damage [by his father] in childhood."[4]

But Wilson's desire for power was mitigated by "a simultaneous need for approval, respect and, especially, for feeling virtuous." Fortunately, in his drive for power and his desire for approval, Wilson developed the "highly constructive strategy" of espousing "reform projects which already enjoyed considerable support and were within reasonable possibility of achievement."[5]

After a good many more such observations, the Georges

---

[4] *Woodrow Wilson and Colonel House: A Personality Study* (New York: John Day; 1956), p. 320.

[5] Ibid.

reach the conclusion that Wilson's personality flaws—rigidity, self-righteousness, the desire to have his own way, and the refusal to compromise—doomed the League of Nations to rejection by the Senate. All very well, but hardly a revelation. Any scholar familiar with Wilson's character is aware of the traits enumerated by the Georges. Indeed the Georges quote a statement of a friend of Wilson, Thomas Woodlock, which, one is tempted to remark, says everything the Georges say, and better: "The nemesis that Woodrow Wilson vainly fought was within himself, but it was as unchangeable, as inexorable as the Greek Fates. In the last few years of his life there was something Promethean about him. The eagle's beak and claws were in his vitals as he lay bound and helpless on his rock of sickness, but he was grimly enduring and coldly defiant to the last. In the lonely citadel of his soul, proud in his conviction that his cause was wholly just, utterly intolerant of criticism, utterly ruthless to opposition, he could not compromise with his daemon. Tragedy if it is not noble is not tragedy, and no one will deny to Woodrow Wilson elements of nobility"[6] Nobody, that is, except the Georges, with their psychoanalytic technique. And what, after all, have they told us that is purely and simply the result of their use of Freudian tools? Only some shaky speculations about Wilson's relations with his father which do not in the end add to our understanding of his triumphs and his ultimate tragedy. The virtues of the book derive from the fact that the Georges are conscientious historians and skillfully explicated Wilson's political career.

Two other biographies of superior quality which profess to employ psychoanalytic insights might be cited. Emery Battis in his biography of Anne Hutchinson makes specific mention of his attempt to follow the injunctions of Professor Langer referred to earlier in this chapter: "I only hope

---

[6] Ibid., p. xv.

that I have adhered to the spirit of these appeals. . . ."[7]

Battis's book is an informed and well-written examination of the Antinomian Controversy and of its central figure, Mistress Hutchinson, but his psychoanalysis hardly gets beyond the most elementary level. Anne's father, Francis Marbury, we are told, "was a father of such a cast as to render his impress determinate. . . . Being as well a man of high ideals and precise scruples, he would have imposed exacting standards of behavior for his children. If he could scale these heights, why not they? Little by little Marbury's salient traits—his obduracy and independent carriage, his contentiousness and high sense of principle—became part and parcel of Anne's own individuality." On the other hand, Anne's husband, mild and malleable, represented "a reprieve from the dominating qualities of her father."[8]

While Battis makes other attempts throughout his book to apply psychoanalytic concepts to the contest between Anne and the Puritan leaders, he is too good a historian to venture more than mild and tentative suggestions, tucked away here and there quite inoffensively, and it can be said with confidence that his modest application of Freudianism does not add materially to nor subtract from the quality of his work.

Another case in point is Fawn Brodie's excellent biography of Thaddeus Stevens. Mrs. Brodie states that her book "attempts to explain Steven's radicalism not only in terms of his active role in what Clemenceau called 'the second American revolution' but also as an outgrowth of his own desperate inner needs."[9] Stevens is a tempting enough subject for an analytically oriented writer. He was born, as Mrs. Brodie tells us, into "a blighted family." His father was a

---

[7] *Saints and Sectaries* (Chapel Hill: University of North Carolina; 1962), p. ix.

[8] Ibid., pp. 8–11.

[9] *Thaddeus Stevens, Scourge of the South* (New York: W. W. Norton; 1959), p. 10.

ne'er-do-well who ran away and abandoned wife and children. He had an older brother with two club feet and Stevens himself was born with one. In the absence of the convenient authoritarian father, Stevens had a strong and capable mother to whom he was devoted all his life.

Mrs. Brodie's quite obvious and perfectly proper commitment to Stevens as a human being is kept well in check by her scrupulous regard for the intractability of historical materials. Like Battis and the Georges, she makes a point of her awareness of psychoanalytic theory; yet, like Battis, she uses such theory with the greatest restraint, and the virtues of her book, which are considerable, are quite independent of such use. At the most, she gives the knowing reader a sense of being "in on" certain Freudian truths.

The most notable exception to these strictures on the usefulness of psychoanalytic theory to the practicing historian —which so far comes down, as Donald Meyer has pointed out, to biographical history—is Erik Erikson's study of the young Luther. Subtitled A *Study in Psychoanalysis and History*, Erikson's work suggests the possibilities of psychoanalytic theory in the hands of a brilliant psychoanalyst who has thoroughly mastered history and can use it with subtlety and penetration. Thus his notion of the identity crisis raises the book, as a psychoanalytic study, far beyond the level of the works we have just discussed. No one, however, could be more Rhadamanthine than Erikson in his judgments on popularized Freudianism. The followers of Freud, Erikson argues, developed "a habit of thinking which reduces every human situation to an analogy with an earlier one, and most of all to that earliest, simplest, and most infantile precursor which is assumed to be its 'origin.' " He is most critical of the tendency in psychoanalysis to "subordinate the later stages of life to those of childhood. It has lifted to the rank of a cosmology the undeniable fact . . . that apparent progression can harbor partial regression, and firm accomplishment, hidden childish fulfillment. . . . We must grudgingly admit that even as we were trying to devise, with scientific determinism, a therapy for the few, we were led to promote an ethical disease among the many."[1]

It is difficult not to suspect that the power of Erikson's study of Luther lies far less in his application of the Freudian system to his subject than in his use of Luther to break with sterile and outmoded psychoanalytic concepts. Such being the case, Erikson's spectacular performance offers no hope for the practicing historian. Erikson's book, after all, is not a biography of Luther in the conventional sense; it is a study of a particular period in the life of the young Luther, the period of his "identity-crisis," which Erikson examines with extraordinary insight and perception. It is a case study, far more than a biography.

The basic question for the historian may well be whether Freud's view of history is not, in fact, antithetical to the concepts of historical process held by the vast majority of working historians (which is not to say that they are right and Freud is wrong, but only that psychoanalysis as a tool of historical interpretation presents considerable problems for historians unless they modify their views or modify Freud). Philip Rieff argues rather persuasively that Freud's notion of the *kairos*—the moment when that which is external to human history breaks through into history—was not, as in Christian thought, a moment full of potentiality and genuine newness, but was rather the single moment before the dawn of human history when the murdered father was deified, a moment which is recapitulated throughout time. For Freud the future, as Rieff puts it, "is an illusion. ... The only end of life is life. One can only hope to survive."[2] Freud put forth an essentially biological model of

---

[1] Erik H. Erikson: "The First Psychoanalyst," *Yale Review* (Autumn, 1956), pp. 18–19.

[2] "The Meaning of History and Religion in Freud's Thought," *The Journal of Religion*, XXXI, No. 2 (April, 1951), pp. 114–31. One of the most striking recent works on psychoanalytic theory is Helen Merrell Lynd's *On Shame and the Search for Identity* (New York: Science Editions; 1961).

history as a cyclical process not unlike that of the Greeks. He could conceive of nothing genuinely new happening in history; the past dominated the future. Understood at the level of consciousness, history could thus hold no surprises: "In this particular way . . . men have always known . . . that once upon a time they had a primeval father and killed him."[3] What has ensued has been simply re-enactments of this event in various forms that are themselves of little importance.[4]

Another reason that psychoanalytic theory is basically antithetical to history is that its central event is the father-son conflict (the Oedipus complex). This, if taken seriously, would destroy history; written history is, in essence, the effort to pass on to the sons the wisdom of the fathers, and thus to preserve, rather than destroy, the continuity between generations. Freudianism sees the crisis of the individual primarily as the effort of the son to free himself from the incubus of the father, that is, of history. If the son does not love his father (while understanding his imperfections and human limitations), and wish to pass on to his own children

---

While accepting much of the Freudian system, Mrs. Lynd is especially caustic about the "reductionism" practiced by most orthodox Freudians. She defines reductionism as the "tendency to think that understanding results from reducing complex phenomena to their simplest elements, or to a single basic principle of explanation. Wholes tend to be reduced to parts, qualitative or organizational descriptions to quantitative statements, human strivings to compensations for frustrated primary needs, human development to response to reward and punishment, human relations to need-satisfying human objects, human society to its here-and-now, history-free structure and function." A healthier and more accurate view of life, Mrs. Lynd argues, sees "wonder, curiosity, interest, thought, sympathy, trust, love" as "characteristic human attributes, not simply as secondary, derived aims. Reality becomes something capable of yielding knowledge, interest, and fulfillment instead of being mainly a threat to be coped with." *Shame*, pp. 114, 141. See also Ernest Schachtel: "The Development of Focal Attention and the Emergence of Reality," *Psychiatry*, XIII, No. 1 (February, 1950).

[3] *Moses and Monotheism* (New York: Alfred A. Knopf; 1939), p. 161.

[4] "The man who reduces this encounter between the cosmos of history and its eternally new chaos, between Zeus and Dionysos, to the formula of the 'antagonism between fathers and sons,' has never beheld it in his spirit." Martin Buber: *Between Man and Man*, p. 93.

his father's spirit and his father's teaching, there can be no history, but only an endless, agonizing process of rejection.[5]

On the other hand, some of the so-called neo-Freudians are currently offering interpretations of the past that pose direct challenges to the professional historian. For example, Herbert Marcuse in his *Eros and Civilization* combines Freudianism with Marxism and looks toward the healing of human society that will take place when man's instinctual life is freed from the repressions of social custom. This is to be accomplished primarily through the cultivation of the aesthetic sense and the abolition of private property. Marcuse presents us with the symbolic figures of Orpheus and Narcissus as reminders of the " 'Great Refusal' to serve reality and reason at the price of libidinal freedom and pleasure."

Norman Brown is another of the "Utopians" who offers us a "way out of the human neurosis" which is history through emancipation from "the sense of possession." Then "the humanity of the senses and the human enjoyment of the senses will be achieved for the first time." Again Marx is invoked to complement Freud, and we are assured that "the life instinct . . . demands a union with others and with the world around us based not on anxiety and aggression but on narcissism and erotic exuberance."[6]

These neo-Freudians hope to cure man from the disease of history. History, for most of them, is too painful to bear; they must find for mankind some escape from its

---

[5] Since it is, generally speaking, the young who feel most keenly the burden of history, it is not surprising that they should eagerly follow the example of their elders in trying to escape it. Their innocence and good will invite corruption. (In a recent high-school essay contest on the subject of "Hamlet and the Oedipus Complex," one student wrote: "An Oedipus complex is when you love your mother." Surely this is a corruption of innocence.) One suspects the neo-Freudians have a special attraction for young people in their late adolescence, who can readily identify the reconstruction of society with the unmasking and rejection of parental authority.

[6] *Life Against Death* (New York: Vintage edition; 1961), p. 318.

burdens and from the fearful neurosis which it imposes upon the race, just as primitive man with his notion of recurrence and his archetypes sought to escape from the "terror of history."

Since Freudianism, in effect, absorbs human history into nature, much of the work of the neo-Freudians involves an effort to free man from that blind and insatiable nature into which Freud thrust him, and with this impulse we can certainly sympathize. But not if it must be done at the cost of accepting Utopian systems which, in effect, annul history. Here Freud himself is perhaps preferable since he insists that we accept our "fallen" nature, and this acceptance is the principal requirement for living in history.[7]

When psychoanalytic theory becomes, gradually, less dogmatic and more sophisticated, it should, like any other area of psychology, provide the historian with useful insights. But as a *system*, orthodox or neo-Freudian, it will not give him the key to an understanding of individuals or of the general course of history. The historian must concern himself with the psychology of the age he is investigating. But in most cases he will do this best if he waits in silence and with a degree of humility for the age to disclose its secrets to him—and does not come armed with systems and arrogant in his modern knowledge, to divest the past of its mysteries. Patience is requisite to establish contact with the individuals, long dead, who compose history. At the

---

[7] Hans Meyerhoff, defending Freud's view of the ambiguity of man's nature and history, gives a most effective analysis of the psychoanalytic "Utopians" who offer "prophetic visions of rebirth, resurrection, and the new life in eternity" that are, in fact, "ultimately illusory phantasms, born of an undying [and in Meyerhoff's view quite unacceptable] faith in the omnipotence of thought and nourished by the romantic longings of the perennial child in man." "Freud and the Ambiguity of Culture," *Partisan Review*, XXIV, No. 1 (Winter, 1957), pp. 117–30. In a different spirit, Karl Stern says: "We feel alarmed . . . when a particular discipline of science assumes a *monistic* tendency, becomes all-explanatory, and even hints at utopian developments." *The Third Revolution: A Study of Psychiatry and Religion* (New York: Doubleday Image Book; 1961), p. 50.

moment, what psychology, and perhaps more especially psychoanalysis, has accomplished with regard to the historian is to extend appreciably his "area of awareness"—and that, perhaps, is enough.

The authors of *The Social Sciences in Historical Study* also leave something to be said about the relevance of sociology to history. In this relationship, it might be argued that history is more sinned against than sinning. Most competent historians have no bias against sociology *in principle*, but many sociologists *in principle* reject the notion that history is relevant to sociological investigation. It is not the subject but the products of sociology that offend the historian. Indeed, he cannot afford to be indifferent to sociology since he must of necessity deal with society, past if not present; the questions that the sociologists ask about class, status, mobility, etc., are of immediate concern to him.

While the editors of successive Social Science Research *Bulletins* have been issuing pretentious and confusing pronouncements, practicing historians have gone about their work, making use of those sociological investigations which best illuminate their own researches. Ignoring exhortations to embark on interdisciplinary projects, these historians have nonetheless often used sociological straw to make historical bricks and will presumably continue to do so. One can readily make up a long list of contemporary historians whose writing is informed by insights derived from sociology. Such a list would, in fact, include most of the able younger historians in the country—Oscar Handlin, Richard Hofstadter, William Taylor, Donald Meyer, David Potter, Daniel Boorstin, C. Vann Woodward, Charles G. Sellers, Jr., Henry May, Marvin Meyers, and Sigmund Diamond, to name only those who come most readily to mind.

No list could be compiled of equally outstanding sociologists who have a strong orientation toward history or even a conviction that the historical dimension of sociology is crucial. Here we can cite the testimony of the sociologists themselves. In the words of Helen Lynd, "recognition of the necessity of including the time dimension does not appear to anything like the same extent in the study of social groups and of society as in the study of individual personality."[8] Mrs. Lynd suggests that the sociologists' "nonhistorical, or even antihistorical, attitude is the natural outcome of the reaction against the oversimplified evolutionary schemes of the eighteenth and nineteenth centuries, as well as of the current emphasis on empiricism and operational methods." But this does not obviate the danger of ignoring history. Too many sociologists "take the attitude that historical data are unnecessary or positively misleading." It is Mrs. Lynd's hope that "recognition of the hazards of the future in a time of social change . . . may lead to the realization that we can have no adequate understanding even of the present moment, or ability to predict its possible outcomes, without having understanding of its history. . . . The attempt of psychology and social science to exclude history in the interests of abstract method, logical completeness, and a timeless objectivity, may result in missing the concrete realities that these disciplines are attempting to understand."[9]

The late C. Wright Mills expressed himself even more strongly on the subject. Mills referred to the ideal "sociological imagination" as that quality of mind which "enables us to grasp history and biography and the relations between the two within society."[1] History is, for Mills, "the shank of social study," without which it is impossible to understand "the problems of our time—which now include the problem

---

[8] *On Shame and the Search for Identity* (New York: Science Editions; 1961), p. 107.
[9] Ibid., pp. 107–12.
[1] *The Sociological Imagination* (New York: Oxford University Press; 1959), p. 6.

of man's very nature." Sociologists must "develop further a psychology of man that is sociologically grounded and historically relevant" and they cannot do this "without use of history and without an historical sense of psychological matters. . . . All sociology worthy of the name is historical sociology."[2]

Similarly, history contains a considerable element of sociology. Few historians would argue with Mills's assertion that "when we understand social structures and structural changes as they bear upon the more intimate science and experiences, we are able to understand the causes of individual conduct and feelings of which men in a specific milieu are themselves unaware. . . ."[3] But at the same time it must be confessed that the professional sociologist is of limited use to the historian. The historian, seeking illumination, finds himself confronted by what Mills called the Grand Theorists and the Abstracted Empiricists. The Grand Theorists are sociologists such as Max Weber, Pitrim Sorokin, and Talcott Parsons who are concerned with vast systems that comprehend the greater part of man's social behavior. The Abstracted Empiricists, generally the younger generation, are preoccupied with carefully controlled statistical studies of very small segments of contemporary social life. The historian can draw far more constructive ideas from the Grand Theorists, when he can penetrate their language, than he can from the Abstracted Empiricists. Weber's examination of the relationship between what he called the Protestant ethic and the rise of modern capitalism has

---

[2] Ibid., pp. 143–6.

[3] *The Sociological Imagination*, p. 162. See also Peter L. Berger: *Invitation to Sociology: A Humanistic Perspective*, (New York: Doubleday, Anchor Books, 1963): "Openness to the humanistic scope of sociology . . . implies an ongoing communication with other disciplines that are vitally concerned with exploring the human condition. The most important of these are history and philosophy. . . . Disregard of the historical dimension is an offense not only against the classic Western ideal of the civilized man but against sociological reasoning itself. . . ." (p. 168).

perhaps had more influence upon historians than upon sociologists, and the same is probably true of David Riesman's treatment of the inner-directed and the other-directed individuals. Most contemporary sociologists deal with generalizations that are too crude or with studies that are too detailed and too limited to be of much interest to the historian. However, the major sociologists, from Comte on, have asked questions that are of the greatest importance to historians, questions about the relations of institutions to ideologies, about the anatomy of an elite and the role of the middle class in an industrial society. To the not inconsiderable extent that historians have, as a consequence, a wider consciousness of these and related problems, all historians are sociologists. But historians have the advantage of not having to subscribe to any of the currently fashionable dogmas and of not having to use the highly formalized language which has become characteristic of sociology.

Seen in this light, the argument as to whether the historian should be a sociologist, and to what degree, appears quite pointless. The historian does not take seriously the claim of the sociologists that they are "scientists," any more than he accepts the similar pretension of the psychologists. The practitioners of both these disciplines are concerned with various aspects of man—man as an individual and man as a member of society—just as the historian is concerned with man as an actor in the drama of history. The study of man, fortunately, cannot be reduced to, or contained within, the categories of any one or any combination of social "sciences." Once this is understood, the expectations of scholars concerned with the study of man will be more modest and their labors more fruitful.

It might indeed be argued that the various "insights" of psychology and sociology will ultimately have to establish their validity on the basis of the degree to which they correspond to, reinforce, or illuminate the accumulated experience of man, and they will do this on history's terms, not their own. History is and must remain pre-eminent among the social sciences, for it is history that brings together the results of the inquiries that the various social sciences carry on and shapes them into a comprehensive account related to the course of historic events. History, in short, by telling its much-abused "story," mediates between the social sciences and the larger community of man; it is primarily through historians that the social sciences themselves may enter history.

II

Academic History

It might be well to restate our general (and by no means original) thesis that the Age of Revolution which ended the eighteenth century in such dramatic fashion gave birth to the modern notion of history and that World Wars I and II mark the end of the historiographical assumptions which had dominated Western thinking for a century and a quarter; the American and French Revolutions signified the destruction of a society characterized by custom, class, and tradition. Secularization was accelerated and democratic aspiration expressed itself in an erosion of the established orders and an intensification of nationalism. Since the individual no longer received his sense of order and direction from Scriptural or Papal authority, he must find it in the destiny of his nation or his class. Historians were thus confronted with the task of creating national histories out of the ill-matched lumber of the past. Nations could no longer have divine justification, so they demanded historical justification. The historians responded with histories which traced the ancestors of the particular nation to the most ancient times and which demonstrated that its citizens were of a singularly pure racial stock. It was a short and perhaps inevitable step from the germ theory of Anglo-American historians who professed to find the peculiar excellence of their respective nations in the Teutonic tribes of the German forests to the racial theories of Adolf Hitler or the new Imperial Rome which Mussolini sought to create. With the loss of authority of the Christian Church, men sought to find a meaning and purpose to life in devotion to the nation as defined by the nation's historians. All the needs that had once been served by faith and tradition had now to be satisfied by the state. Moreover, since philosophers and historians had invested the state with many of the attributes of divine power, among them eternal life and the amelioration of evil in the form of poverty, the citizens of the Western nations, in which an attenuated Christianity survived, were inclined to see God in history or, more explicity, history as God. If a progressive teleology, expressed in the nation state, was at work in the world, one could serve the grand design by serving the state and one could thereby endow one's life with meaning. Thus history was essential to the modern nation, just as the nation was essential to the development of present-day notions of historiography; the nation could not have taken the form it did as a replacement of the universal church if historians had not been at hand to justify and rationalize its past and its future. By projecting the history of the nation back into the past and clothing it in mythic garments in the process, the historian made it possible for his nation to look toward a future in whose name it could organize its people for the important political and social tasks that lay ahead.

As we have seen, it was the particular notion of many historians in these centuries to fancy themselves scientists. The principal effect of this illusion was to make them more dogmatic and doctrinaire than they might otherwise have been, since they imagined that they were acting under the aegis of the "scientific spirit."

The two world wars of the twentieth century, accompanied by the return to the barbarism of the modern dictatorships, more especially that of Hitler, showed with the inescapable logic of events that the optimistic expectations of the nineteenth century were doomed to frustration. The devotion of modern man to the myth of nationhood generated by statesmen and their handmaidens, the historians, is seen clearly enough in the tenacity with which the citizens of the various states of the Western world have clung to illusions which history itself has made untenable—the principal one being the viability of the independent, aggressive, expansionist, self-centered state whose microcosm was the independent, aggressive, self-centered individual, indivisible and autonomous. The First World War and its traumatic by-product, the appearance of a communized Russia, did not shake the West from its century-long dream. Spengler's brilliant obituary sent a thrill of dismay through the intellectuals of the West. There was a terrible fascination about his great symphony of civilizations rising and passing away, to litter the shores of history with their bleaching bones. Arnold Toynbee's vast survey of the cycles of civilization too owed its inspiration to the Greek historians.

But Spengler and Toynbee, although not by any means alone in their pessimistic appraisal of European culture, failed to disturb seriously the system of ideas which was rooted in the eighteenth and nineteenth centuries and wedded to the concept of the modern nation. The shock of the war led a generation of theologians and philosophers to re-examine the underlying assumptions of their respective disciplines, more especially as they related to historic man, but it did not affect the masses of the people, nor did the anxious, if not despairing ruminations of Toynbee and Spengler break through the crust of liberal optimism. The reason for this was undoubtedly the rise of Soviet Russia as the exemplar of Marxist Communism. The intellectuals of the West were too habituated to the categories and modes of thought of science to be immune to the claims of international Communism. The dialectic seemed to have triumphed. Science as a way of looking at man and at society might still prove itself valid in Marxism. In that case it would be evident that science was not at fault, nor the Utopian social expectations to which it had been harnessed, but simply that the wrong science had been used, a science poisoned by the fallacies of capitalism. Many American intellectuals seized eagerly on this explanation of the "time of troubles" which had been ushered in by events of 1914–1918.

Among them, a number of historians were seduced by the notion of dialectical materialism; to a profession already aspiring to scientific credentials, economic determinism seemed to offer a splendidly objective tool for making sense out of the disorder of history. So while the most sensitive individuals—the artists (Dadaists), writers (Proust, Ford Maddox Ford, Jacob Wasserman, Kafka), poets (T. S. Eliot, Rimbaud, Rilke)—revealed a world in agony and disintegration, the majority of professors, ministers, and politicians continued to act as if the world war had been an unfortunate but temporary interruption in the orderly and progressive march of history. And those who allowed the true state of affairs to penetrate their consciousness and touch their consciences ascribed it, with the astonishing glibness that characterizes Marxist theory, to the death throes of capitalism.

The professors of history were trapped in the institutional arrangements of the academy, which had taken shape during the nineteenth century. History at that time had been divided chronologically and geographically. The chronological arrangement prevailed in ancient and medieval history; thereafter, in honor of the modern nation states, it became primarily geographical—the history of Germany, France, England, Italy, etc. These segments were further divided into periods (early modern, late modern) and sometimes into centuries and even generations. Today many history departments in major universities offer courses in the Federal Period of American History, the Age of Jackson, the Civil War, Reconstruction, the Progressive Era, the New Deal, and so on. It is not unusual for one department to have seven or eight instructors in American history, each with a carefully demarcated preserve in which he does research, writes monographs, and teaches undergraduate and graduate students. Professional status, in fact, depends on a high degree of specialization. Every ambitious younger professor who must for a time teach a freshman survey course aspires to "his own" highly specialized course, and if half a dozen of his departmental colleagues are in the same field it takes a great deal of ingenuity to mark out a new subdivision in an already crowded tract. Such a system is defensible only if history is, indeed, a science or is like a science, that is to say, if the accumulation of monographs and the painstaking preoccupation of hundreds of historians with minutia can be relied on to bring us "nearer the truth" about the past. If this is not the case, then there is very little justification for "more and more research into less and less." Great history, the history that has commanded men's minds and hearts, has always been narrative history, history with a story to tell that illuminates the truth of the human situation, that lifts spirits and projects new potentialities. The detailed, analytical history that is the standard product of our academies has little to say to the ordinary man. Indeed, it often seems to have only contempt and scorn for him. *Popular* means, in the academic lexicon, meretricious. It can hardly be otherwise, for in the asceticism which modern-day historical scholarship imposed upon itself lies the implication that excellence cannot be understood or appreciated by the layman. It is a rite for the initiate, not a means of communication with those "outside."

But the simple fact is that a society lives by its power to define the tasks which need to be done, not by "understanding" itself through an endless process of analysis. History without the capacity to project common goals, to discriminate between that part of the past which must be preserved and that part which must be abandoned, serves society ill.

A concomitant of the notion that history is scientific (which I would say is no longer believed but is still practiced as a consequence of intellectual sloth, inertia, and the strength of existing academic arrangements) is the concept of historical perspective. This is one of the most familiar illusions of the modern historian. It might be stated thus: in the heat of particular events, the contemporaries of the events, who may also be the participants, are too involved emotionally to be able to judge fairly and wisely what is happening (the more common term would be *objectively*, but we will have more to say about this unhappy word; let us avoid it for the time being). It is necessary to wait for the passions of the moment to die, for another generation, further removed in time, to make those even-handed and impartial judgments to which the historian is pledged. Official archives must be opened, relevant papers collected, monographs written before we can really say what happened and what its import was. If this postulate be granted (it cannot be proved), it thus follows that the further removed in time the historian is from the events he is dealing with, the better will be his perspective and the more clearly will he see and understand the motives and the passions which moved his ancestors. One metaphor might see him standing on a mountain from whose noble summit the distant events of another age are seen through a telescope fashioned by the dedicated researchers of the intervening generations. This notion is especially congenial to the historian who fancies he stands on the mountain top, that is, to the historian of the present day. He is content to imagine himself on a pinnacle of wisdom, while modestly acknowledging, as the price for enjoying this eminence, that his successors will enjoy an even more comprehensive view.

The fact of the matter is that the modern historian from his lofty perch can see very little of what went on in an earlier age. His vision is distorted by a vast accumulation of ideas, values, and subsequent events, which, to pursue the metaphor, have so altered the lenses through which he regards the past that it is extremely difficult, if not impossible, for him to recapture any very clear picture of past events. But surely, the champion of historical perspective replies, he is less involved, less emotional than the people who lived through the event he has marked out for investigation. By no means. I recall a debate over the respectability of contemporary history waged some years ago between the British historian Herbert Butterfield and the American historian Arthur Schlesinger, Jr. Schlesinger maintained with considerable persuasiveness that the only events in the past about which we could be impartial were those involving issues about which we no longer cared, issues that were unimportant to us today. At first thought, one might assume that such issues and events make up a rather large portion of the recoverable past, but a moment's reflection will suggest otherwise. Ancient Greece? The history of Israel, the Middle Ages, the Reformation and the Counter-Reformation? The Enlightenment and the Age of Democratic Revolutions, to borrow R. R. Palmer's phrase? The rise of Communism? Since the historian directs his attention primarily to those events of the past which seem to him important, and these are apt to be important, directly or indirectly, as they are relevant to the present, it thus follows that the researches of the vast majority of historians involve issues about which they care very much indeed. A little reflection will make this eminently apparent. And even in the study of long-dead civilizations whose relevance for our own day seems remote, one can readily observe the bitter disputes and contentions between historians with different points of view. Time may bring perspective and dispassionate judgment, but this is nowhere reflected in the acrimonious wrangles common among academic historians debating the character of an ancient Chinese dynasty or the institutions of feudal India.

There is, of course, the matter of research. The material relating to a past age must be collected, collated, examined, digested. The contemporaries had no chance, or little chance, to do this—to perform the laborious tasks of historical methodology. Their standards of critical judgment were unrefined, they had taken no graduate seminars in method, in the assessing of documents of dubious authenticity, in the comparison of sources, in the preparation of bibliographies, in the scrupulous annotating of texts. Today research has become a god; everyone wishes to do research and everyone who does it enjoys high status. The club lady does research on travel in Mexico; the toddler in grammar school does research on the Indians of Lower California; the advertising agency does research on customer preferences. Research, along with creativity, as Jacques Barzun has so engagingly suggested, rules our world. Much of it, however, is spurious, and much that satisfies the formal canons is ultimately meaningless. The mountain and the mouse are fixtures of the academic world. Mountains of honest and conscientious research produce a progeny of mice-like monographs. Research is too often a substitute for thought, for bold speculation, for enlightening generalization. "What original contribution do you feel your dissertation makes?" an examiner often asks a doctoral candidate. "Well," the candidate replies, "nobody has really made a thorough study heretofore of the influence of newspaper comics in the decade between 1885 and 1895." A perhaps aprocryphal story is told of the professor who, informed that a doctoral candidate's bulky thesis was on the dairy industry in Wisconsin between 1875 and 1885, observed dryly that he must have covered the subject "teet by teet."

Our veneration of research is a formalism as stultifying, and as remote from real life, as the proverbial scholastic speculations about the number of angels that could be accommodated on the head of a pin. A historian has recently suggested, not entirely facetiously, that a moratorium be declared on all research for ten years and that in that interval historians be required to reflect on the research that has already been done. One of the particular burdens that our modern notion of research imposes on the historian is the obligation to read *everything* that has been written upon his particular subject. "I woke up last night in a cold sweat," a colleague who had just finished an ambitious study of literary criticism told me recently. "I dreamed that I had overlooked an important monograph and a reviewer called attention to it in the *Modern Language Quarterly*."

To be sure, only an obscurantist would attack research indiscriminately. One of the principal contributions of the Western world has been the concept of research as the thorough investigation of all relevant evidence. No one would want to relinquish this basis for all knowledge in the humanities and social sciences. Yet some of the illusions engendered by our devotion to research are patent. One such is that a case may be proved by the sheer volume of data mustered in support of it; or that fifty footnotes are more conclusive than five. Professional historians know, or should know, that they have often been persuaded against their better judgment that such-and-such was true by the sheer weight of evidence paraded before them. In many cases, subsequent study has overturned a thesis accepted as fact by a majority of scholars in the field simply because they allowed themselves to be overborne by the weight of research offered to "prove" the hypothesis. One of the most spectacular instances is that of the French historian Henri Vignaud, who by vast labors managed to convince many of his contemporaries that Columbus was not looking for a route to the East Indies but rather for legendary islands in the Atlantic. Similarly, Charles Beard "proved," to the satisfaction of at least a generation of historians, that the Founding Fathers framed the Federal Constitution to protect their personal interests in continental securities. And recently, when Beard has been challenged, it has generally been on the grounds that his research was faulty.

The most painstaking and orthodox researches do not relieve the historian of the responsibility for exercising thoughtful discrimination. The historian's own prejudices and preconceptions, it is now accepted, determine in a very large degree what he finds in his research. This is not to say that he should abandon his researches but rather that he should recognize and admit that the truth is less in his sources than in himself. The sources will reveal no more to him than he has the wisdom to elicit from them. His problem is complicated, moreover, by the fact that it is not simply his own prejudices that he is contending with; he wears glasses, so to speak, that are colored by the general assumptions in his field. The individual historian can hardly be blamed for these, but they do blind him, to an extraordinary degree, to any bit of evidence that does not fit the existing and generally accepted generalizations.

This may be best understood by reference to the field of nuclear physics. Two physicists, Tsung-Dao Lee and Chen Ning Yang, won a Nobel Prize in 1957 for making an important breakthrough in nuclear theory. Modern physics had for some years accepted as a basic proposition the law of parity conservation, or mirror symmetry, as it is sometimes called. The law of parity conservation states, in essence, that two particles, as the mirror image of each other, should behave in exactly the same manner. It had been observed in numerous experiments with high-velocity particles that the respective particles, when split, decayed at the same rate; these experiments reinforced the authority of the law of parity conservation. However, in the early 1950's certain experiments indicated that some low-velocity particles did not have identical lifetimes. Yang and Lee, puzzled, as were many of their colleagues, by this phenomenon, concentrated on the theta and tau mesons, which seemed clearly to represent an anomaly in terms of the law of parity conservation. If these two weak interactions did not conform to the law, then it followed that the law was not as comprehensive as it had been taken to be.

The proposition seems simple enough to a layman. What was accepted as a law describing the behavior of nuclear particles apparently did not cover a portion of the phenomenon which it was supposed to cover. This had been noted and had caused some uneasiness and some tentative speculation. But the nuclear physicists did not know what to make of this discrepancy. If not exactly ignored in the hope that it would go away, the theta-tau puzzle remained apparently insoluble until Yang and Lee turned their attention to it. The breakthrough which won them the Nobel Prize consisted essentially in their daring to question directly the applicability of parity conservation to weak mesons. After long reflection and discussion, Yang and Lee arrived at a conclusion that a nonphysicist, not committed to a law which offered aesthetic as well as practical advantages, would perhaps have come to much sooner. Their revolutionary discovery—that parity conservation did not apply to weak-interaction particles—was possible only after they had freed themselves of existing preconceptions.

Once they had convinced their fellow physicists of the validity of parity nonconservation, it was discovered that experiments performed as far back as 1928 had demonstrated a clear violation of parity symmetry (this was a year after a Hungarian-born physicist had devised the first mathematical formulation of parity conservation or symmetry in quantum theory).

The case of the nuclear physicists can be taken to illustrate a problem common to all fields of human knowledge. Laws and principles are formulated, and myths created, which profess to explain the human or the natural world. In order to be accepted, these laws and myths must correspond, at least in part, with what can be observed of the behavior of matter or of human beings, as the case may be. The original formulation is an act of genuine creativity; it involves the penetration of a barrier imposed by an earlier and outmoded concept, law, or myth. The new formulation, often bitterly resisted at first, eventually exerts a pervasive influence, especially upon the professional—the expert —who always opposes anything that threatens the principles to which he has given his loyalty, on which his professional career may, to a large degree, be founded, and whose overthrow must leave him adrift upon uncertain seas. In the field of history, we might take Frederick Jackson Turner's frontier thesis as a case in point. Turner wrote his famous essay on the significance of the frontier in opposition to the germ theorists of New England who dominated American historiography and who considered the history of the United States as an extension of the history of England. In this interpretation, the West, which reached from the Alleghenies to the Pacific, counted for very little. Turner offered a view of history which made the frontier experience, and thus the West, the crucial experience in the development of the United States. Its appeal was irresistible. It had, as has been suggested, a naturalistic base—the notion that environment shapes society—which made it most congenial to a science-minded age. At a time when European historians were busy discovering for their respective nations unique attributes generally rooted in pre-history, the Turner thesis permitted America to put forth a claim for a special and unique experience. The Turner thesis was to America what the Magna Charta was to the British, Charlemagne to the French, and the Teutonic tribes to the historians of a recently unified Germany. It appeared to explain certain aspects of the American story which were otherwise inexplicable. It was, nonetheless, a myth, albeit a useful and appealing one and one which provided a framework for a host of American historians. But the point is that once this law, or principle of interpretation, had been formulated, it closed the eyes of most historians to any facts which did not conform to it. Honest scholars went to the sources and found what in most instances was not there, namely, confirmation of Turner's thesis. The frontier did *not* make men more liberal; if anything, it made them more conservative. Moreover, it did *not* attract the independent, liberal spirits, but rather the aggressively orthodox who did not hesitate to subordinate the individual to the community.

Perhaps we can best understand the Turner thesis as the declaration of independence of that part of the United States which lay west of the Mississippi, or indeed west of the headwaters of the Ohio River. In his most basic assumption—that the West was an enormously important part of America—Turner was indisputably right. In almost all the arguments he used to support this proposition, he was wrong.

Much the same thing can be said of Charles Beard's interpretation of the Federal Constitution. The critical problem of any healthy society is to distinguish between those elements of the past that must be preserved in order to prevent chaos and decadence and those which must be abandoned in order to prevent rigidity and stultification. The greater part of the public to which Beard addressed his seminal work, *An Economic Interpretation of the Constitution,* regarded that document as sacred writ, perfect, unchanging, divinely inspired. Beard argued that the framers of the Constitution were human, indeed all too human, and that they had devised a government which would protect their own privileged position and make their property inviolate. While most historians acknowledged that Beard went much too far in assigning motives of self-interest to the men who drew up the Federal Constitution, he did make his basic point—that they were men and not gods and that their handiwork had to stand under constant judgment by posterity and prove itself sufficiently flexible to provide for contingencies that the framers could not have foreseen. To many historians of Beard's generation, it seemed that he had buttressed his argument with irrefutable facts, with thorough and conscientious research that led ineluctably to his conclusions.

But in recent decades, when Beard has been attacked by a new generation of scholars, he has been criticized for the inadequacy of his research. He did not dig deep enough into the evidence (as he himself had confessed); he was not rigorous enough with his facts; he shaped the facts to support his thesis rather than modifying his thesis in accord with the facts. His self-righteous successors fancy that they are better men than Beard, that their improved methodology will preserve them from the errors into which he fell.

Thus the comedy is played out: "My research is better than yours," declares one historian. "No," the other answers, "my research is better than yours. I have more footnotes and a bigger bibliography than you do." And so on they go, mounting toward the truth over the fallen bodies of their colleagues. But to return to the atomic physicists, Yang and Lee: the problem in history, as in nuclear physics or any other science, is to free oneself of the existing generalizations that have served to organize knowledge and have thereby made it possible to deal with the raw materials of the discipline in an orderly and systematic manner.

While we are on the subject of research, we might pause

to examine the importance of research to the historian as a teacher—which is, after all, his primary function. Here again he is inclined to comfort himself with unexamined assumptions. He is working in new areas, discovering new truths or refining old ones so that he can pass this improved knowledge and understanding on to his students. They will then be better informed about their world, past and present, and thus think and act more effectively. This is at least the way historians are inclined to put it, if pressed.

Let us for the moment concede that the scholar-historian, decade by decade, is approaching more closely to the truth. How much of this truth can be conveyed to undergraduate students? Let us assume what is manifestly impossible, that by dint of heroic reading the scholar-teacher, in addition to doing his own research and teaching, "keeps up" with the research in his field, that is, reads all the books and articles that bear directly on his primary area of interest. How much of this appears at once in his undergraduate instruction? How much can? Does the teacher rewrite his lectures every few years to incorporate the latest research? Perhaps he should, but he does not. He may occasionally freshen stale fare by reference to some recent study which amplifies or refutes a traditional interpretation. Moreover, most contemporary research is so specialized, so detailed, that it is irrelevant to undergraduate instruction. One might ask how important it is that an undergraduate student be informed at once, or indeed at all, of some change or modification in an accepted view or interpretation. Certainly, it would be irresponsible and pointless to misinform the student. But let us say a new monograph has appeared which suggests that General Horatio Gates performed more effectively at the battle of Saratoga than historians have generally given him credit for. Generations of students have been given an unfavorable view of that unhappy soldier's role in the Revolution—without, presumably, any impairment of their understanding of the conflict as a whole. The obligation of the teacher-researcher to inform himself of the new interpretation and pass it on to his students is, at the least, arguable. It would be difficult to maintain that the student will have a better grasp of the meaning of American history as the result of being brought up to date on the most recent estimates of General Gates's military talents, or even of a considerable number of similar items. It might well be argued that the opposition still must be heard from, and the older interpretation may ultimately prevail.

This may be said of the many minor adjustments that are constantly being made by historians tinkering with the model they offer as a reasonable replica of the past. But it is not applicable to the larger reinterpretations, the sweeping revisions, which are so much a part of the present historiographical scene. These more extensive modifications or revolutions in interpretation, however, are not the work of a day or a year. They make headway gradually against the determined rear-guard action of the old views; they penetrate slowly and deeply the successive layers of historical consciousness, as did the germ theory and later the environmentalist school of the nineteenth century and the economic determinism of the twentieth. In these instances, even the most isolated scholar is aware of major readjustments and is very well able to pass them along if he wishes, as he certainly will if he believes in progress and in "scientific" history. Unfortunately, as I have indicated at greater length elsewhere, the new interpretations are often no better than the old, and not infrequently a good deal worse.

The rationale underlying the standard system of passing on the newest "knowledge" has been that there is some magic in the newer data, that it would reach the soul of the student and make him somehow a better man, that simply knowing the more recent "truth" entails a heartening, inspiring victory over the older "error."

This belief is indeed magical. It is not susceptible of proof, and nobody has ever tried to prove it. It would require some ingenuity to show conclusively that a man who had been taught that the American Revolution was caused by the desire of the colonial merchants to protect their profits against their British rivals was wiser or better than the man who had been taught that the Revolution was fought over the abstract principle of the right of taxation. The rationale is that the student who was given the interpretation based on self-interest would have a more realistic grasp of human behavior and thus a better understanding of himself and his motivations. But such a thesis assumes that people act from self-interest rather than principle, and that indeed principles are only rationalizations offered by interest as a cover for its actions. These propositions may, for all I know, be true, but at least at the present stage of knowledge in the behavioral sciences they are not provable. We might indeed go further and say that they will never be, because they have to do not with provable postulates but with the way men conceive of their relationship to the world; they can never be successfully transmuted from matters of value to matters of fact.

What I have been saying, then, is that the basic assumptions about the role of the historian as a teacher, as the conveyor of information about history, rest on seldom-examined academic customs, practices, and conventions which over the years have become highly formalized and relatively empty of meaning.

Another much-worshipped and false god is "objectivity." The analogy to science is again made: the observer is presumed to view the material neutrally, without emotional commitment, coolly, impartially, disinterestedly. To be sure, objectivity has been annihilated by a hardly more worthy foe, relativism or historicism, but its ghost lingers on, crying out to be exorcised and laid to rest once for all. Objectivity does not correspond to any human experience, except perhaps utter disinterest. As we have seen, even the scientist who deals with dead matter is very far from being "objective" in any strict sense of the word, and for the historian the word is quite irrelevant. Its background may be briefly given. When, in the nineteenth century, history began to consider itself a science and make an analogy between the "method" of the historian and the method of the scientist, objectivity was held up as the scholarly ideal. By the end of the century, the relativists had made serious inroads in the notion of objectivity, having pointed out that the individual historian was so conditioned by the culture of which he was a part and the time in which he lived that he could not achieve any real detachment. Faced with this unhappy fact, the historian found an ally in the sociologists of the Mannheim school, who argued that it was possible to create a "sociology of knowledge" in which the scholar made a highly sophisticated analysis of his own involvement in "classes, interests, and periods." The historian was thus encouraged to hope that he might learn to peel off successive ideological skins until he came at last to a hard core of objectivity. The hope proved illusory. Indeed, the formulation of the idea of objectivity turned the whole problem on its head and led to the most serious misunderstanding of the function of the historian. Instead of debating the degree of objectivity that the historian might hope to attain, it would be far better to conceive of the task of the historian as one of sympathetic understanding of his subject, a matter of attachment rather than detachment, of love rather than aloofness. Most of the great histories are animated by the devotion of the author to his subject. His insight is the consequence not of lack of involvement but of the deepest commitment to the people, the period, and the events about which he is writing. Such a devotion does not, of course, preclude honesty, fairness, and balance. It rather makes these qualities essential if the work is not to degenerate into a simple panegyric. Honesty in the treatment of sources and judiciousness in the assessment of individuals, parties, and partisans must of course be exercised—and these may be achieved through patience and the determination to subdue one's prejudices. If we imagine that such attributes are the product of a "scientific" spirit or of "objectivity," we should recall that the Bible offers us a classic example of history without whitewash: David, Solomon, the kings and the prophets of Israel are depicted with all their human vices and follies. The whole issue of objectivity is perhaps best summed up in Reinhold Niebuhr's words: "The ability to judge friend or foe with some degree of objectivity is, in the ultimate instance, a moral and not an intellectual achievement, since it requires the mitigation of fears and prejudices, envies and hatreds, which represent defects, not of the mind, but of the total personality."

Fairness, intelligence, honesty, compassion, judiciousness, painstaking workmanship, and, most hopefully, wisdom do not by any means depend on one's being objective and even less on one's being scientific, at least in the sense in which that word is generally used. Objects are dead, inanimate things; subjects are alive. *Subjective* has been, generally, an opprobrious term; *objective*, a complimentary one. Both are perhaps irrelevant. To say that a historian is subjective is simply to state that he is a living human being who grasps the past through a kind of extension of his sensory apparatus, with the help of his critical faculties—which is the only way in which the past can be properly grasped. To say that he is objective suggests that he exists somehow outside of time, outside of the flux of human events, and thus views mankind with cold, Olympian detachment.

Even if objectivity, in any deep sense, is unattainable, there is probably a certain detachment in the historian's attitude as a consequence of his being "outside" the events he is dealing with. And although history at its noblest may be narrative in form, the primarily critical and interpretative elements are certainly present as well. Here the historian may profit from the coincidence of being, to a degree, removed from his subject. The simplest and one of the most familiar forms of detachment is political exile. Thucydides is an excellent example: his exile from Athens gave him a perspective on the Peloponnesian War that he might not otherwise have attained. A historian might derive a broader perspective, too, from the fact that he is part of a declining culture which in maturity and worldly wisdom is superior to the new culture with which he is preoccupied. Polybius might be taken as a case in point.

The "outsideness" may also be ideological. Marxist historians, starting with Marx himself, have written brilliant critical history because of their alienation from a predominantly middle-class capitalist society. This alienation gives them perspective that has often enabled them to penetrate the surface of prevalent ideologies and institutions which they have rejected and which they regard as dying or as deserving of death and are therefore able to view with the detachment of an anatomist. But such insights are provisional and coincidental. They are achieved at the price of uncritical devotion to an "outside" ideology, which in turn produces distortions quite as gross as any it exposes in "the others." And they cannot be planned or taught or learned; they are the by-products of an individual's view of the world. Psychotics, for example, have insights which are inaccessible to normal people. A member of a submerged proletariat, the representative of an alienated minority, a political refugee may, as a result of his existential situation, see the dominant society from a fresh and revealing perspective. But these insights cannot be called in any sense objective, since they are the consequence of deep devotion to a particular ideal. This kind of historical insight may be lik-

ened to the view of a scene through a narrow aperture
which, because of the narrowness of perspective, allows the
viewer to focus on an aspect of the scene hidden from those
with a wider vision, those who, let us say, are in the scene
itself.

Let us return for a moment to the discussion with which
this chapter opened. I described the modern illusion of the
historian's time perspective in terms of a man on the mountain top of the present viewing the past through a telescope.
A more accurate image might be that of the man on the
mountain top laboriously sinking a shaft through the heart
of the mountain, past successive layers of the debris deposited by the intervening ages, until at last he approaches a
genuine understanding of the people and events which he
has chosen as the subjects of his investigation. The longer
the time that has intervened between the historian and his
subject, the greater the effort required to dig back to the
truth or a near approximation of it.

This metaphor represents more truly the historian's task
and his inevitable limitations. However, we shall make some
modification of it at a later point in the discussion.

In any event, it is neither to research, objectivity, or the
perspective of time that we can turn with confidence in our
search for the meaning of historical study. Research, ab-
surdly pretentious as it has become, is nonetheless an essential part of the historian's work. Objectivity, on the other
hand, is without meaning for the historian. We understand
quite well those scholarly virtues which it is supposed to
comprehend, but it gives rise to so much misunderstanding
about the "methods" of the historian that we can banish
it without a qualm and still retain, under their proper names,
honesty, scrupulousness, balance, and so on—its positive
attributes.

As for the "perspective of time," perhaps the most deeply
ingrained and least challenged notion of modern historical

scholarship, we shall demonstrate in the next chapter how feeble a reed this is for the historian to lean upon.

One of the direct results of the concept of history as a science was the preoccupation of historians of the last generation with causality—with a sequence of cause and effect traced through successive events. The appeal of such a notion is obvious. The disorder and complexity of history could be reduced (once the causal connections had been pointed out by historians) to a simple and easily followed line of development in which certain consequences were shown to have flowed inevitably from certain causes and to have become, in turn, the causes of subsequent events. The so-called Whig historians read English history as the unfolding of certain liberal political ideas throughout the course of the seventeenth, eighteenth, and nineteenth centuries; American historians interpreted American history in much the same spirit, seeing it as a pure stream of democracy rising with Roger Williams and flowing from him to Thomas Jefferson, to Andrew Jackson, and finally, Franklin Roosevelt.

The simpler notions of causality gave way in time to what we might call "multiple causality." As each new claim to have discovered *the* cause of the American Revolution or the War of 1812 or the Civil War was attacked and discredited by rival historians who had causes of their own to advance, the professional historian became more and more inclined simply to list all reasonable causes (and some unreasonable ones) and leave it to the student to decide which cause or combination of causes might best account for the events. This increasingly popular practice, often referred to as "the problem approach," was (and is) usually justified on the grounds that it encourages the student to think for himself. In fact, it often leaves the student as confused as the professor and prompts him to pass the buck back by listing the various "causes" and giving the provenance of each. As professors have become coy about "causes," we find them speaking of "factors," a more modest, if more ambiguous, word.

An increasing number of historians avoid such problems by concentrating their attention on a rather narrow field— let us say intellectual or cultural or social or constitutional or political history. These academics ("tunnel historians," in the phrase of J. H. Hexter), by abstracting one thread from the fabric of history, have, in many instances, enriched our understanding of history in general, but they are also peculiarly vulnerable to the charge of overspecialization.

The shift from a rather naïve causal orientation to a more sophisticated emphasis on "factors" has had one widely observed consequence: a diminishing of the dramatic quality of history. There is, of course, some gain in moving away from simple blacks and whites, from a good-guys and bad-guys approach, but unfortunately the "new" historian seems often to be working with a palette of neutral grays. In the field of American history, for instance, much has been made in recent years of the fact that in our past there has been no real struggle between liberal (i.e., good) ideas and conservative (bad) ideas; that, instead, American society has always been distinguished by a "consensus." Americans have been predominantly liberal and what has been sometimes seen as a dramatic struggle between proponents of change and proponents of the *status quo* has been in fact a family quarrel over how liberalism should best be interpreted and applied.

The genius of American politics, the proponents of consensus argue, has been a lack of any real ideological divisions, and indeed of any ideology at all. We have been especially blessed in having, instead of alien European dogmas, a set of vague working principles inherited from our British progenitors, the most conspicuous and effective of which is a healthy pragmatism—a willingness to judge something on whether it works rather than on whether it conforms to a particular ideological system. Undoubtedly there is much worth in such a view, but, if carried to an extreme, it reduces the role of individuals and of ideas in history; the uneasiness of some historians in the face of the present popularity of the doctrine of "concensus" is understandable.

But the feeling persists that these are minor and on the whole relatively unimportant skirmishes: causality versus factors; concensus versus sharply defined opposites. The ills of contemporary academic history lie deeper, in the very notion of the meaning of the historical enterprise.

One of the most unfortunate institutional by-products of academic history is the textbook. The trouble with textbooks is not that they are illustrated in color, that they are "written down," that they are fuzzy and mealy mouthed and an insult to the intelligence of the teacher and the student. The inadequacy of the textbook goes much deeper. It is a reflection of the basic philosophy or nonphilosophy of the upper echelons of the profession—the scholars whose views, to a large degree, dominate our thinking about the central problems of historiography.

The textbook is, among other things, a monument to the assumption that history is a cumulative "social science" in which today's views are necessarily better than yesterday's, in which the truth about the past can be comprehended in a series of facts and formulas which in turn can be learned, and the past, as a consequence, understood.

The king pin in this system is the examination, or "quiz," in which the student is expected to give the correct answer. In some more backward institutions, this answer is extracted in the mechanical form of "true" or "false" or the slightly more sophisticated multiple-choice tests, and these are graded by machines. That this degradation of the nature and meaning of history usually destroys any interest the student may have in the past or any feeling that the past is relevant to the present or essential for the future is hardly to be wondered at. The miracle is that a few students retain their interest despite such an offensive treatment of the subject. If a student wishes to be a chemist or an engineer, he must be required to memorize a considerable body of fact—though I gather that even in the sciences the emphasis on memorizing formulas and theorems is far less than it once was. But the sciences deal with matter and history deals with human beings. The techniques of teaching, study, and examination that are appropriate to one are not appropriate to the other. Indeed, if one wished to kill history as a humane study, it is hard to imagine a better system than the one currently in use in our schools and colleges. It is rather as though we were to substitute courses in anatomy for courses in literature as an avenue to the understanding of man. (And we have come perilously close to doing just that by anatomizing the creators of literature by means of the "tools" of psychology, sociology, and history.) One has at times the feeling that the humanistic disciplines are intent on borrowing from the social or behavioral sciences surgical instruments with which to dissect themselves. They do not understand that there is a fine line between explaining and explaining away. In many instances, the brilliant young professor's critical analysis, dazzling as it may be as a virtuoso performance, serves only to demonstrate to his students that they need not take the subject seriously: it is less a record of the profounder stirrings of the human soul than the expression of neurotic compulsions of various kinds.

In the same spirit, I confess that I am much less interested in the Progressives of the early twentieth century when they are presented to me simply as members of a "displaced elite" than when I am able to view them as intelligent and dedicated men and women who were contending with many of the important social issues of their day. If they were simply a "displaced elite" trying desperately and a little pathetically to compensate for their loss of power and authority by agitating for certain limited and more or less meaningless reforms, they have very little to say to me since I am not a member of a displaced elite. I am, however, a member of a displaced something else. Perhaps I am an alienated, upwardly mobile academic and my apparent concern for the future of mankind is only compensation for this sense of alienation, a kind of acting out of frustrations and anxieties, an attempt to relate them to wider social and political problems and thus give them dignity and importance.

This may be an exaggeration, but I fear not. It is rather characteristic of the tone of intellectual life in America today, and it produces, as its depressing antidote, the superpatriotism and mad activism of the John Birch Society.

But we were talking about the classic deficiencies of the history textbook. One conspicuous quality is that it is more or less indiscriminate. As a consequence of the flirtation of history with science, historians have lost the power to discriminate. All facts are more or less equal. Once we submitted to the compartmentalizing and fragmenting of historical knowledge, it was difficult, if not impossible, to find a principle of selection. We thus yielded without a struggle to the autocracy of the fact. We are obliged to "cover" a certain body of material; we must avoid "gaps." But, as we know very well, the essence of teaching (and of scholarship) is selection. Older generations undertook to teach the younger because they were convinced that certain things which gave order and dignity to life must be communicated; it was necessary to learn these things. Today we are more enlightened. To insist that certain things must be learned would be considered authoritarian or would be denounced as injecting value judgments into the educational process, which should, ideally, be neutral—simply the passing on of information, data, etc., to the student, who uses these bricks and lathes to construct his own intellectual home. If the more responsible and enlightened members of a society do not dare to say what must be done, what must be kept and what must be discarded, what is good and what is evil, the least responsible elements will insist on elevating an individual or a class to perform this function, however badly. Modern history provides an abundance of such examples. The textbook, however, by its deceptively bland offering up of the "facts" or of equally limp generalizations, deprives us of the most essential reality of history—that it is unfinished and imperfect, always being challenged to yield up answers to new dilemmas as well as to the recurrent questions posed by every age.

Academic history is not the detached and objective pursuit of Truth. It is the product of a particular moment in the political and intellectual history of the Western world, the moment of birth of the modern nation state and of the exaltation of "science" as the god of that world. Its future is, in consequence, quite uncertain: having no objective reality, it is dependent on the fragile loyalties of men who live in a world of revolutionary upheaval.

A Case in Point: the American Revolution

It is perhaps easiest to make the point—that the "perspective" provided by the historian's distance in time from the particular events with which he is concerned does not insure better understanding—by taking a specific case, in this instance, the American Revolution.

A re-examination of the attitudes of successive generations of historians toward the causes of the American Revolution poses most explicitly the problem of historical method. The thesis of this chapter is that the best interpretation of the causes of the Revolution was made in the decade following the treaty of peace in 1783 and that thereafter, as we moved further in time from the dramatic events of the Revolution and brought to bear on the problem all the vast resources of modern scholarship, we moved further and further from the truth about our Revolutionary beginnings.

Among the generation of historians who themselves lived through the American Revolution, David Ramsay is pre-eminent, though by no means atypical. Ramsay (1749–1815) was born in Pennsylvania of Scottish Presbyterian parents and attended the College of New Jersey, where his friend Benjamin Rush said of him that he was "far superior to any person we ever graduated at our college . . . I can promise more for him, in every thing, than I could for myself."[1] After graduating from Princeton, Ramsay moved to Charleston, South Carolina, where he began to practice medicine. He was a prominent patriot, served in the Continental Congress, and took an active part in the political life of his state.

Ramsay, a participant in those violent times, should have written in an extreme and partisan spirit. Caught up in the excitement and emotionalism of the Revolutionary crisis in which England appeared as tyrant and oppressor, he had none of that perspective in time supposedly requisite for an objective and impartial treatment. He had no training as a historian and made no boast of impartiality. The passions which the war aroused had had little time to cool when he began his work. His *History of the American Revolution*, moreover, had a frankly didactic purpose: completed just as the delegates to the Federal Convention finished their work on the Federal Constitution, it was designed to awaken Americans to their responsibilities as citizens under the new government. Finally, he, like many of his fellow eighteenth-century historians, drew heavily and without specific citation from the *Annual Register*. Yet, with all these handicaps (from the viewpoint of orthodox historiography), Ramsay's history is a remarkable

---

[1] *Letters of Benjamin Rush*, edited by Lyman Butterfield (Princeton University Press, 1951), I, p. 220.

achievement. In his analysis and interpretation of the events culminating in the Revolution, he showed unusual insight and a keen sense of proportion.

In considering the causes of the conflict between Great Britain and the colonists, Ramsay went back to examine the Puritan attitudes toward church and state and found in Puritan theology a tradition of opposition to tyranny— which it considered contrary "to nature, reason, and revelation."[2] More important in nourishing a spirit of independence in the American colonies, however, was the fact that "the prerogatives of royalty and dependence on the Mother Country, were but feebly impressed on the colonial forms of government." In charter and proprietary colonies, the crown delegated broad powers, and even in the royal provinces the king exercised no more control over the colonists "than over their fellow subjects in England." Thus, "from the acquiescence of the parent state [in the growth of self-government], the spirit of her constitution, and daily experience, the Colonists grew up in a belief, that their local assemblies stood in the same relation to them as the Parliament of Great Britain to the inhabitants of that island. The benefits of legislation were conferred on both, only through these constitutional channels." In this situation, the colonists claimed as part of their birthright all the benefits of the British constitution, chief among which was that "the people could not be compelled to pay any taxes, nor be bound by any laws, but such as had been granted or enacted by the consent of themselves, or of their representatives."[3]

England, also, had not markedly interfered with the economic welfare of the colonists. Indeed, "the wise and liberal policy of England towards her Colonies, during the

---

[2] David Ramsay: *History of the American Revolution*, 1st ed. (Philadelphia, 1789), I, pp. 8–9. This edition is cited throughout this chapter.

[3] Ibid., I, p. 20.

first century and a half after their settlement," had exalted
them to the pre-eminence they enjoyed when the crisis
with the mother country broke out. England had given the
Americans "full liberty to govern themselves by such laws
as the local legislatures thought necessary, and left their
trade open to every individual in her dominions. She also
gave them the amplest permission to pursue their respective
interests in such manner as they thought proper, and reserved little for herself, but the benefit of their trade, and
that of political union under the same head."[4] Great
Britain, Ramsay added, "without charging herself with the
care of their internal police, or seeking a revenue from
[the colonies] . . . contented herself with a monopoly of
their trade. She treated them as a judicious mother does
her dutiful children. They shared in every privilege belonging to her native sons, and but slightly felt the incon-
veniences of subordination. Small was the catalogue of
grievances, with which even democratical jealousy charged
the Parent State" prior to the Revolutionary crisis. It was
Ramsay's conviction that "the good resulting to the Colonies, from their connection with Great Britain, infinitely
outweighed the evil."[5]

Among the causes that contributed to the breach with
Great Britain were such subtle factors as "the distance of
America from Great Britain [which] generated ideas in the
minds of the Colonists favourable to liberty." Moreover,
the religion of the great majority of the colonists "nurtured
a love for liberty. They were chiefly Protestants, and all
Protestantism is founded on a strong claim to natural
liberty, and the right of private judgment." There were, in
addition, intellectual currents in the age which encouraged
libertarian ideals. "The reading of those Colonists who
were inclined to books, generally favoured the cause of

---

[4] Ibid, I, pp. 17–18.
[5] Ibid., I, pp. 42–3.

liberty. . . . Their books were generally small in size, and few in number: a great part of them consisted of those fashionable authors, who have defended the cause of liberty. Cato's letters, the Independent Whig, and such productions, were common in one extreme of the Colonies, while in the other, histories of the Puritans kept alive the remembrance of the sufferings of their forefathers, and inspired a warm attachment, both to the civil and the religious rights of human nature."[6]

The social development of the colonies was likewise, in Ramsay's view, congenial to "a spirit of liberty and independence. Their inhabitants were all of one rank . . . from their first settlements, the English Provinces received impressions favourable to democratic forms of government. . . . A sameness of circumstances and occupations created a great sense of equality, and disposed them to union in any common cause from the success of which, they might expect to partake of equal advantages."[7] The vast majority of the colonists were farmers. "The merchants, mechanics, and manufacturers, taken collectively, did not amount to one fifteenth of the whole number of inhabitants," Ramsay pointed out, adding in characteristically Jeffersonian terms that while "the cultivators of the soil depend on nothing but Heaven and their own industry, other classes of men contract more or less of servility, from depending on the caprice of their customers."[8]

Against this background of the maturing colonies, constitutional usage, libertarian ideas, and social equality, the British ministers undertook to tighten the lead strings by which the colonists had heretofore been so loosely guided. The decision of Parliament and the ministers of the crown to attempt to raise a revenue in the American colonies

---

[6] Ibid., I, pp. 29, 30.
[7] Ibid., I, pp. 31, 32–3.
[8] Ibid., I, p. 33.

destroyed at one blow "the guards which the constitution had placed round property, and the fences, which the ancestors of both countries had erected against arbitrary power."[9]

The reaction of the colonists to the Stamp Act was prompt, if unexpected. Although the tax worked no considerable hardship on the colonists, public resistance was widespread and apparently spontaneous. The issue was not primarily an economic one, but one of principle—the principle of no taxation without representation, for which the Revolution would eventually be fought. The Stamp Act aroused the sentiment of liberty among the Americans as no other pre-Revolutionary issue had, and, in Ramsay's words, it became "evident, from the determined opposition of the Colonies, that it could not be enforced without a civil war. . . ."[1]

With the repeal of the Stamp Act, the colonies, "instead of feeling themselves dependent on Great Britain . . . conceived that, in respect to commerce, she was dependent on them." They were thus "inspired with such high ideas of the importance of their trade, that they considered the Mother Country to be brought under greater obligations to them, for purchasing her manufactures, than they were to her for protection and the administration of civil government." The upshot of repeal was that "the freemen of British America . . . conceived it to be within their power, by future combinations, at any time to convulse, if not to bankrupt, the nation from which they sprung."[2]

In America, the Revolutionary stage was set. What of England after the Stamp Act? In Ramsay's history we do not find what we have every reason to expect—a devil theory of the Revolution in which George III and his

_____

[9] Ibid., I, p. 47.
[1] Ibid., I, p. 71.
[2] Ibid., I, pp. 74–5.

ministers appear as the malevolent instruments of tyranny and oppression. Pride and inflexibility were the principal shortcomings of the British. " 'What,' said they, 'shall we, who have so lately humbled France and Spain, be dictated to by our own Colonists? Shall our subjects, educated by our care, and defended by our arms, presume to question the rights of Parliament, to which we are obliged to submit?' . . . The love of power and of property on the one side of the Atlantic were opposed to the same powerful passions on the other."[3]

The task facing Britain was, at best, not an easy one. "Great and flourishing Colonies . . . already grown to the magnitude of a nation, planted at an immense distance, and governed by constitutions resembling that of the country from which they sprung, were novelties in the history of the world," Ramsay pointed out. "To combine Colonies, so circumstanced, in one uniform system of government with the Parent State, required a great knowledge of mankind, and an extensive comprehension of things. It was an arduous business, far beyond the grasp of ordinary state[smen], whose minds were narrowed by the formalities of laws, or the trammels of office. An original genius, unfettered with precedents, and exalted with just ideas of the rights of human nature, and the obligations of universal benevolence, might have struck out a middle line, which would have secured as much liberty to the Colonies, and as great a degree of supremacy to the Parent State, as their common good required: But the helm of Great Britain was not in such hands."[4]

Ramsay here offers us no evil George III, no tyrannical ministers, no demons and oppressors, but simply well-meaning men caught in a situation too complex and demanding for their very average talents. His wise and

---

[3] Ibid., I, pp. 52–3.
[4] Ibid., I, pp. 54–5.

temperate assessment of the British failure has not been improved on. This is due not to vast research labors but to Ramsay's unusual sense of proportion and keen power of analysis.

Remarkably sensitive to all currents in the tide of Revolutionary agitation, Ramsay paid due attention to the economic motif. Many Americans, he pointed out, especially among the merchant class, found it profitable to oppose British measures. The reaction of the merchants to the threatened importation of East India tea was, in his view, motivated by their fear of losing a profitable trade in smuggled tea. "They doubtless conceived themselves to be supporting the rights of their country, by refusing to purchase tea from Britain," Ramsay wrote, "but they also reflected that if they could bring the same commodity to market, free from duty, their profits would be proportionately greater." Hence the merchants took the lead in denouncing the dutied tea. But, "though the opposition originated in the selfishness of the merchants, it did not end there." When the Tea Act of 1773 was passed, the majority of the colonists opposed Great Britain on the ground of "principle." They saw the Act as a scheme "calculated to seduce them into an acquiescence with the views of Parliament for raising an American revenue."[5] In accepting the cheaper tea, they would be accepting the tea tax.

The South Carolina doctor also knew that the motives of the patriots, like the motives of all men, were mixed. He did not present a picture of a united country rushing to arms in defense of its liberties. "The inhabitants of the Colonies . . . with regard to political opinions," he wrote, "might be divided into three classes; of these, one was for rushing precipitately into extremities. They were for immediately stopping all trade, and could not even brook the

---

[5] Ibid., I, pp. 95, 97.

delay of waiting till the proposed Continental Congress
should meet. Another party, equally respectable, both as to
character, property, and patriotism, was more moderate,
but not less firm. These were averse to the adoption of any
violent resolutions till all others were ineffectually tried.
They wished that a clear statement of their rights, claims,
and grievances, should precede every other measure. A
third class disapproved of what was generally going on. A
few from principle, and a persuasion that they ought to
submit to the Mother Country; some from the love of
ease, others from self-interest, but the bulk from fear of the
mischievous consequences likely to follow. All these latter
classes, for the most part, lay still, while the friends of
liberty acted with spirit. If they, or any of them, ventured
to oppose popular measures, they were not supported, and
therefore declined farther efforts. The resentment of the
people was so strong against them, that they sought for
peace by remaining quiet. . . . The spirited part of the
community being on the side of liberty, the patriots had
the appearance of unanimity. . . ."[6]

To the summary analysis of the temper of these three
classes, Ramsay added a detailed accounting on the basis
of section and interest. That three million loyal subjects
"should break through all former attachments, and unani-
mously adopt new ones, could not reasonably be expected.
The revolution had its enemies, as well as its friends, in
every period of the war. Country, religion, local policy, as
well as private views, operated in disposing the inhabitants
to take different sides. The New-England provinces being
mostly settled by one sort of people, were nearly of one
sentiment. The influence of placemen in Boston, together
with the connections which they had formed by marriages,
had attached sundry influential characters in that capital to
the British interest, but these were but as the dust in the

------

[6] Ibid., I, pp. 125–6.

balance when compared with the numerous independent Whig yeomanry of the country."[7] The Quakers of Pennsylvania and the Tory farmers of the Carolina frontier were treated by Ramsay with as much sympathy and understanding as the independent yeomen of New England or the gentlemen planters of the Southern colonies.[8]

"The age and temperament of individuals," Ramsay continued, "had often an influence in fixing their political character. Old men were seldom warm Whigs; they could not relish the changes which were daily taking place; attached to ancient forms and habits, they could not readily accommodate themselves to new systems. Few of the very rich were active in forwarding the revolution. This was remarkably the case in the eastern and middle States; but the reverse took place in the southern extreme of the confederacy. There were in no part of America more determined Whigs than the opulent slaveholders in Virginia, the Carolinas, and Georgia. The active and spirited part of the community, who felt themselves possessed of talents that would raise them to eminence in a free government, longed for the establishment of independent constitutions: but those who were in possession or expectation of royal favour, or of promotion from Great Britain, wished that the connection between the Parent State and the Colonies might be preserved. The young, the ardent, the ambitious, and the enterprising, were mostly Whigs; but the phlegmatic, the timid, the interested, and those who wanted decision were, in general, favourers of Great Britain, or at least only the lukewarm, inactive friends of independence."[9]

Economic factors exerted a strong influence: "The Whigs received a great reinforcement from the operation of continental money. In the years 1775, 1776, and the first

---

[7] Ibid., II, p. 310.
[8] Ibid., II, pp. 312–13.
[9] Ibid., II, p. 314.

months of 1777, while the bills of Congress were in good credit, the effects of them were the same as if a foreign power had made the United States a present of twenty million of silver dollars. The circulation of so large a sum of money, and the employment given to great numbers in providing for the American army, increased the numbers and invigorated the zeal of the friends to the revolution."[1]

Even after Lexington, Ramsay pointed out, the colonial leaders, like the great mass of people everywhere, showed the greatest reluctance to take the decisive step toward independence. Thomas Paine's *Common Sense,* more than anything else, nerved the colonies to declare themselves independent of the mother country. In an excellent analysis of Paine's pamphlet as propaganda, Ramsay concluded that "in union with the feelings and sentiments of the people, it produced surprising effects. Many thousands were convinced, and were led to approve and long for a separation from the Mother Country. Though that measure, a few months before, was not only foreign from their wishes, but the object of their abhorrence, a current suddenly became so strong in its favour, that it bore down all opposition."[2]

Despite Ramsay's sensitivity to the more subtle problems of colonial psychology, to self-interest, chance, and the inflexibility of the British government as elements in the Revolutionary crisis, he grasped firmly that the heart of the conflict lay in the constitutional principle. "This was the very hinge of the controversy. The absolute unlimited supremacy of the British Parliament, both in legislation and taxation, was contended for on one side; while on the other, no farther authority was conceded than such a limited legislation, with regard to external commerce, as would combine the interests of the whole empire." "In

[1] Ibid.
[2] Ibid., I, pp. 336–7.

government," Ramsay added, "as well as in religion, there are mysteries from the close investigation of which little advantage can be expected. From the unity of empire it was necessary, that some acts should extend over the whole. From the local situation of the Colonies it was equally reasonable that their legislatures should at least in some matters be independent. Where the supremacy of the first ended and the independency of the last began, was to the best informed a puzzling question."[3]

David Ramsay's *History of the American Revolution* has been treated at some length in order to provide a base point of interpretation against which the views of later historians may be measured. In addition, Ramsay can be considered an excellent representative of the first generation of Revolutionary War historians. He outstrips his contemporaries in the depth and perception of his analyses, but he stands with them in the main outlines of his interpretation.

The absence of rancor against Great Britain that characterized the histories of Ramsay and William Gordon was apparent in most first-generation histories of the Revolution. Many were journeymen jobs; yet, almost without exception, they contained fair and balanced narratives of the events that led to the Revolution. One looks in vain for mention of the "long train of abuses and usurpations" or the dark designs "to reduce [the colonies] under absolute despotism" referred to in the Declaration of Independence.[4]

---

[3] Ibid., I, p. 136; see also I, p. 48: "As the claim of taxation on one side, and the refusal of it on the other, was the very hinge on which the revolution turned, it merits a particular discussion."

[4] Some of Ramsay's contemporaries who, like him, wrote Revolutionary history of unusual breadth and balance are William Gordon: *History of the Rise, Progress and Establishment of the Independence of the United States of America* (London, 1788); Charles Stedman: *History of the American War* (London, 1794); John Marshall: *Life of George Washington*, 5 vols. (Philadelphia, 1804–07). At the end of the nineteenth century, Orin Grant Libby attacked Gordon and Ramsay as plagiarists, discrediting them as reliable sources on the Revolution: "A Critical Examination of William Gor-

The ablest representative of the second generation of American historians who dealt with the Revolution was George Bancroft. Bancroft allowed his Jacksonian principles to color his interpretation. In him, we find an openly polemical tone. To Bancroft, the era of the Revolution was the golden age, the time of giants, the opening act of the extraordinary drama of American democracy. There is in his mammoth history much that appears to modern eyes as rhetorical embellishment. Whereas his predecessors had been content to describe the events they had observed, Bancroft was unconsciously a mythmaker. He was also the first American historian to bring to a study of the Revolution the research techniques of modern scholarship. He was an insatiable collector of source materials and combed European as well as American archives. And although he wove these materials into a narrative tapestry of vivid colors, he subscribed wholeheartedly to the ideal of scholarly objectivity. "The chronicler of manners and events," he wrote, "can alone measure his own fairness, for no one else knows so well what he throws aside. Indiscriminate praise neither paints to the life, nor teaches by example, nor advances social science. . . . The historian, even more than philosophers and naturalists, must bring to his pursuit the freedom of an unbiased mind."[5]

Yet Bancroft's characters emerge somewhat larger than life and often, one feels, without those human flaws that would make them readily identifiable as real people. The compulsion to create myths was stronger than the good resolutions of the scholar. By the time Bancroft wrote, the

---

don's History of the American Revolution," *American Historical Association Annual Report*, 1899 (Washington, 1900), I, pp. 367–88; and "Ramsay as a Plagiarist," *American Historical Review*, VII (1901–02), pp. 697–703. See also William A. Foran: "John Marshall as a Historian," Ibid., XLIII (1937–38), pp. 51–64; R. Kent Newmyer: "Charles Stedman's *History of the American War*," Ibid., LXIII (1957–58), pp. 924–34.

[5] George Bancroft: *History of the United States* (Boston: Little, Brown; 1876), V, pp. 69–70.

War of 1812 and England's growing power, coupled with
her air of arrogant superiority, had exacerbated American
feelings. (Bancroft spoke of the "haughty feeling" of the
Englishman for his American cousin which had outlasted
the "period of revolutionary strife" and which, to Bancroft's own day, hung "as a heavy bias on the judgment . . .
of Englishmen.")[6] In addition, the United States had
grown further apart from Great Britain, and the sense of
Englishness that had softened the animosities generated by
the Revolution had been largely dissipated by the 1830's.

History, for Bancroft, was the working of Divine Wisdom, and God's eternal principles were discoverable
through its study. History traces "the vestiges of moral law
through the practice of the nations in every age . . . and
confirms by induction the intuitions of reason."[7] Seen in
this light, the Revolution appeared as part of God's plan:
it was intended for the edification of man and the improvement of society; it ushered in a new and brighter age of
human progress.

What in earlier histories had been presented as essentially a misunderstanding between two power systems became, in Bancroft's interpretation, a conscious plan to
subvert liberty. George III, in the perspective of a triumphant Whig tradition, was a relentless authoritarian with
a "hatred of reform, and an antipathy to philosophical
freedom and to popular power."[8] Under his leadership,
"Great Britain, allured by a phantom of absolute authority
over the colonies, made war on human freedom." If the
British Parliament had succeeded "in establishing by force
of arms its 'boundless' authority over America," where
would "humanity find an asylum?"[9] The struggle was thus
a contest between progress and reaction for the soul of

---

[6] Ibid., V, p. 73.
[7] Ibid., V, p. 70.
[8] Ibid., IV, pp. 197–8.
[9] Ibid., IV, p. 308.

man. The Revolution sounded the death knell of "the ages of servitude and inequality" and rang in "those of equality and brotherhood." America's feet were, thereby, set on a "never-ending career of reform and progress."[1]

Bancroft fixed the image of a wicked king which was to have a long life in American historiography, and his political ideals led him into what became in time another classic error. His sentiments in favor of free trade induced him to count the Acts of Trade and Navigation, some of which dated from the middle of the seventeenth century, as one of the principal causes of the Revolutionary crisis. He was a good Democrat and an advocate of a low tariff, and he concluded that mercantilism, as expressed in Parliamentary statutes, must have been a bitter grievance to the American colonists. In the years that followed, this interpretation led to the listing of mercantilism as one of the primary causes of the Revolution.

We see in Bancroft's history the optimism and self-confidence of Jacksonian democracy allied with the eighteenth-century conception of an orderly universe governed by natural law. His history was drawn from wide sources; it was based on scrupulous research and was written with passion and insight. Yet it was transformed by a mythos too strong for Bancroft to resist. Already historians were moving away from the realistic appraisal of the first generation; history was beginning to serve the social needs and aspirations of an explosively expanding nation. The image of America's past fixed by Bancroft was a polestar during the tumultuous middle decades of the nineteenth century.

If Bancroft had vices, they were the counterpart of those virtues which won him thousands of readers. His love of the colorful and dramatic, his devotion to democracy and progress, his fine, if to modern tastes overelaborate, prose

---

[1] Ibid., IV, pp. 311, 308.

style entitle him to a continued hearing by students of American history.

By the turn of the century the ideals of "scientific" history had penetrated the historical profession. Nurtured in the German seminars of Leopold von Ranke and Barthold Niebuhr, the champions of the new history cast a cold eye on Bancroft's patriotic effusions. The task of the historian was to recount with dispassionate objectivity "what had happened," ruthlessly suppressing personal prejudices and loyalties wherever possible, so that the facts could speak for themselves.

Sydney George Fisher's *The Struggle for American Independence* (1908) was the first detailed treatment of the Revolution since Bancroft's history, and the first, as Fisher was at some pains to make clear, written under the new scholarly dispensation. Previous historians, Fisher wrote, had never made "any attempt to describe, from the original records, England's exact position with regard to ourselves at the outbreak of the Revolution, except the usual assumption that the Tory statesmen who were in power were either ignorantly stupid, and blind to their own interests, or desperately corrupt and wicked, and that the Whig minority were angels of light who could have saved the colonies for the British empire."[2] Fisher directed his fire primarily at Bancroft and John Fiske, but such a Rhadamanthine judgment was certainly not fair to Bancroft and missed the mark entirely with the first generation of Revolutionary historians.

In attempting to correct what he considered the anti-British prejudices of his predecessors, Fisher stressed the "mildness" of Great Britain and her "spirit of conciliation." "Modern readers of history," he wrote, knew nothing of "the conciliatory measures Great Britain adopted" or

---

[2] Sydney George Fisher: *The Struggle for American Independence* (Philadelphia: J. B. Lippincott; 1908), I, p. vii.

"her gentle and mild efforts to persuade us to remain in the empire."[3] The Revolution was "not a contest between a dragon and a fairy," not "a mere accidental mistake on the part of England" resulting in a war brought on "by the king alone against the wishes of the English people." It was, on the contrary, a path "entered upon by the English nation as deliberately and intelligently as any other imperial expansion they have undertaken and upon principles which for them are still unchangeable."[4]

Fisher's emphasis in explaining the Revolution was primarily on the character of colonial life, which had shaped the New World settlers and in so doing had made independence inevitable. He thus shifted his focus from the immediate causes, such as the Stamp Act, to underlying changes in outlook and ideology. If England was to be exonerated, it was necessary to neutralize the moral and political conflict and, in place of the traditionally offered explanations of the Revolutionary crisis, to stress the "characterological divergence" that had developed between England and her colonies. Forces thus take the place of issues. The action of individuals is of little significance except as a response to these forces and it is obviously pointless to try to apportion praise or blame for events which move onward, ineluctable and impersonal as the slow passage of a glacier.[5]

While the story of the Revolution lost, by such treatment, much of the drama with which Bancroft had invested it and, perhaps more important, lost its didactic quality—its power to teach patriotism to the young by inspiring example—it gained a greater breadth and a wider tolerance. Moreover, it was recognized that "forces" did indeed exert great influence upon the behavior of indi-

---

[3] Ibid., I, p. vii.
[4] Ibid., I, p. xiii.
[5] Ibid., I, p. 104.

viduals and the course of history. The dignity and significance of the individual may have been lessened thereby,
but as partial compensation a deeper awareness of the
complexity of historical events was recaptured.

That Fisher took such a position was, at least in part, a
result of the increasing complexity of American society.
The sense that America exercised control over the course
of history, which had been a by-product of the Enlightenment and which during the years of America's buoyant expansion had seemed to find confirmation in our experience
as a nation, had declined sharply as the cruel inconsistencies
of American capitalism became more apparent. The American dream at times seemed more of a nightmare. Historians
such as Fisher began to see the individual in a diminished
role, because the individual himself began to feel his role
diminished as he became aware of the harsh shadow of
reality that fell across the classic dream.

The strongly pro-British inclinations of Fisher, which
wore the mask of dispassionate objectivity, appeared even
more forcefully in the work of many of his contemporaries.
There is no question that these Anglophile sentiments were
stimulated by the growing world crisis. In the rivalry between Germany and Great Britain for power and empire,
the sympathies of many Americans and virtually all historians were with the British. The enthusiasm of Americans of German ancestry for the cause of a nation to which
they still looked with pride and affection only served to
increase the ardor of the Anglophiles.

It would be wrong, of course, to label as pro-British all
American historians who wrote about the American Revolution in the early decades of the twentieth century. Yet it
is unquestionably true that such sympathies crept into the
"scientific" investigations of the Revolution that were made
in these years. We have already seen that Fisher explicitly
rejected any devil theory, being determined to exculpate

George III as well as his ministers and the English people as a whole.

What had been implicit in Fisher—that the underlying causes of the Revolution were primarily economic—was boldly stated by a young historian from the Midwest. Arthur M. Schlesinger, in *The Colonial Merchants and the American Revolution, 1763–1776*, spelled out in impressive detail his thesis that the colonial merchants brought on the Revolutionary crisis, albeit unwittingly. Two rival systems of capitalist enterprise, England's and America's, developed inevitable conflicts of interest, which precipitated the war for independence. Schlesinger stated this thesis forthrightly in 1919 in an article summarizing his views on the causes of the Revolution. "In the first years of the republic," he noted, "the tendency of the popular histories and text-books was to dwell almost exclusively upon the spectacular developments of the struggle and to dramatize the heroism of the patriots."[6] The real explanation of the movement for independence, however, was to be found in the "clashing of economic interests and the interplay of mutual prejudices, opposing ideals and personal antagonisms—whether in England or America." These "made inevitable in 1776 what was unthinkable in 1760."[7]

Schlesinger lost no time in presenting his credentials as a historian of the new school. "The shock of American entrance into the Great War," he wrote, brought the American people "to seek a new orientation for the revolutionary struggle," to view "the conflict from the standpoint of scientific detachment."[8] (It apparently did not

---

[6] Arthur M. Schlesinger: "The American Revolution Reconsidered," *Political Science Quarterly*, XXXIV (1919), p. 61. Schlesinger's *The Colonial Merchants and the American Revolution, 1763–1776* (New York, 1917), like Charles A. Beard's *An Economic Interpretation of the Constitution of the United States* (New York, 1913), made historians aware of the importance of economic factors in the Revolutionary era.

[7] Schlesinger: "The Revolution Reconsidered," p. 63.

[8] Ibid., p. 61

occur to Schlesinger that this formula might contain a paradox. He offered no explanation of how, in logic, the intense emotions aroused by our participation in World War I could be expected to result in "scientific detachment.") He displayed his particular orientation even more when he wrote: "At the same time that publicists were questioning the foundations and practices of our modern economic system, a band of devoted research students . . . were employing the ruthless methods of modern scholarship in an effort to make possible a reappraisal" of the Revolution.[9]

If, in the view of American liberal reformers, industrial capitalism had gone sour, all the presuppositions upon which it claimed to be based must be re-examined. The ideals parroted by exploiting entrepreneurs and vulpine politicians must be subjected to the disinterested scrutiny of modern scholarship. That this reappraisal might itself be influenced by the reformist zeal of the reappraisers seems not to have occurred to them. They were secure in the methods and techniques of scientific research, which, they seemed to feel, must carry them inevitably to conclusions untainted by personal prejudice or by the liberal temper of their own times.

Against this background, Schlesinger advanced his highly influential analysis of the Revolutionary crisis. His conclusions were that the merchants, hit in the pocketbook by the tightening of England's imperial policy, promoted the early agitation against Great Britain. It was they who encouraged the leaders of the radicals to whip up mobs of angry patriots. Their purpose was to exert, thereby, countervailing pressure against their English rivals and thus win relief from measures which placed their trade under crippling inhibitions. "As a class they [the merchants] entertained neither earlier nor later the idea of independence,

---
[9] Ibid., p. 62.

for withdrawal from the British empire meant for them the loss of vital business advantages. . . ."[1]

At each stage of the colonial resistance, the merchants stood in the background, manipulating the Sons of Liberty. The rhetoric of the radical leaders meant nothing to them; their concern was with profits, not principles. But they had calculated without the ambitions of patriot champions and the ardor of the people. The agitation against Great Britain gathered a momentum that swept it onward with a force of its own. Too late the merchants realized that they had summoned up a whirlwind they could not ride. They found it impossible "to reassert their earlier control and to stop a movement that had lost all significance for hard-headed men of business."[2]

The talk of "no taxation without representation," the appeals to Magna Charta, the heated debate over the authority of Parliament—all this was simply flotsam which showed where deeper currents were flowing. "The popular view of the Revolution as a great forensic controversy over abstract governmental rights," Schlesinger wrote, "will not bear close scrutiny."[3]

In a historiography which disclaimed heroes and villains in the name of scientific objectivity, heroes and villains nonetheless crept in. To Schlesinger, a liberal idealist, those without ideals, that is, the colonial merchants, were the villains. It was not coincidence that Schlesinger's book—in which the colonial merchants were represented as narrow, self-seeking men who, in their blind devotion to pounds and shillings, rent the fabric of the British Empire—appeared at the same time that modern-day American captains of industry were blandly testifying before Congressional committees as to their ruthless repression of

---

[1] Ibid., p. 66.
[2] Ibid., p. 71.
[3] Ibid., pp. 76–7.

labor and their callous exploitation of the public. Even George III is depicted in his familiar role of wicked tyrant. With all his professions of scientific objectivity, Schlesinger, like Bancroft, charges the king with trying to convert the British government into "a personal autocracy."

Having identified the villains, we do not need to look far for the heroes. They are the "proletarian element," the workers in the colonial towns, who were "for the most part unenfranchised," and the sturdy frontiersmen, who "brought to the controversy a moral conviction and bold philosophy which gave great impetus to the agitation for independence"—presumably more moral conviction than could be found among the self-interested elite of the seacoast towns. In Schlesinger's work, tidewater radicals and back-country farmers march side by side toward independence. Exploited by the cunning merchants, they finally seize control, and the Revolutionary initiative passes "into the hands of the democratic mechanic class"—in other words, the workers.

In this formula of Schlesinger's we have a significant union of Turner's frontier thesis, which credited the frontier with all that was liberal, progressive, and uniquely American, and the twentieth-century liberals' idealization of the industrial worker—whose spiritual ancestor they perceived in the mechanic class of colonial towns. This was a "modern" analysis of the causes of the Revolution, and in it for the first time the case for an "economic interpretation" was explicitly stated. The argument from "principle" was swept away and Great Britain was thereby freed from any taint. Above all, this account carried the imprimatur of "scientific" history, self-stamped to be sure, but hardly the less impressive for that.

Arthur Schlesinger's liberal formulary was carried further by Claude Van Tyne in his book *The Causes of the War of Independence*, published in 1922. Like Schlesinger, Van

Tyne saw himself as one of a company of courageous historians, guided by scientific principles and bent on presenting the facts about the Revolution to a people long misled by the distorted accounts of men who put patriotism ahead of the search for objective truth. "For nearly one hundred years after the awakening of the 'spirit of '76'," Van Tyne wrote, "the story of the Revolution was told much as the contemporaries had told it, bitterly, with no effort to be impartial or judicial, and no emphasis upon the fundamentals. Men like Bancroft conducted amazing researches in the archives, but rose out of heaps of musty records only to write again of the cunning, malevolent King George and his wicked minister, Lord North, enemies of the human race, oppressors of America."

Finally, "here and there a scholar, an investigator," appeared, and "it was these trained investigators who began to get at the truth as to the Revolution. With no aim but to understand, with no desire but to know the truth they worked for forty years—as long as the Chosen People searched for the Promised Land—rewriting the story of the founding of the American Republic. New records, new points of view, new principles of research made new generations of investigators see the Revolution in a new way."[4]

Van Tyne's history is the fruit of all this enlightened industry. In it we find a strong emphasis on the frontier thesis adapted from Turner. On the frontier, "the English race" experienced "a rebirth, the first of these destined to occur perennially as the race marched westward toward the setting sun."[5] In the raw environment of a new continent, "townbred men became denizens of the wilds." Van Tyne accepted without question Schlesinger's picture of the merchants guiding the early stages of colonial re-

---

[4] Claude Van Tyne: *England and America: Rivals in the American Revolution* (New York: Macmillan; 1927), pp. 3–6.

[5] Van Tyne: *The Causes of the War of Independence* (Boston: Houghton Mifflin; 1922), p. 15.

sistance and then dropping out, as "radicals everywhere, from Samuel Adams at the North to Christopher Gadsden in the South, seized the moment of high feeling to carry America beyond the point where there could be any going back." The conflict became a class struggle. In Massachusetts, as in Pennsylvania "the masses [were] pitted against the great merchants." "Thus, in 1776, came the climax in the struggle between rich and poor, East and West, those with a vote and those who were voteless, between privilege and the welfare of the common man."[6]

The terms have shifted, but we find, nonetheless, familiar echoes of Bancroft in Van Tyne's insistence that the Revolution was "one of the glories of British history," since the colonists, as heirs of all the political accomplishments of England, were simply carrying forward the fight for democracy and political liberty which "England had fostered beyond any other country of the world."[7] And, as in Bancroft, we find an unscrupulous George III drawing on "an inexhaustible treasure of corruption" to obliterate the liberties of the colonists, despite the warnings of Burke, Pitt, Fox, and Camden. The cast has changed somewhat, but the final curtain rings down on the same stirring patriotic note.

Two years after Van Tyne's book appeared, Charles McLean Andrews surveyed *The Colonial Background of the American Revolution* in a notable collection of essays. Andrews accepted what had by now become the general view of the Revolutionary crisis: that the basis of the dispute lay in a conflict of interests. The question of colonial rights was "a subject of more or less legal and metaphysical speculation. . . . There is nothing to show," he wrote, "that the somewhat precise and finely spun reasoning of these intellectual leaders had any marked influence on the popu-

---

[6] Ibid., pp. 416, 421, 425.
[7] Ibid., p. 478.

lar mind."[8] Andrews, like Van Tyne, emphasized the role of the frontier, which encouraged individualism and independence, but the conflict remained in its broader outlines a struggle over trade and commerce. We find in Andrews, it must be said, in addition to the residues of many earlier interpretations, a tentativeness and an absence of the doctrinaire.

Under the surface of historical investigation, the economic interpretation of history had been moving like a subterranean current, influencing individuals in many areas of American history. It was discernible in Arthur Schlesinger's study of the colonial merchants and in the works of a number of his contemporaries. As applied to the Revolution, however, it was persistently modified in the works we have been concerned with by the naturalistic and romantic gloss of the frontier thesis, and by the fact that even skeptical historians of the scientific school found it extremely difficult to disengage themselves from the mythic elements of the Revolution. However resolutely they started out demolishing, as they boasted, the biased and partisan accounts of earlier historians, they all ended up sounding remarkably like George Bancroft.

In 1954, Lawrence Henry Gipson's *The Coming of the Revolution, 1763–1775* was published in the *New American Nation Series*. In the introduction, the editors of this series wrote: "During the past half a century the lapse of time and the uncovering of much new evidence have made it possible for scholars to pursue their investigations into the causes of the American Revolution in an atmosphere far less partisan than had prevailed in earlier generations. As a result of this more objective handling of the period of mounting tension that preceded the War of Independence, the rights on both sides of the controversy are more gen-

---

[8] Charles McLean Andrews: *The Colonial Background of the American Revolution* (Yale University Press, 1924), p. 135.

erally conceded." It is Gipson's argument "that the causes of the Revolution stem first from the effort of the British government, faced with vast territorial acquisitions in North America at the end of the Great War for Empire, along with an unprecedented war debt, to organize a more efficient administration on that continent and to make the colonies contribute directly to the support of the enlarged Empire. . . . Secondly, the causes of the breach can be traced to the radically altered situation of the colonies after 1760, by which date they were at long last relieved of the intense pressure previously exerted along their borders by hostile nations."[9] The heart of the issue was a clash of "interests."

From the time of Sydney George Fisher to that of Lawrence Gipson, an interpretation of the causes of the American Revolution had slowly taken form. By the early 1950's, its outlines seemed, generally speaking, clear and stable and satisfyingly impersonal. The Revolution was the outcome of forces rather than "the result of the actions of wicked men—neither of the King or Lord North, on the one hand, nor of American radicals on the other." The forces were primarily economic and social—the clash between rival systems of mercantilism and the differentiation of the colonists from the citizens of the mother country as a result of the influence of an agricultural frontier. The problem of human motivations, decisions, aspirations, and illusions was thus solved by submerging them in the larger currents of history.[1]

---

[9] Lawrence Henry Gipson: *The Coming of the Revolution, 1763–1775*, in *The New American Nation Series*, ed. Henry Steele Commager and Richard B. Morris (New York: Harper; 1954), pp. ix, xii.

[1] Nineteenth-century historians who dealt with the Revolution, such as George Washington Greene in *Historical View of the American Revolution* (Cambridge: Riverside Press; 1876) and John Fiske in *The American Revolution* (Boston: Houghton Mifflin; 1896), wrote the tradition of George Bancroft. Limitations of space have compelled me to omit consideration of the influence of Sir Lewis Namier and his revisionist school. The Namierists, by rehabilitating George III, reinforced the view of the Revolution as a clash of "forces" or 'interests." See Morgan: "American Revolu-

On to this settled and orderly scene burst Edmund and Helen Morgan's *The Stamp Act Crisis: Prologue to Revolution*.[2] Their argument, like that of David Ramsay a hundred and sixty-five years earlier, hinged on the decisive character of the Stamp Act and threatened at once to undermine the whole painstaking, if jerry-built, structure of interpretation that had been erected by a dozen twentieth-century historians. The Morgans reminded their readers that the Stamp Act had aroused an instant and entirely unexpected wave of protest and of determined resistance in the colonies—resistance which could have led to revolution. Never again were the colonists to be so united in opposition to a British measure. The actual cost of the stamp tax to the colonists would have been relatively light. In most places it was not even put into effect, and the colonists experienced no material hardship as a result of the Act. The opposition was thus almost entirely on the grounds of abstract principle—the constitutional principle of no taxation without representation.

Moreover, most of the leaders who came forward at the time of the Act to direct colonial resistance maintained their position of resistance up to the Revolution and beyond. Of the twenty-six members of the Stamp Act Congress, "only two . . . are known to have become loyalists in 1776. . . . Others who took no part in the congress but led the resistance to the Stamp Act within their own colonies were likewise conspicuous in the revolutionary movement. It seems particularly significant that the parties which brought on the revolution in the two leading colonies, Massachusetts and Virginia, gained their ascendancy at the time of the Stamp Act."[3]

Even more important than the appearance, at the very

tion" for an excellent discussion of the Namier position and some effective counter-arguments.

[2] Edmund S. Morgan and Helen M. Morgan: *The Stamp Act Crisis: Prologue to Revolution* (University of North Carolina, 1953).

[3] Ibid., p. 293.

outset of controversy, of able and aggressive leaders who
continued to lead was "the emergence . . . of well-defined
constitutional principles." The colonial assemblies in 1765
"laid down the line on which Americans stood until they
cut their connections with England. Consistently from
1765 to 1776 they denied the authority of Parliament to tax
them externally or internally; consistently they affirmed
their willingness to submit to whatever legislation Parliament should enact for the supervision of the empire as a
whole."[4]

In the Morgans' view, far too much had been made of the
shifts in the colonial position in regard to the powers of
Parliament. Historians of the Schlesinger school had pointed
to these shifts—from no power to impose internal taxes,
to no external taxes for revenue, to no internal or external
taxes of any kind, to no right to legislate for the colonies in
any case whatever—as an indication that material self-
interest, rather than principle, motivated the colonial
actions. On the contrary, the Morgans argued, the colonists
did not move from one position to another under the pressure of Parliamentary enactments. In actual fact, the Stamp
Act brought at once a denial of the right of Parliament to
tax the colonies "without representation." All official statements, such as the resolves of the Stamp Act Congress,
asserted this principle; they only conceded acquiescence in
the Acts of Trade and Navigation in force in 1763. Moreover, a number of colonial leaders at the time of the Stamp
Act crisis, or soon afterwards, came to the conclusion that
Parliament had no constitutional authority to legislate for
the colonies. But they knew that to press such a view would
rouse the deepest suspicions of Parliament and its sup-
porters and alarm all colonial moderates, and so they kept
their peace.

Like Ramsay, the Morgans expressed the conviction that

---

[4] Ibid., p. 295.

the growing conflict "was not irretrievable, but that to retrieve it would have required an understanding on each side
of the exact limits of the other's claims." While "the English
thought that they saw the Americans inching their way
toward independence, the Americans thought that they saw
a sinister party in England seeking by gradual degree to
enslave them."[5] So the crisis moved to its denouement.

If the Morgans' argument in its main outlines is granted,
it modifies those interpretations which see the Revolution
as the more or less inevitable result of a slow process of
economic, social, cultural, and political differentiation between the colonies and the mother country. The Schlesinger
thesis that the merchants used the radical leaders and the
mobs simply to gain redress of specific grievances becomes
likewise untenable, and the frontier thesis loses much of its
force. The Morgans' position, in addition, diminishes the
importance of class conflict as an element in the Revolutionary crisis. Class and sectional frictions undoubtedly
existed in some of the colonies, but they did not become
sharply defined until the later years of the war and the
postwar period. They were, in no sense, determinants in the
development of the Revolution.

With the Morgans' book we have come full circle, back
to the position of Ramsay and the historians of the first
generation. After a century and a half of progress in historical scholarship, in research techniques, in tools and methods, we have found our way to the interpretation held,
substantially, by the historians who themselves participated
in the Revolution or lived through that era. As Morgan suggests, "George Bancroft may not have been so far from the
mark as we have often assumed"; and Ramsay was closer
still.

Once we have picked our way throught the bewildering
variety of intepretations that successive generations of his-

---

[5] Ibid., pp. 291, 290.

torians have offered us, we would do well to go back and re-read David Ramsay. We cannot fail, I think, to be both puzzled and impressed. How account for the remarkable insight, the proportion, and the "objectivity" of this historian who was himself a Revolutionary politician? The historical profession is so deeply committed to the belief that objectivity, or perspective, is a product of distance in time from the events with which the viewer is dealing that we find it hard to accept that Ramsay offered us a wiser and better balanced interpretation than the most expert and "scientific" of his successors. And we cannot write off Ramsay as a sport, an exception, or an oddity. He may be the best of his generation, but he is by no means exceptional in his general attitude toward the events of the Revolution or in his interpretation of those events. It seems to me that we must accept the proposition that, generally speaking, the first generation of historians gave us a more "objective" view of the Revolution than historians have managed to do since.

In justice to later historians, it should, of course, be pointed out that the historian's task in interpreting the American Revolution has been more than ordinarily difficult. The America that emerged from the War of Independence had no pre-history in the traditional sense. Having won their independence, the rather loosely knit United States had to find myths and symbols to reinforce and give substance to the national unity, which for the first eighty years was so precariously maintained. Myths perforce had to be created around the moment of birth. What Homer and the siege of Troy had been to the Greek states of the Periclean Age, George Washington and the campaigns of the Revolution were to nineteenth-century America. What Romulus and Remus and the Twelve Tables of the Law had been for Imperial Rome, the Founding Fathers and the Federal Constitution were for the United States, searching in the midst of extraordinary social and economic transformations for unifying symbols.

The American Revolution is encrusted with mythic elements and residues which have vastly complicated the task of the historian who wishes to state the truth of the events that took place then. The historian, being human and ineluctably partaking of the ideas and values of his day, has been under the strongest pressure to make the events of the Revolution conform to the particular spirit he himself consciously and articulately represents. He has been not simply the enemy of the myths, as he would like to see himself, but quite as often the victim, in the sense that he has seldom escaped the temptation to make the Revolution prove something about his own society or the society which he wishes to see evolve in the future.

It is only fair to add that the aims and aspirations of the generation of historians of which Ramsay was a member were ideally suited to the writing of balanced and judicious history. Federalists, or at least deeply imbued with Federalist doctrines, these historians were friends of the new Federal Constitution. They were enemies of factionalism and party rancor and sought to write history that would draw the states together. It was Ramsay's wish that each state might have "an ingenious learned and philosophical history," so the knowledge of sister states might be widely diffused and the union correspondingly strengthened. As reconcilers, the first-generation historians had the particular responsibility to write accounts so broad and generous that patriot and Tory, planter and merchant, Northerner and Southerner could find therein common ground and, joining forces, move forward to the bright future that awaited the new nation. "We are too widely disseminated over an extensive country and too much diversified by different customs and forms of government to feel as one people which we really are," Ramsay wrote his friend John Eliot. "Had we Belknaps in every state we might become acquainted with each other in that intimate familiar manner which would wear away prejudices, rub off asperities, mold us into an homogeneous people loving esteeming and rightly appreciating each other."[6] Approaching their task in this missionary spirit, Ramsay and his fellows were under the strongest compulsions to write fair and unbiased history. Disunity was the sharpest danger which faced the country; unitary history was its best remedy.

In addition, and perhaps most important of all, the historians of the eighteenth century made no distinction between fact and interpretation. Unaware of, or unconcerned with, such divisions, they had not succumbed to the illusion that facts and interpretations were different orders of reality—that if the facts were diligently searched for and assembled, the proper intepretation would somehow follow from them. That Ramsay and a number of his contemporaries drew largely from the *Annual Register* suggests a good deal about their attitude toward facts. These, if generally reliable (and there was no better source in the eighteenth century than the *Annual Register*), were of secondary importance. By far the most significant part of the process of writing history was the application of principles of interpretation, or, perhaps better, moral judgment, to the events with which the historian was dealing. The position that the historian took in regard to the treatment of his material did not rest upon "facts" but rather upon an awareness of his responsibility to do justice to the rival groups and conflicting aspirations involved in his story. Ramsay's generation would have spoken of this as a concern with "first principles." If first principles were wrong, all subsequent steps, however rational, systematic, or scientific, would simply compound the error. It would not have occurred to an eighteenth-century historian to sanctify the facts under the illusion that they contained some measure of saving grace.

---

[6] Ramsay to John Eliot, Charleston, August 11, 1792, Massachusetts Historical Society.

Whatever imperfections there may be in Ramsay's facts (and his detractors have argued not that the facts were at fault but that, in a number of instances, they were taken from the *Annual Register*), it was a poor bargain to get, in place of his work, histories which were factually impeccable but which lost sight of the essential meaning of the Revolutionary experience.

On the basis of this brief survey of interpretations of the Revolution, it would be very difficult to demonstrate clear and consistent progress in the interpretation of historical events as the result of the longer time-perspective of successive historians. Neither do we find that the opening up of untapped archives and the discovery of new documents (beyond a certain point, of course) results in notably improved or (in any final sense) more acceptable interpretations.[7]

Indeed, in regard to the Revolution, the most extreme distortions appeared in the work of historians who made the loudest claims to being "scientific" in their approach. Perhaps these men, believing implicitly in the authority of the data—the "facts," as disclosed by their researches—have been less sensitive to the nature and extent of their own prejudices. The older, "pre-scientific" historians realized that there was no way of evading judgments and were thus quite conscious of any distortion produced by their personal loyalties and allegiances. The scientific historian, comforted by the illusion of a vast amount of supporting data, might fall victim (and obviously in many instances did) to his own predispositions disguised as the objective results of research.

---

[7] Herbert Butterfield, in an essay entitled "The Reconstruction of an Historical Episode; the History of an Inquiry into the Origins of the Seven Years War," *Man on His Past* (Cambridge University Press, 1955), pp. 143–67, has shown that Leopold von Ranke, writing not many years after that war, gave a better analysis of its causes than anyone else has done with a longer perspective in time and far greater access to documentary materials.

Beyond all this, an intelligent contemporary has a particular advantage over all later investigators. He was there.
He saw it happen, felt it, experienced it on many levels. It
was part of the complex fabric of his life. Like a seismo-
graph, he recorded through the channels of his nervous system and stored in his brain (rather than in a filing cabinet
or archive) the emotions, ideas, realities of his era. And he
recorded these, if he was a person of sensitivity and judgment, in roughly the proportion in which they were present
in his environment. He could, in addition, widen his environment as far as the breadth of his mind and his ability
to extrapolate from his own immediate experience would
allow. Furthermore, he did not have to mythologize the
events or view them through the lens of a later generation
with its very different needs and aspirations.

The story of the successive interpretations of the American Revolution seems then to bear this moral: There is, or
has been so far, no panacea (such as the scientific method)
which can perform for the historian the functions of judgment and analysis. Whatever the historian gains in time
perspective or new materials or specialized monographs, he
may well lose through distortions that result from his own
Zeitgeist. He does not necessarily approach in an orderly,
systematic way the truth in the form of some final or,
often, some better interpretation or understanding of the
events he is concerned with. We would do well, therefore, to
show more respect for the best contemporary history and
abandon the professional pieties with which we have solaced
ourselves in the past. In the struggle for historical understanding, there are no final triumphs. Insights, once gained,
will not automatically sustain themselves but must be rediscovered time and again. We cannot solve problems of
historical interpretation and then, having reduced the solutions to formulas, pass on to new problems, for the
"solved" problems are remarkably full of life, tenacious,
and enduring.

This being the case, the responsibility is clearly placed where it belongs—on the individual historian. He cannot escape making judgments by taking refuge in techniques. And his judgments will be no better than his capacity for wise insight and human understanding.

13

Categories
of
Historical Reality

One of the perennial curses in all discussions of the nature of historiography is the notion that there is only one proper form of historical research and writing. Much of the debate over history as the record of man's past has floundered on this shoal of either/or. We would argue for a plurality of historiographies; indeed, we could do worse than to recall the "methods of treating history" listed by Hegel and Nietzsche.

Hegel divided historical scholarship into three types: *original history* (documentary sources such as official documents, letters, diaries, public monuments and inscriptions, etc.); *reflective history*, which is concerned with fashioning the materials of history into a coherent narrative and interpreting their significance; and *philosophical history* (meta-history, in Toynbee's term), which speculates about the greater human meaning of the historical process.

Nietzsche's divisions are *monumental, antiquarian,* and *critical history.* Monumental history involves a preoccupation with "the rare and classic"; it is a source of strength through the examples and precepts it provides, but it is full of danger because it exists "by false analogy" and encourages illusions and fanaticism in its adherents. Antiquarian history is the history favored by "the man of conservative and reverent nature, who looks back to the origins of his existence with love and trust; through it he gives thanks for life." The antiquarian historian is the custodian of the values and traditions of the past, which he honors. The danger of antiquarian history lies in the fact that, for the antiquarian, life is mummified rather than enhanced. "Antiquarian history," Nietzsche wrote, "degenerates from the moment that it no longer gives a soul and inspiration to the fresh life of the present."[1] Critical history is devoted to "the service of life." Since "man must have the strength to break up the past," as well as to apply it in order to live, the critical historian brings "the past to the bar of judgment, interrogate[s] it remorselessly, and finally condemn[s] it."[2]

All these forms of history have their validity and their place—the monograph and the universal history as well. We should ask of them only that they avoid the perversions they are subject to and pay proper tribute to Clio, their muse.

Is "progress" discernible in historical interpretation, or is one historical fad doomed to follow another in endless procession? We cannot even begin to answer this question until we recognize an error historians often make. They assume that all the elements which make up history are more or less autonomous, equal particles of reality—a kind

---

[1] *The Use and Abuse of History,* translated by Adrian Collins, introduction by Julius Kraft (New York: Liberal Arts Press; 1949), pp. 24–7.

[2] Ibid., p. 28.

of simplified atomic view. There are many different elements, to be sure—battles, ideas, civil wars, religious and social movements, class struggles, royal dynasties, inventions, books, people, machines—and all are related. But the techniques of historical investigation, based on "method," on accumulation of evidence, on sources and citations, on authorities and documents—these techniques are equally relevant in all areas and aspects of history. We do not, for instance, prefer one method for intellectual history, another for social history, another for political history, another for military history. We are aware that different problems are involved in the application of the traditional methods to different historical elements. But we tend to forget that we are dealing, among such a variety of subjects, with quite different classes of historical reality.

It is my purpose here to suggest some of the ways in which our understanding has been impeded by historical phenomena grouped together indiscriminately. There are in fact two distinguishable classes of historical phenomena: the first we shall call *existential history*, and the second, *symbolic history*.[3] Existential history is the history of the most dramatic and sharply defined episodes of the past. Under this heading we would include such events as the American Revolution, the destruction of Rome, the American Civil War, the French Revolution, World Wars I and II, the Peloponnesian War, and so on. In other words, the majority of the dramatic crises of world history belong in the existential category. They involve large numbers of people in particular events that have a discernible form, and by engaging these individuals on all levels of experience, they

---

[3] I use *existential* with some reluctance because the word is encrusted with so many meanings that are irrelevant here. "Contemporary," although close, would be inappropriate; it, too, has misleading connotations. "Experiential," suggested by a friend, is an uncouth word. So I can only ask the reader to divest himself, as far as he can, of the notions that may be called to his mind by the word *existential*. It will, I trust, become clear enough in the context of this chapter what I wish to convey by its use.

achieve a reality that clearly transcends the scholarly researches of the historian. Even if historians did not exist,
these events would have been preserved in the collective
memories of their respective societies.

Symbolic history, on the other hand, is quite clearly the
creation of the historian. It has no existence, no reality,
other than that given it by the researches of the professional historian. It is clearly a product of the modern post-
Renaissance temper with its techniques of investigation,
comparison, analogy, analysis, and its remarkable capacity
for generalization based upon vast accumulations of empirical data. Events in this category are not given names by
those involved in them; they are named, and thus called to
life, by the historian. The people of the Renaissance lived
out their age; historians, examining the age and reflecting
upon its meaning, gave it a name that by its very appro-
priateness increased enormously its power over the lives of
future generations. The name was, in effect, a symbol. It did
not correspond to any particular identifiable reality; rather,
it symbolized a style, a value, an ideal. The Industrial Revolution, the Reformation, the Westward Movement, the
Middle Ages—all these are symbolic names that depend for
their power, not on specific, clearly defined episodes, but
on their ability to evoke broad generalized movements,
long-range trends and developments.

This power to give symbolic names was unknown in the
ancient world; it constitutes the chief difference between
the historiography of Greece and Rome and that of the
modern world. The ancients knew only existential history,
which they handled with a deftness that has been the wonder and despair of later generations of historians. Symbolic history, which rests upon generalization from observed
facts, was alien to them. The ability to compare modes of
existence, to identify change in its subtler and more comprehensive forms, was not part of the historian's craft. In-

deed, their cyclical view of the historical process precluded the development of what we have here called symbolic history. It remained for Machiavelli to indicate for modern historiography the rich potentials of symbolic history, which since the sixteenth century increasingly challenged existential history.

It is unlikely that we can point to a clear and steady progression (or even to a cloudy and unclear progression) in our understanding and interpretation of the events of existential history. With existential history, we are conscious of the validity of the best contemporary accounts. It is here that we are most dependent on the judgments and evaluations of the actors in the drama—the wisest observers— individuals whose accounts provide us, in many instances, with the substance of what we know or think we know about the particular event. The reasons are obvious. At the epoch-making moments in history, the critical and analytical faculties of the participants are sharpened and intensified. The issues, heightened and dramatized, are presented in vivid form; the degree of self-consciousness of those involved in the crisis is raised to a higher level. The existential situation of the groups, classes, states, or nations engaged in the struggle is developed to the fullest. In such a moment there is, of course, the attendant danger of partisanship and deep emotional and irrational involvement. But at the same time, for the wise and perceptive individual who endeavors to see the broader implications of the issues, there is an unparalleled opportunity to tell the story "definitively." As crises often call forth the best resources of a people, elevate and frequently ennoble those caught up in their storms, so they often call forth the best efforts of those who undertake to chronicle them.

We see this fact clearly demonstrated in Thucydides, Xenophon, Polybius; we can see it in Clarendon's account of the English Civil War and, as I have already indicated,

in David Ramsay's *History of the American Revolution.*
In the case of Xenophon or Thucydides, we may modify or amplify their accounts, correct them in specific detail, balance them against "opposition" accounts, where
they exist, but we cannot argue convincingly that we have
thereby presented a story that is substantially truer to their
experiences. Neither can we count these and other such
contemporary histories as exceptional or credit their long
life primarily to their qualities as great literature. The more
attention we give to the contemporary narrators of history,
the more we are impressed by the number of histories which
display an abundance of those qualities that we have come
to think of as the consequence of "the perspective of time"
and of modern research techniques.

"Definitive' ' existential history may be written very soon
after the termination of the event, and will perhaps be better the closer it is to the events themselves, allowing always
for a "cooling-off" period—a time long enough for the participant-historian to have second thoughts, to see the dimensions of the conflict which extend beyond his own
partisan involvements. It may also be written some years
after the event. But then the difficulty of re-creating faithfully the events and their causes will be greater and demand
a more powerful effort of the will and the creative imagination than that demanded of the participant-historian. In
both cases, the successful historian must be an individual
of far more than ordinary insight and intelligence. With
existential history, there is no clear advantage in being at a
remote distance in time from the event. In fact, the reverse
is more apt to be true. Neither the opening of new archives,
nor the detachment presumably brought about by a greater
distance in time (and thus, presumably, a greater psychic
distance) from the events described, nor new techniques of
investigation, nor new methods of handling materials, afford
the later historian any explicit advantage. And if they do,

this advantage is counterbalanced by serious disadvantages —the disadvantages, indeed, of which the historical relativist is so well aware, the most notable of which is the distortion of vision produced by the *Zeitgeist* of the later historian. Thus, while interpretations change from generation to generation, whether they move toward or away from the truth is largely coincidental. It depends primarily on whether or not their own *Zeitgeist* is congenial to that of the age in which the events they are dealing with are embedded.

Latter-day formulations, moreover, cannot be more true than the statements of the men who lived, believed, acted, and in many instances died in the name of certain principles and ideals. Individuals in history achieve authenticity through their actions, and historians cannot arbitrarily deprive these lives of their meaning by judgments imposed long after the event. That we should ever have accepted any convention which held the contrary is monstrous. Only a particular kind of intellectual formalism could have persuaded us to deny our forebears their essential humanity. We did not understand that by diminishing them we diminished, rather than exalted, ourselves; that by exposing, as we thought, the crasser motives of the actors or the hidden currents in these great dramas which shaped the modern world, we compromised our own character as free and responsible men. We may examine, criticize, analyze, and pass judgment upon the actors in these events. We may scrutinize their motives and speculate upon the sincerity of their aims, but we must accept the "conceptual framework" which, *in their view*, gave meaning to their actions.

Clearly, we cannot have it both ways. We cannot live off the fruits of their commitments while demonstrating by means of the latest research techniques that they were quite unaware of what they were doing or that they were moved by motives quite different from those which they professed.

Much of this material is intractable, simply there, and we have no choice but to accept it. We cannot truly transcend the explanations of participants as to why they were involved in these momentous episodes; the unity of the actors and their actions has a kind of inviolability that makes it difficult and precarious to separate the two and intrude between them the conclusions of a historian writing many years or cultures after the event.

It thus follows that existential history is remarkably resistant to reinterpretations. Turn and twist which way we may, we must come back at last to an acceptance of what the contemporaries said they were up to. We have, perforce, to take them at their word. This is not, of course, to say that the historian cannot profitably devote himself to existential history. He may examine details, reconstruct important episodes which have been dealt with in a brief or cursory fashion; he may study individuals and their motives, trace complicated interrelated actions, illuminate developments which heretofore have been obscure. But he will be well advised to do so within the general framework of the original interpretation, rather than trying to make his name by unveiling a new and improved interpretation which discards the most emphatically stated assumptions of the participants. We cannot delve far into these or substantially alter them for reasons that are tied directly to the nature of reality, of human experience and man's perception of it. We expect to be as well treated by the men who come after us. But if we accept this dogma—that later interpretations are, almost inevitably, better and that those who come after us can state better than we ourselves the purpose and meaning of our actions—we surrender, it seems to me, our belief in ourselves, in the integrity of our own lives and the intimate relation between intention, action, and purposive result. We may still acknowledge the highly fortuitous and contingent character of such sequences of thought-action-result. But, barring the kind of abdication which I do not think many historians would be willing to make, I confess I do not understand the logic by which we can profess to a better grasp than the actors themselves of the true nature of the events which constitute existential history.

The impulse to reinterpret the events of existential history is relatively new. When symbolic history developed, it brought with it, as part of its critical and comparative method, a universal skepticism which it applied indiscriminately to the past. Symbolic history rested, quite clearly, on generalization and interpretation. Dazzled by the success of this approach, historians undertook to apply it to all history, existential and symbolic alike, with a heavy-handed uniformity. Moreover, once the so-called critical spirit had established itself in the university, fortified itself with "method," and taken up the emblem of science, a kind of independent force was generated which impelled scholars to conceive of themselves as ruthless searchers after a kernel of truth that was obscured from (or by) the participants and could only be unearthed by the diligent researches of later historians. This led to an increasing subtlety and complexity in interpretation. But it soon became evident that an excess of subtlety in the analysis and interpretation of the causes of events that fall in the category of existential history resulted, almost invariably, in obscurity and confusion rather than illumination.

Interpretation has followed upon interpretation in bewildering succession until it seems there are no stable marks in the landscape of history. A good many older scholars have simply withdrawn to vast editorial projects where interpretation is unnecessary and where they can practice their refined and immaculate scholarship undisturbed.

This indeed is the situation in most areas of American history, the only history about which I am at all competent to speak. We thus have an absurd and paradoxical situation altogether different from what we had imagined would follow upon our vast and laborious researches: more and more scholarship has resulted in growing uncertainty about the causes and significance of some of the most important episodes of our past. An increasing tentativeness, hesitancy, and qualification has brought about a strange kind of impotence, the "homogenized history" about which John Higham has recently written.

It seems clear, moreover, that in addition to the pressures inherent in the institutional arrangements of American colleges and universities there are tendencies at work in society in general which encourage the effort to break down the decisive events of history into merely dramatic aspects of long-range trends, hidden forces, and generalized social developments—in short, to obscure their existential character and subsume them under the broader categories of symbolic history. Such interpretations—which inevitably diminish the roles of individual actors—are, like every human creation, fashioned against a background of contemporary prejudice about the nature of the historical or, rather, the social process. Prevalent attitudes toward the role of the individual in society color the historian's conception of change in history. If, looking around him, he sees a highly conditioned, relatively passive, in a certain sense "nonpolitical," populace, he is inclined to extrapolate from these observations and offer us a history in which, as in present-day American society, the individual seems to be acted upon by forces, rather than playing a creative role in his society. Hannah Arendt has traced the shift from an ethic of "action" to one of "behavior" and has discussed its implications for our world. Needless to say, a mass society will almost inevitably derogate the value and relevance of individual action. The twentieth-century American doubtless finds some solace in the assurance that he has not suffered an acute loss of effective power in the theater of human affairs but that in fact every generation has been more or less powerless in the face of historical process and any contention to the contrary is simply a romantic illusion whose deceitfulness is now apparent to sophisticated observers.

Professional historians have carried out their mission in this general "transvaluation of values" by purporting to show that the actors in the great dramas of history were not as effective or meaningful as they thought themselves to be and as we have sometimes naïvely credited them with being. Put in a familiar perspective, the issue is, in essence, one of free will and necessity. The categories of historical reality that have been described herein correspond to this classic human experience. We are quite conscious today of the conditioned nature of our lives, that we are "social animals" whose "behavior" follows patterns that can be traced by the social scientist. Evidence of this modern preoccupation is not hard to come by. It is manifest in contemporary sociology and cultural anthropology—indeed, those disciplines are to a degree postulated on the existence of recognizably patterned responses to specific stimuli. We see this interest reflected in the popular acceptance of books such as Vance Packard's *The Status Seekers* and William Whyte's *The Organization Man*, works which offer us a picture of individuals conditioned by social and economic forces, behaving in a way which suggests an ant-like mass culture rather than a society of free and responsible individuals. Indeed, modern man is extremely sensitive to the conditioned character of his situation on earth—in short, to necessity. Western man has had, historically, a conviction of free will within the limits of the necessary—a conviction that he had the capacity to make meaningful choices. Deeply imbedded in the *Weltanschauung* of the Western world has been the idea of individual responsibility, based on the assumption that man was creator as well as creature; that he could affect process as well as being affected by it; that he was an actor in a drama which, in terms of classic Christian theology, involved an interplay between God's plan and man's response.

Even in times when devotion to one doctrine of determinism or another has blurred or diminished the sense of free will, people have nonetheless continued to act as though it was reality in fact, if not in theory. The Marxist belief in the inevitability of the triumph of Communism has not, for example, lessened the vigor or the resourcefulness with which its adherents have sought to advance the day of that triumph. While our present-day culture has been particularly ingenious in fostering a sense of powerlessness, of conditioning, of necessity, and relentless determinism, the greater part of mankind still continues to act as though choices were meaningful and action purposive. Within sociology itself, Karl Mannheim and the apostles of sociology of knowledge have tried to provide for an intellectual elite a secure base outside the fluctuations of changing ideals and values.

Perhaps we have overly belabored a proposition that can hardly be disputed: that freedom and necessity are the dichotomous principles, the poles, which correspond to Western man's most basic apprehension of his relation to his world. This being the case, it is noteworthy that historians have given such slight attention to the relation of this basic apprehension to the problems of historical research and interpretation. Certainly the expectation of making the discipline of history into a science implies, however loudly its champions might deny it, a determinism, a complete conditioning. Unless by scientific history they mean calculable patterns of individual and social response based on man's behavior under similar conditions in the past, they do not mean *science* and had better abandon the term once and for all. If they simply mean methods of research and investigation that are as painstaking, as thorough, and as accurate as possible, they have no more claim to the word *science* than any honest and careful intellectual craftsman. To pre-empt for historical studies the term *scientific*, it is not enough simply to refer to method alone—a sense in which apparently a good many historians are prone to use the phrase. This is true for a number of reasons. Here it is perhaps sufficient to point out that no historical method can ever be precise enough, or subject to strict enough controls, to qualify as "scientific."

Moreover, the fact is that to argue against the possibility of scientific history or to protest the phrase is, today, to beat a dead horse. Very few historians can be found who are willing at this hour to assert that the study of history is a science or can ever have the character of a science in any proper sense of that word. What is far more important is that many, if not most, historians think and write about the historical process as though it is very largely determined. Hence our concern with general trends, long-range developments, and vast social movements, where the role of the individual is clearly subordinated to mass transformations. In these studies—of the Westward movement, the rise of cities, the growth of industrialism, the triumph of technology—the element of the conditioned or the necessary predominates, although the processes described are more often shaped by individual wills and by purposive action than most historians are inclined to acknowledge. Nonetheless, it is clearly the case that topics of this kind, topics in the area of symbolic history, are concerned, in general, with the more conditioned aspects of man's behavior in history.

At the same time, it seems patently true that the dramatic and crisis events of existential history correspond most directly to man's experience of free will. We have thus in the interrelation of existential and symbolic history a representation of the interplay between free will and necessity. To extend the techniques appropriate to symbolic history to existential history, as we have persistently done in the last half century or so of historical study, is an obvious perversion; in so doing, the historian tries to force all historical reality into what is essentially a pattern of conditioned response, of behavior rather than action, of necessity rather than free will.

If, indeed, the experience of mankind consists of both free will and necessity, our treatment of history must reflect this fact. The alternative is to declare that necessity is overriding and that, for all practical purposes, man is conditioned, *not* free—rather than, as our tradition has held, conditioned, *and* free. If modern man freely chooses the former option, that is his right, but the terms of the capitulation should be clearly stated and generally understood; if the historian is determined to write history based on the assumption that the story of mankind is predominantly one of necessity, that should be explicit.

The dangers such a conception of the social process poses for what we speak of so glibly today as "Western civilization" are obvious. We might say that he whom the gods would render impotent they must first convince of his impotence. History is our greatest reservoir of self-images, ideas, and "life-styles"; it is of vast importance therefore that we preserve a clear vision of our past. If we create and promote as the truth an account of the past which reinforces our modern sense of powerlessness and anomie, we encourage this trend. If we see history more truly as the creation of man's effective will and action—and this is what historical investigation shows it to be—we can find the heart, as other generations have done, to act as men; to assert boldly, if not our complete dominance over process, at least the dignity and validity of human action, and, in so doing, to reduce "behavior" to its proper status as an interesting and important but minor aspect of our earthly predicament, always subordinate to intelligent and purposeful action.

To revert to the analysis of the two categories of historical reality: let me emphasize once more that the events of existential history as recounted by contemporaries have about them a kind of definitiveness that makes them unrewarding subjects for the ambitious reinterpreter. Yet they offer fascinating fields of study for the scholar who approaches them with the desire to learn what they have to teach, rather than to wrest from them some obscure and hidden and often, in the end, depressingly mundane secret.

Has the historian then no function? By no means. He can, as has been pointed out, devote himself profitably to existential history. It is not possible, nor indeed desirable, to rule out reinterpretation entirely. Certain aspects even of crisis events, for a variety of reasons, will have a somewhat different significance for posterity than they had for the individuals involved in the historical episodes. But the frame of reference within which the actors moved, their basic assumptions, their stated aims and ideals must be respected by subsequent historians. We cannot assume that the "objectivity" afforded by a longer time perspective, or the improved methods of historical investigation, will reveal broad truths that were inaccessible to the participants. In addition, the whole field of symbolic history lies ready to hand. The themes and topics of symbolic history, as distinguished from those of existential history, are susceptible of progressive development. These day-to-day trends move through a series of crises and, with their slow changes and their complexity, are generally beyond the comprehension of contemporaries; they move too slowly, lie too deeply buried, involve too wide a range of phenomena to be fully grasped by the individuals who are borne along on their slow tide. They involve ideas, inchoate mass movements, social change, modifications in economic systems, new conceptions of the role of the individual or of institutions.

Research in these areas constitutes a genuine expansion of the human consciousness, of our awareness of the components of man's social life—which, viewed in the past, we call history. Such researches reveal us more clearly to ourselves and make us more fully aware of our nature, our limitations, and our potentialities. They quite readily satisfy the requirements of the relativists that historical research cast light on contemporary problems and issues. In addition, since they represent at best a widening of our consciousness, they do involve a kind of progress "on and up"; the insights and understandings derived from them cannot be lost by later generations, whereas understandings and insights in the field of existential history can be lost. Of course, the interest of historians in particular themes and topics in the general area of symbolic history will vary from generation to generation, because the urgent contemporary problems will change. Thus the researches of one generation of historians into the role of religion in American history, stimulated, let us say, by the prevalent feeling of uncertainty and anxiety over religious values, may be put aside in a time of greater religious security. But although these earlier insights may be subjected to changing interpretations or shifting emphasis, they are cumulative in a sense that interpretations of events in existential history are not. An insight, say that of Max Weber into the relationship between Protestantism and capitalism, may be severely modified, but there is no way, short of the obliteration of the mind, that our awareness of the relevance of this relationship can be lost. Along this line, I am prepared to argue that our understanding of American Puritanism, for example, is greater (and of a different kind, of course) than that possessed by the Puritans themselves, greater than that possessed by nineteenth-century historians, and of a nature that unquestionably represents an advance in our knowledge of the Puritans. There is, to be sure, no reason to believe that this knowledge will continue to expand in the future at the rate it has in say the last thirty years, but what has been gained cannot very

well be lost—although, as I have suggested, its relevance
for another generation may well be different. While the
vast majority of American historians have rejected all the
major premises on which Frederick Jackson Turner's frontier thesis professed to rest, one element has remained inde-
structible—that the frontier experience was of transcendent
importance in American history. That is Turner's per-
manent gift; it has enlarged our understanding of our history
by drawing our attention in a most dramatic way to one of
its essential ingredients.

The events of existential history have the character of
dramatic art—the capacity to recover their original form
even after they have been hacked to pieces by the busy an-
alyzer. The themes of symbolic history lack this dramatic
unity. They depend on rational coherence. They are not
irresistible by virtue of a mustering of facts but rather
through their power to convince and illuminate. They make
sense (or a larger sense) out of our collective experience.
They seek admittance to Clio's domain by their relevance,
by their powers of persuasion. In the realm of symbolic
history, moreover, it quite clearly becomes necessary for the
historian to be familiar with and to seek to exploit effectively the insights of sociology, social psychology, and cultural anthropology.

We have argued for a recognition of the dual nature of
historical reality—the existential and the symbolic. Existential history commands the historian, sets limits to his free-
ranging imagination (or to his slavish subordination to what
he assumes to be the facts) by reminding him that the
classic events of history have an independent life of their
own; it deals with man in the concrete fullness of his existential situation, in action, at the height of his powers,
and it imposes on the historian the obligation to be faithful
to the authentic events.

Symbolic history, on the other hand, challenges the historian to make sense of the broader developments of social man, to impose, like the artist, a meaningful and revealing order upon the disorder of the past (and, thereby, of the present). It may truly be said that we live by our ability to keep these two classes of history viable and relevant. A society preserves its form and coherence by virtue of the image of it projected out of its past. Therein lies the crucial nature of the historian's task. By blurring or dimming that image, the historian may corrupt or cloud a people's consciousness of its identity. And this is generally the first step on the road to social disintegration.

Existential and symbolic history represent two poles of man's common experience; a healthy humanity will live in the field of force between them.

14

Unity of History

❀ ❀ ❀

To distinguish between existential and symbolic history is not enough to preserve the historian from error and futility. Since World War II dozens of new nations, the great majority of them former colonies of European powers, have come into formal, if extremely precarious, existence. This fact of history has had its effect upon historical study in the colleges and universities of the nation. American institutions of higher learning have perhaps been especially responsive to the problems posed by "emergent nations." Dozens of institutes have been established to sponsor post-doctoral work in Near and Far Eastern History, in the histories of Africa, Latin America, and Southeast Asia. This is all commendable. Honest and systematic efforts are being made to study the social, political, and economic problems of these nations, so new and so tenuous. But the emphasis, not unnaturally, is contemporary, as indeed it must be, since many of these countries have very little history in the sense in which the Western world has used the word.

In the emergent nations themselves, native historians have already begun to write histories; histories of the colonial period are popular in countries which, like the Latin American nations, are far enough removed from their beginnings so that their colonial past has taken on an aura of glamour and adventure and where, as a general rule, the dominant class is descended from the settlers sent out by the colonizing power.

More popular in the recently emerged nations are histories of an ancient golden age before the appearance of the European invaders. That this golden age is generally illusory is less important than that the new nations need such a fabricated history to define themselves as a people. Certainly the West should not be surprised at this development, for it was the West which, in the nineteenth century, discovered this means of self-identification. As much myth as fact was mixed into the early histories of the nation states of Europe. Yet the history of the European states in the last century—armored with an aggressive arrogance which was based, in part at least, upon spurious history—does not make us wish to see the experiment repeated by a host of new nations.

If there is an overriding theme for the century ahead, it is the unity of mankind. Such a goal cannot be served by the production of particularistic histories in which truth is submerged in legend. The new nations need, above all, to see themselves and their neighbors as free as possible of illusion and gross error. But the problem is not easily dismissed. The Western nations, confident and poised, are able to affect considerable sophistication about their respective histories. They have shown a commendable rigor in reducing overblown histories to their proper proportion, in separating myth from fact, in criticizing their own excesses of nationalistic zeal. With all this, their histories are still cast in an essentially nationalistic and parochial mould. They can hardly be surprised (nor should they be supercilious) that new nations which are struggling desperately to achieve some sense of national identity employ the means invented by their former colonial overlords. Most of the new nations have been propelled out of pre-history into history by the West. The experience has been traumatic and irreversible (unless indeed the whole world is to return to barbarism, an eventuality which is by no means to be ruled out). However primitive, crude, naïve, or presumptuous these newcomers may be, they must be integrated into the community of nations. The alternative is chaos.

It is we who have burdened the primitive and traditional cultures of the world with "the terror of history." Most of them have evaded history for thousands of years by means of the techniques Mircea Eliade has described—astral analogies, archetypes, repetition, cosmogonies of creation, and so on. They have been wrenched out of the womb of the eternal present or, as in the case of India, out of a complex but consoling cosmogony, and delivered raw and naked into a historical world. It is not surprising that Marxism, which offers a prospective release from history, should have great appeal for them; that it does not have more is due less to its attractiveness than to the fact that a vast majority of these newly modern peoples still cling to remnants of their anti-historical theologies. Certainly their very tentative acceptance of a historical world in the Western sense may be withdrawn at any time, particularly if the tragedies of history place too heavy a burden on psyches ill-prepared to cope with them. Moreover, we should remember that in the United States the millennial Protestant sects, with their expectation of Christ's more or less imminent reign on earth, offer a tempting avenue of escape within the framework of fundamentalist Christianity. These forces, so different in origin, may combine to overwhelm the historic consciousness of twentieth-century man if we fail to recover and then dramatize the human meaning and relevance of history, thus using history as a means of creating the true unity of mankind.

In this primary task (one shared, incidentally, by Russia), historians must surely take part. As we have noted, institutes have been established on many university campuses to carry on research in the problems of the emergent nations. But these programs will not satisfy the deeper needs of the new countries for a place in the family of nations. If the avenue to national respectability seems to lie in an insistence upon a unique and glorious history, they will, inevitably, follow this path. Western historians can forestall such intellectually disreputable and politically dangerous enterprises by emerging from their national preserves and writing universal history; that is to say, the common history of mankind in which new nations and old nations take their proper place. It is entirely conceivable that the citizens of newly independent Nigeria will be satisfied to see themselves as part of the general history of the human race; that they and their sister states will then waive their rights to particularistic and largely mythical histories. The experiment is worth trying—the more so since national histories are, in any event, obsolete. Unfortunately, the idea of historians in England, France, Germany, and, above all, the United States, abandoning their primarily nationalistic orientation is, on the face of it, wildly Utopian. It runs counter to all the tendencies and prejudices of our day. Specialization and compartmentalization are everywhere in the ascendency. The Toynbees are viewed with suspicion or contempt; the monograph reigns supreme and virtually unchallenged.

Yet suppose the notion that the sum total of monographs with each passing year can come closer and closer to the truth; suppose this notion, in which we have in fact lost faith, should suddenly fall to the ground. Suppose that, like the one-horse shay, it were to disintegrate before the astonished eyes of the onlookers. What would then occupy the attention of historians?

To take another tack, let us consider the number of Ph.D's in institutions of higher learning in the United States who are engaged in research in American history. The vast majority of historians who have received the doctorate in this country since 1873 have concentrated on American history. There are between five and six thousand Ph.D's in history in the United States, and the ranks are growing at the rate of some three hundred a year. Of these, approximately fifty-five per cent—or between twenty-five hundred and three thousand—are working in the field of American history. And perhaps seventy-five per cent are specialists in some aspect of the so-called national period— roughly the hundred and seventy-three years since the formation of the Federal Constitution. In other words, there are about fifteen trained and presumably productive scholars for every year of our history as a nation. And as the passage of time adds about a hundred and fifty Ph.D's a year for every additional year of our history, the "historian explosion" has rather serious implications. Technological unemployment may be as much of a threat to American historians as to the assembly-line workers of Detroit.

Despite the fond expectations and periodic exhortations of department chairmen, colleagues, and deans, most of these Ph.D's produce very little in the way of so-called scholarly work. And that, under the circumstances, is a blessing. Nonetheless, there are so many productive historians and so few years to cover that the same field is constantly being replowed. This is known as offering "new interpretations," and each new interpretation, hopefully, brings us nearer the truth. In earlier chapters I have suggested that this is too optimistic an expectation. Often the new interpretations are fleeting indeed and do more to confuse than to enlighten the undergraduate students to whom they are revealed immediately by instructors anxious to "keep up" with the latest scholarship. One cannot but wonder what this consists of. A Rip Van Winkle student familiar with David Ramsay's interpretation of the causes of the American Revolution who subsequently fell asleep and awoke a hundred and seventy years later would find the Revolution being interpreted very much as it had been in Ramsay's day. This would be reassuring to him until he discovered that at least three quite different interpretations had been considered "true" before the contemporary view once again prevailed.

We have reached the point of diminishing returns in the research and writing of American history.[1] If anyone doubts this, he has only to compare the quality of articles which appeared in the early years of the *American Historical Review* with those of, say, the last decade. We have better training, more resources, more monographs, more historians, and, generally speaking, worse history. American historians need a new concept of their task. They have trampled around in their own back yard too long, stumbling over one another and working and reworking an increasingly arid soil. It may thus be hoped that they will be favorably inclined toward a new orientation.

All they need to do is to recapture the generous and cosmopolitan spirit of the first generation of American historians. The word *universal* came readily to the minds of these gentlemen. Jedediah Morse wrote a *Universal Geogra-*

---

[1] It might be well to recall Burckhardt's warning about the dangers of national history: "Bias . . . is particularly prone to make its appearance in the guise of patriotism, so that true knowledge finds its chief rival in our preoccupation with the history of our own country. . . . There are certainly things in which the history of a man's own country will always take precedence, and it is our bounden duty to occupy ourselves with it. Yet it should always be balanced by some other great line of study, if only because it is so intimately interwoven with our desires and fears, and because the bias it imparts to our mind is always towards intentions and away from knowledge." *Force and Freedom*, p. 88.

phy with special emphasis on the United States of America, and David Ramsay, at the time of his death, was at work on a *Universal History; or, an Historical View of Asia, Africa, Europe, and America, from their Earliest Records to the Nineteenth Century; with a Particular Reference to the State of Society, Literature, Religion, and Form of Government, in the United States of America*. In the years after the Revolution, Americans were very conscious of their relation to the rest of the world. Nationalistic zeal had not yet caused them to become provincial, to speak with increasing stridency of American this and American that, of American wealth and power, American wisdom and virtue, American uniqueness and American rectitude.

With a United Nations and a European Economic Community, it is perhaps not too much to hope that historians might once more become part of a world community. Of course, when one speaks of universal history to a scholar who has spent the better part of his life mastering a decade of American history or a generation of European history, one arouses the profoundest anxieties and suspicions. And, indeed, it might properly be asked: Is everyone suddenly to start writing universal history? Is the historian who feels incapable of encompassing a decade to be asked to venture into the broad stream of time which includes all human societies? Such a notion is inconsistent with all the canons of conscientious scholarship, and we are not naïve enough to recommend it. What is involved, essentially, is a new frame of mind in which the historian's study of a single period or event in a single nation is broadened to include the whole spectrum of similar events in other nations. We might well recall the words spoken in 1890 by Herbert Baxter Adams, the dean of American historical studies. He wanted, Baxter declared, "a fair field for comparative studies in Church and State and the Institutes of Education, without being regarded as an American provincial." A review

of the statements and the scholarship of this generation of
historians will disclose a much greater concern for the history of man in general than is found among their present-
day heirs. It is this spirit, deepened and extended, which
we would call universal history. The historian will still have
his specialty, but it will be related to problems common to
segments of society larger than his own nation.[2]

In an age when astronauts orbit the earth in little more
than an hour and by doing so give dramatic emphasis to
the common destiny of man, it is an anachronism for historians to confine themselves to an intellectual orbit that
fails to carry them beyond the borders of their own nation.
What is demanded as the price for this wider range is that
the historian do what by the nature of his craft he has been
most reluctant to do, that is, distinguish between that
which is important and that which is unimportant. The
monograph, which includes everything of any conceivable
relevance to its subject, is the model of indiscriminate history and involves the abdication of the process of selection
and arrangement that is the essence of good history.

C. Vann Woodward has enumerated some of the specific
tasks with which modern history has presented the historian.
These are, primarily, tasks imposed or suggested by the manifestly interdependent relationship of the nations of the
world: military and diplomatic history, the history of science
and technology, the relation of America to Europe, etc.[3]
All these are relatively new fields for investigation. In addi-

---

[2] C. Wright Mills has written: "You cannot understand or explain the
major phases through which any modern Western nation has passed, or
the shape that it assumes today, solely in terms of its own national history.
I do not mean merely that in historical reality it has interacted with the
development of other societies; I mean also that the mind cannot even
formulate the historical and sociological problems of this one social structure without understanding them in contrast and in comparison with other
societies." *The Sociological Imagination*, p. 151.
[3] C. Vann Woodward: *The Age of Interpretation* (Washington, D.C.:
Service Center for Teachers of History; 1961), No. 35.

tion, epic political history, which has been the backbone of all history, will doubtless reassert itself. In the fields of social and intellectual history, as indeed of what we have called symbolic history, work of considerable insight and sophistication is being done. Such work only needs, in most instances, to be broadened to yield enormously fruitful results. It is concerned, generally, with analysis and needs to be balanced by better existential history.

Science claims to be predictive. Indeed, if it is not, it is not science. The historian's desire to work toward prediction or to attain the power of prediction is a measure of his longing to share in the dazzling nimbus of the scientist. But the yearning has deeper roots. The historian, as we have suggested, is vitally concerned with the future. In fact, it is his concern for the future which induces him to turn his attention to the past. The future can only take place when that portion of the past which must be preserved has been distinguished from that portion which must be abandoned, and this can only be done by reference to a future which commands the deepest faith and the highest aspiration of the present. For this reason, history is important; for this reason, we pay heed to it. As science, as antiquarianism, as history-for-history's sake, it is quite unimportant. As a means of survival, as a means of making possible a decent future for all mankind, it must be told and must be heard. Santayana has said that the nation which will not remember its history has to repeat it. Historians are the custodians of the common memories of mankind. In a very real sense it is upon their wisdom and resolution that the destiny of man depends. The Hebrews discovered history; the Christians made it the heritage of all men. The secular mind of the Western world put it in the service of modern nation states without at the same time destroying its power to unify mankind through its ability to evoke the universality of man. This is its present task. The yearning of many historians to make history a predictive science degrades the prophetic power of history. History is not concerned with predicting: the ability to predict would mean a closed and determined universe or, perhaps worse, a managed one. And if we know anything from our observation of the drama of history, it is that history is open, full of extraordinary potential and inexplicable turns and changes.

Egon Friedell, writing in 1920 of the future, professed to find "just these five possibilities: that (1) America will triumph materially, which would mean world-domination by the United States and, at the end of this interim empire, the fall of the West through over-technicalization; (2) America will triumph spiritually by becoming sublimated, this implying the rebirth of Germany, whence alone this sublimation could be derived; (3) the East will triumph materially, bringing about world-Bolshevism and the interim reign of anti-Christ; (4) the East will triumph spiritually, reviving Christianity through the Russian soul; and (5) the fifth eventuality is—chaos. These five possibilities present themselves and no others, whether political, ethical, or psychological. It will, however, be clear, we hope, to the intelligent reader that none of these eventualities will materialize, for world history is not an equation, not even one with several solutions. Its only real possibility is the unreal, and its only causality irrationality. It is made by a higher mind than the human."[4]

When we say that the proper role of history is prophetic, we use the word in its Old Testament sense. The prophets of the Hebrews did not try to predict the future from any position "outside" their tribe or kingdom. The called their people to judgment because they loved them only less than they loved the Lord and they were, in consequence, compelled to remind the people constantly of what they wished

---

[4] *Cultural History of the Modern Age* (New York: Alfred A. Knopf; 1932), III, p. 478.

to forget: the requirements of Jehovah. The responsibility of the modern historian, like that of the prophets of Israel, is to speak of those things which must continue to claim our loyalties and engage our faith (Robert Frost has defined faith as our power to dream the future into existence); the future is given shape by our faith, or condemned to drift and disaster by our indifference.[5]

The relativism which has so distressed present-day historians and which most of them have come to accept finally as an unfortunate but inescapable fact of their human condition might be better translated as *commitment*. Because the historian is himself involved in history, or should be; because he is a participant in the struggles and crises that now quite clearly shape man's common destiny, his history is relative—which is not only as it must be, but as it should be. In this context, *relative* might also be translated *relevant*. It is only by being relevant to his day and age that the historian has the remotest chance of being relevant to any future day. All his whoring after objectivity is a death wish in disguise—disguised as a desire for a kind of immortality to be won, hopefully, by escaping from history, by getting "outside" and thus being as true tomorrow as today, by being, in other words, like God Himself. But such an expectation is the vanity of all vanities. Out of the vast legions of the past, the few souls who have won earthly immortality—whether in history or in literature—have done so because of their power to universalize the particular, to involve themselves so deeply and percipiently in their own time or in an earlier time that they transcend time by

---

[5] "History, without qualification, is the process of the civilizing of mankind. It is world history, always something more than a collection of stories of independent states and nations, or collations of these. History is mankind expressed over time, inching on in the production of a single civilization where men flourish in peace and justice fulfilling themselves together as wills, bodies, minds and persons." Paul Weiss: *History, Written and Lived*, p. 130.

the power of their love. Their passion speaks with such
accuracy and insight of the men and events that moved
them that others are equally moved and stand in spirit
with them at the pass of Thermopylae or at the ruins of
Carthage.

The historian must recognize that history is not a scientific enterprise but a moral one. It is the study of human
beings involved in an extraordinary drama, and its dramatic
qualities are related to the moral values inherent in all life.
History is in large part the story of the men and women
who have suffered and sacrificed to create the world in which
we live. In this sense, it is selective rather than democratic.
In history, all men are *not* created equal. The general is
more important than the private; the king, in most instances,
is more important than his subject. History is concerned
with the actions of individuals and social groups, and since
such action almost invariably has been undertaken in the
name of certain values and ideals, the historian must make
judgments on the actors and their actions. He must discriminate, furthermore, between that which must be preserved and that which must be discarded. If he is dealing
with the American Civil War, for instance, he must implicitly or explicitly take a position on slavery. And this
position will have very little to do with objectivity; it will
be based on certain moral assumptions about the nature of
involuntary servitude. And so on, throughout history. Sometimes the values will be, as we are so fond of saying, "relative," but they will nonetheless be present. Judgment is a
continual part of the dialogue of the historian—although,
if he is true to his muse, he will temper his judgment with
understanding and compassion. There is nothing more irri-
tating than the complacent and insensitive boor who tramps
through the past, meting out praise and blame with a heavy
and dogmatic hand. It is this type that is so ready to indict
an individual or an age for failing to be as enlightened in

its social, political, or religious practices as he is. To abuse the Founding Fathers for favoring suffrage based on property, for example, is not only stupid but gratuitous. On the other hand, we should hardly be inclined to propose such a basis for suffrage as a panacea for present-day political ills.

Historians have hotly debated the question of "present-mindedness" as opposed to "history-mindedness"—whether the historian should exploit the past in behalf of the present, or whether his primary responsibility is to try to detach himself from the present and immerse himself in the past. Either course, pursued single-mindedly, invites disaster. Present-mindedness may result in the most superficial and jejune treatment of the individuals and events of earlier ages—in adapting the past, as Nietzsche expressed it, "to present trivialities." These are the "thoughtless folk who write history in the naïve faith that justice resides in the popular view of their time, and that to write in the spirit of the times is to be just."[6]

History-mindedness may equally well result in antiquarianism, in a stultifying devotion to the imagined charm and quaintness of the past. The truth lies somewhere between. Almost inevitably, the historian's attention is directed to those aspects of the past which are relevant to his own day. Once that assumption is granted, it must be said with equal emphasis that the historian is under the heaviest obligation to extend his own sympathy and understanding to those who, in other times, loved and aspired, believed and fought, suffered and died—actors, like the historian himself, in the universal drama of mankind.

Above all, the historian must cease to think of himself on the one hand as standing "outside" history, as explaining to youthful and immature minds the "way things happened," and on the other hand as carrying on an esoteric

---

[6] *The Use and Abuse of History*, p. 44.

conversation with his colleagues about the finer points of interpretation. The historian is existentially involved in history, or he is nothing. His task is to awaken the minds of his students and to inspire them with a vision of the future which will make sense of the past.

15

History and the Search for Identity

The classic search of our time is the search for identity. But we cannot ask "Who am I?" and expect to find an answer without asking Kant's question "What is Man?"[1] We might well recall Heidegger's famous diagnosis: "No age has known so much, and so many different things, about man as ours. . . . And no age has known less than ours of what man is."[2]

---

[1] "What we once were, how we developed and became what we are, we learn from the way in which we acted, the plans which we once adopted, the way in which we made ourselves felt in our vocation, from old letters, from judgments on us which were spoken long ago. . . . We understand ourselves and others only when we transfer our own lived experience into every kind of expression of our own and other people's life." (Wilhelm Dilthey, from "The Peculiar Nature of the Human Studies," in *Wilhelm Dilthey: An Introduction*, translated and edited by H. A. Hodges (London: Routledge & Kegan Paul; 1949), p. 142.

[2] From *Kant and the Problem of Metaphysics*, quoted by Buber in *Between Man and Man*, p. 181.

In earlier chapters[3] we touched on the modern impulse to escape from history. Here we propose to carry the matter somewhat further and suggest a number of ways in which the attenuation of the historical sense is impoverishing modern society and thwarting the "self" in its search for identity.

One of the most conspicuous characteristics of our society is oversensitivity. This oversensitivity deprives modern man of the deeper emotions—love, hatred, compassion, loyalty.[4] The relation between sensitivity and sentiment corresponds on the one hand to the moment and on the other to the historic. Sentiment has its roots in the past, in memories and associations, loves and loyalties that command our allegiance. Sensitivity presses upon the immediate and has little or no power to sustain itself in the absence of the present objects which evoke it. Sensitivity, without the counterbalance of sentiment, progressively destroys the capacity of the individual to be deeply engaged. Moreover, oversensitivity produces sentimentality, which is misplaced sentiment, as in one of the classic literary vulgarities of our day, when Salinger's Zooey Glass assures his sister that "Christ is the fat lady." This is gross sentimentality and, as such, has a strong appeal to the deracinated intellectual; it avoids the problems and burdens of historic religion and offers instead a mild and inoffensive religiosity—the liberal doctrine of empathy.[5] In the absence of a sense of the his-

---

[3] See, e.g., the discussion of free will vs. determinism in Chapter 13.

[4] J. D. Salinger is the perfect literary expression of this characteristic. He has explored the psyche of his characters with such an exquisite sensitivity that he has finally destroyed them, for we no longer believe in their power to act in a real world and thus no longer care to read about them. He has refined them out of existence, most typically in the strange case history of Seymour Glass.

[5] Such sentimentality is equally evident in the work of Tennessee Williams, around whose derelicts, psychopaths, and homosexuals a kind of dim religious light plays—the hero of *The Night of the Iguana* is a defrocked Episcopal priest of enormous sensitivity. *The Milk Train Doesn't Stop Here Anymore* features a Christ-like figure as hero. Edward Albee's *The Zoo Story* indulges in the same sentimental vulgarity: "It's just that if you can't deal with people, you have to make a start somewhere. WITH

toric, the oversensitive cannot handle sentiment without having it degenerate into sentimentality.[6]

Contemporary man is often both extraordinarily sensitive and extraordinarily impotent. It is hard not to feel, for instance, that the matter of sensitivity is related to the rapid increase in homosexuality; homosexual relations provide an opportunity for great sensitivity between partners to the relationship, without the risks and complex *historical* demands of heterosexual relations. When a man loves a woman, he faces the possibility of having a child by her —already an extreme and drastic involvement in history— and perhaps even of marrying her—then, together with his wife, he forms a unity that becomes part of history. If he and his wife have a child, the child immediately asserts its place in the continuity of generations by demanding grandparents and great-grandparents and threatening, in turn, to have children of its own one day.[7]

An excess of sensibility erodes all meaning and falls at last into mannered posings. *Last Year at Marienbad* is a cinematic example of such an excess which abandons meaning and coherence for effect. The film is conspicuous for its outspoken rejection of any recognizable historical framework. Whether the unhappy lovers met last year or the year before or, indeed, ever is not clear to them or to the audience; the film offers a calculated ambiguity which serves to annihilate time.

One of the principal causes of the oversensitivity which results in alienation and withdrawal (seen most dramatically, though not necessarily most typically, in the beatnik living a life of rebellious inactivity in some desolate pad)

ANIMALS. . . . WITH GOD WHO IS A COLORED QUEEN WHO WEARS A KIMONO AND PLUCKS HIS EYEBROWS."

[6] It is probably no accident that one of the most robust and prolific writers of our time, William Faulkner, was obsessed by history.

[7] Today one often hears childless couples declare self-righteously that they "would not think of bringing a child into such a frightful world."

is the modern city. It is in the city that history most often
seems nullified. The feverish activity of the metropolis
hangs upon the moment. What yesterday loomed solidly in
brick and concrete is today replaced with steel and glass.
Landmarks disappear almost overnight; children are conspicuously absent and old people are invisible, segregated
in crumbling slums or in senior-citizens developments.
There is little sign of death or birth, and the sequence of
generations which is the backbone of history is hardly to be
observed. The city lives in a kind of prolonged today whose
symbol is the metropolitan newspaper, which tells every
morning of various horrors—deaths, mutilations, terrible
accidents—but seldom makes any subsequent mention of
these tragedies (except where it focuses with morbid sentimentality on the lingering death of a child or a celebrity
from some incurable illness).

The city prides itself above everything else on being up-
to-date and works in a hundred direct and indirect ways to
erode the sense of a historical dimension in our lives. It is,
for example, the citadel of the senses; most of its inhabitants learn to live on sensations of the most transient kind,
a constant and ingenious titillation of superficial emotions.
Daniel Bell, writing primarily about art, has suggested that
our technical civilization, of which the city is the most characteristic accomplishment, has "eclipsed distance"—that
psychic interval which has traditionally existed between the
observer and the object observed. Bell attributes this eclipse
to certain elements of our "style" as a society, which he
comprehends in the terms *"novelty, sensation, simultaneity,
immediacy, and impact."*[8] As Bell puts it, "the loss of
psychic distance means the suspension of time." It is in just
this timeless, a-historical void that modern man wanders,
often hopelessly lost, searching for his authentic self. Time

---

[8] "The Eclipse of Distance," *Encounter*, XX, No. 5 (May, 1963), pp.
54–6.

and space are the walls and roof of the home in which the soul of Western man has grown to its present estate. The eclipse of these dimensions threatens that soul in its innermost being.

Ironically, we are especially susceptible to despair as a consequence of having been able to imagine a better world than the one we live in. We are, in fact, overcome by the discrepancies between the ought-to-be and the is or, more accurately, by the apparent absence of any readily accessible path from the is to the ought-to-be. As the eighteenth century was sustained by faith in reason, the nineteenth was supported by a belief in some form of evolutionary process. The twentieth century, however, is painfully aware that process is no longer to be relied upon. Our century has faced too many horrors to believe that progress is part of the structure of the universe. We are thus left with the grim fact that the progress of the race depends on the good will and intelligence (and, one is tempted to add, luck) with which we solve the crises that seem to press on us from every side. The authority vested in abstract thought induced us to believe that society could be reconstructed according to some planner's blueprint, whereas history, if we would listen, speaks with a somewhat different voice and reminds us of "the risks we have to run, the partial obscurity in which we have to take decisions . . . the state of dispossession, insecurity and hardihood which is the climate of all great action."[9]

It is not accidental that the optimism of the Enlightenment with regard to the power of man over himself and the cosmos has been replaced, in our own day, with the contradictory sense of man's powerlessness over his own psyche and over the social and political arrangements that obtain in the contemporary world. As man's power over nature has

---

[9] Emmanuel Mounier: *Personalism* (New York: Grove Press; 1952), p. 93.

grown, his power over himself seems to have diminished. But the extremes of optimism and pessimism are, to a considerable degree, the consequences of inadequate or faulty history. The Enlightenment was convinced that what seemed evident about man in the past—his superstition, cruelty, and vice—must vanish in the light of reason and thus could not condition the future. This delusion enabled the French to accept the horrors of their Revolution; when you are convinced that you are about to cure the patient (man) from the disease of history, you will stop at no cruelty to effect the cure. In our century Russia was driven by the same terrible lust of idealism that propelled the French Revolution in its course.

Yet, Western man, as we have seen, has dared to hope and the balance of mankind has been infected with this fever of aspiration. Gabriel Marcel has expressed man's universal aspiration: to be in the future "as before but differently and better than before."[1]

While it is doubtless true that the self today has taken much more upon itself than in earlier times—a truly staggering load—it condemns itself to ineptitude if it does not constantly carry the awareness of the darker areas of life back to the active world. In other generations people have known just as vividly the sordidness, degeneracy, and falsity of much of life, but they have also known delights and pleasures that were not purchased at the cost of insensitivity to the desperate needs and frustrations of the world.

At the other end of the spectrum from that excess of sensitivity, which is so sensitive that it rejects the world as misshapen and intolerable and refuses to enter into its dilemmas and crises, are the "overadapted," whose spokesmen tirelessly congratulate us on our technological achievements and exhort everyone to avail himself gratefully of the rich

---

[1] *Homo Viator; Introduction to a Metaphysic of Hope* (Chicago: Henry Regnery; 1951), p. 67.

bounty that this technology has produced. The overadapted gives himself up to bondage to "things"; the bondage itself degrades his "productive or social function to automatism." He is the victim of the transient fads that our society presses on him without end, claiming that some new revelation of the good life is to be found in each one: swimming pool, deep freeze, patio, electric rotisserie, powerboat, color TV, electric toothbrush, motion-picture projector, an endless cornucopia of *things*, an enchanted forest of materiality. Small wonder the oversensitive, who, although he may not know how to save his soul, at least realizes it is in desperate peril, turns away in revulsion.[2] The oversensitive knows in his heart that "man's exploitation of nature was not destined to erect upon the web of natural determinism another network of conditioned reflexes."[3]

The oversensitive suffer from an excess of self-consciousness and indeed from that very narcissism which such neo-Freudians as Marcuse and Brown celebrate; the overadapted are afflicted by a spiritual nullity that is the consequence of being devoured by an omnivorous present. They, who have given themselves so willingly to the fancied delights of an abundant technology, go as restlessly and as aimlessly as butterflies from one gleaming, machine-made flower to another, sucking up a nectar which eventually poisons them. The only thing that can save them from the tyranny of the middle-class standard of living is the knowledge that other people have lived differently and lived better by subordinating "things" to human values. Surely they will not improve by visiting a psychoanalyst, for he will tell them that the solution to their problem lies in freeing them-

---

[2] "The supreme despair," Kierkegaard wrote, "is not to feel desperate."

[3] Mounier: *Personalism*, p. 12; see also p. 85. Speaking of those whom I have called the oversensitive, Mounier writes that their "almost visceral repugnance to commit themselves, and an inability to bring anything to realization, betray the dried-up sources of feeling that underlie their sometimes highly-colored eloquence."

selves of any lingering sense of guilt over their self-indul-
gence.[4] The basic malady of the oversensitive and the
overadapted is indeed the same: they are destroying themselves for want of history.

Another contemporary manifestation of oversensitivity is
subjectivism. The subjective spirit believes that it can heal
the schism between subject and object by absorbing the
objective, but finds that, instead, the objective triumphs.
The unexpected accomplishment of the subjectivists has
been to turn the world, human and material, into objects,
objects which seem to have no relation to one another and
whose symbol is "the now pure lordship of the eye," the
detached, coolly observing gaze, which, like that of Robbe-
Grillet and his school, ranges impersonally over the world.
In the film *Last Year at Marienbad*, the façades, gardens,
and interior details of the hotel are more substantial and
seem to promise more meaning than the wan people who
act out deliberately impenetrable anti-dramas before them.

It is well to recall Paul Weiss's concept of the historic
as that which objectively happened in the past *rather than
simply that which happens in the mind of the historian*.
The working historian is hardly apt to be led astray on this
point, but the theoretical ground may be washed out from
under him by philosophers (Croce, Ortega y Gasset, and
Collingwood are cases in point) or attitudes which, in effect,
destroy the power of the historic. The dimension of the
historic alone prevents us from being crushed by the weight
of the present; it is equally important to hold fast to the

---

[4] It is the fate of the overadapted to "have no secret, no contents, no
background" and, "having no experience of any depth," to have "no respect
for privacy, their own or anyone else's." Mounier: *Ibid.*, p. 35. Marcel writes
of them: "The more we allow ourselves to be the servants of Having, the
more we shall let ourselves fall a prey to the knowing anxiety which Having
involves, the more we shall tend to lose not only the aptitude for hope,
but even I should say the very belief, indistinct as it might be, of its possibility." *Homo Viator*, p. 61. It is this spirit which apparently motivates
many members of the "radical right" in the United States.

objective nature of the historic as a bulwark against the encroachment of the subjective.

Thus, to repeat, it is essential that the objective nature of the historic be insisted upon in all discussions of history, because it is the objective nature of our historic life which offers the means for drawing modern man out of his increasingly sterile subjectivism and back into an inhabitable, if grossly imperfect, world.

In the world of art, abstract expressionism might be called "art without history," an art which undertook to free the painter from the constraints and inhibitions of traditionalism and thus allow him to express his inner, that is, his "true" self.[5] This movement has resulted, ironically, in works that lack individuality—suggesting that all "inners" are curiously alike. This might serve to convince us that the "true," inner man is indistinguishable from his fellows; he is only individualized as he appears in the world—that is, as he acquires a history. Moreover, he does not make that history, nor, more precisely, does he make himself. As Mounier has expressed it: "If every man *is* nothing but what he *makes himself*, there can be no humanity, no history, and no community."[6] The individual acquires an identity by being involved in a common enterprise. If between all individuals there existed that "absolute discontinuity" which is so prominent in much existential thought, mankind could have no history and no real future.

Another area of contemporary life where the impulse to annihilate the past is inescapably evident is in modern architecture. In the brutal and impersonal buildings that

---

[5] In the words of Willard Gaylin, there is "a prevalent tendency to think of the 'inner' man as the 'real' man and the 'outer' man as illusion or pretender. But the unconscious of a man represents *another* view, not a 'truer' one. Though a man may not always be what he appears to be, what he appears to be is always a significant part of what he is." "Psychoanaliterature: The Hazards of a Hybrid," *Columbia University Forum*, VI, No. 2 (Spring, 1963), pp. 11–16.

[6] *Personalism*, p. 30.

sprout like mushrooms all over the urban landscapes there is "no trace of the forms which lived in the centuries before us, none of their arrogance, their privilege, their aspiration, their canniness . . . their vulgarities."[7] They are coldly anti-human monoliths whose promise is death. Indeed, there is a spirit abroad, armed with such cant words as *progressive*, *modern*, *functional*, *dynamic*, which would gladly pull down all buildings with any dignity, with any power to evoke a past, and erect in their places structures as cruel as knives and as graceless as blocks. These banal and monotonous erections are like congealed pieces of the present, and it is for their very contemporaneity that they are prized. Devoid of any suggestion of the richness and variety of the past, they are the perfect monuments of an anti-historical age.

It might be said that the peculiar curse of America has been its preoccupation with individualism, rugged or otherwise. A good many Americans have had the notion, whether they acted upon it or not, that they as individuals could, without study or prayer, recapitulate the experience of the race; they have not hesitated to attempt to found new religions or novel sects. That the self has insatiable appetites was known to Christian theology long before it was discovered by Freud. Moreover, the ingenuity with which the self masks its appetites and the skill with which it uses reason or religion as the servant of its interest is equally well known and is not, in any sense, a modern discovery.[8] These facts make even more dangerous and futile the effort of modern man to escape from history. "Self-expression" and "self-realization" are two of the cant phrases of our time. What is thought to be the ultimate reality

---

[7] Norman Mailer: "The Big Bite," *Esquire*, LX (August, 1963), p. 21.

[8] Reinhold Niebuhr has pointed out that the self's desire "for security or for prestige is, like all human desires, indeterminate. There is no point at which the self . . . can feel satisfied and free to consider others than itself." *The Self and the Drama of History* (New York: Charles Scribner's; 1955), p. 139.

—the self—becomes in fact the ultimate unreality, and the tormented individuals who continue to probe the depths of their psyche become increasingly unreal.

Self-expression and self-realization are, much as their advocates would be repelled by the idea, the lineal descendants of nineteenth-century rugged individualism. Individualism, with its rapacious and exploitative attitude toward the world, is the antithesis of that individuality which is the authentic self realized within a genuine community. One of the principal fallacies of those who pursue individualism in one form or another is the notion that it is achieved by the rejection of all authority, within which history is included. Certainly, history is authoritative. We are capable of saying with reasonable accuracy what happened.[9] The historic appears as form and order, which, while it discloses areas of choice, i.e., freedom (which often, from later perspectives, also appears to be inevitable), also imposes limitations on our actions. But the framework of necessity within which history binds us cannot be escaped by ignoring history. Indeed, it could be said that to ignore it is, ultimately, to turn its authority into tyranny.

The fact is that the individual, per se, is without history; the community is historic. The individual is powerless; the community has the power to re-form its members and the world as well. In the words of Robert Oppenheimer, with the disintegration of the community (the public), "we have had neither the time nor the skill nor the dedication to tell one another what we have learned, nor to listen, nor to wel-

---

[9] "The historian never arrives at certainty; he rarely ends with more than a not altogether sifted totality of plausible, hypothetical, guessed-at and imagined formulations of what had been. One will more likely achieve more truth by turning away from the study of history than by engaging in it. . . . The historian does not find this fact as regrettable as others do, for he is primarily concerned not with achieving pure and well-tested truth but with providing a comprehensive, illuminating account of what had been." Paul Weiss: *History Written and Lived* (Carbondale: Southern Illinois University Press; 1962), p. 45.

come its enrichment of the common culture and the common understanding. Thus the public sector of our lives, what we have and hold in common, has suffered. . . . Our specialized traditions flourish; our private beauties thrive; but in those high undertakings where man derives strength and insight from the public excellence, we have been impoverished. We hunger for nobility; the rare words and acts that harmonize simplicity and truth." Our public life is pre-eminently our historic life, and it is this life that is shrunken and attenuated.[1]

Another serious flaw in the modern psyche is a lack of "patience." We cannot wait for anything; we must snatch with rude violence everything that time might properly withhold in order that it should come to fruition. If the teen-ager must have adult pleasures at once, he can never become an adult. It is a sad fact that "too soon" means "never."

The curse of impatience can be seen in almost every aspect of our lives. Young people cannot wait to get married and once married cannot wait for that deepening of understanding and sympathy which would enhance their sexual relations. Few people are willing to sacrifice today for a prospective joy. The talented young writer sits down at once to write the great American novel and ends up making a hundred thousand dollars a year in Hollywood. The novice actor wishes to be a star long before he has learned his craft. All fail to recognize that without patience it is impossible to achieve anything more than brief sensations. One of the principal sources of patience is to be found in the contemplation of the historic, which teaches us that the most

---

[1] Man's common nature and his historic being are perhaps best seen in the liturgies for the dead that are found in every great religion. In such solemn moments secular efforts to summon up some "personal" or "individual" traits to commemorate the deceased inevitably seem trivial and banal beside the profound religious utterances which bind all mankind in the common bond of death: To try to speak "individually" at this instant is presumptuous and futile.

significant transformations of society are the work of decades and generations. To enter consciously into the great enterprise of carrying history forward is to learn, almost inevitably, the meaning of patience. We might well recall the Pauline injunction to glory in tribulation, "knowing that tribulation worketh patience; and patience, experience and experience hope."[2] History, in this sense, is collective experience. And whoever has known historic man in the hours of his profoundest defeats and triumphs will not easily lose faith in the possibilities of our common future. It is the impatient who most readily abandon hope when their often puerile expectations are frustrated.

Another aspect of the search for identity which is related to history is the tendency of our time to rob life of its dramatic content. Life without drama becomes flat and tasteless; yet today the demolition of the dramatic is pursued with a spirit of almost demonic intensity. We see it, for instance, in the destruction of the various arts by their practitioners. In the realm of ethics, good and bad are dissolved into neutral grays; the devil is banished and God with him; conflict is at all odds to be avoided; adjustment is the national ideal; the case study replaces the imaginative narrative.

One of man's most basic needs is for the dramatic representation of life. It is hard to escape the feeling that much of the senseless violence of juvenile delinquents stems from a desperate effort to endow marginal lives with some dramatic meaning, however perverse. Certainly the names they give their gangs—the Dukes, Royals, Kings, Jets, Earls, Sharks, etc.—suggest this most strongly.

History, as the story of the race, is a tale of unparalleled drama, but today it too is stripped of its dramatic quality and reduced to a series of dreary dates and bland formulas. The supreme importance in written history of the imagina-

---

[2] Romans: 5:3-4.

tive rather than the analytical powers can hardly be over-emphasized. The imaginative reconstruction of the past, if done faithfully and scrupulously through narrative history, involves an extension of the affective life; it trains us to extend our sympathies so as to include the alien and the unfamiliar and thus reproduces in the historical arena that most painful and exemplary of exercises—the enlargement of our capacity for participation in the needs, hopes, anxieties, and expectations of others. The restoration of a sense of the dramatic in history will do much to fortify the individual in his effort to discover his identity, for an essential part of that identity is to be found in the story of his past —his collective "autobiography," as Rosenstock-Huessy has called it.

The point where the historic and the individual most frequently intersect is in the high-school or college classroom. I have spoken at length of the stultifying character of most instruction in history. It does the devil's work by convincing most of the young people exposed to it that it is, at least for them, quite irrelevant. We must admit, I think, the validity of Mounier's criticism of the university as the distributor of "a formal knowledge which predisposes men to ideological dogmatism, or, by reaction, to sterile irony."[3] Martin Buber most effectively contrasts the modern pedagogue with his predecessor: "The 'old' educator represented particularly the historical world, the past. He was the ambassador of history to this intruder, the 'child'; he carried to him, as the Pope in the legend did to the prince of the Huns, the magic of the spiritual forces of history; he instilled values into the child or he drew the child into values."[4] The modern teacher who reduces the encounter between the historic and "its eternally new chaos" to "facts" or "interpretations" destroys the power of history to become

---

[3] *Personalism*, p. 94.
[4] *Between Man and Man*, p. 93.

a part of the student and wrench him out of his self-centeredness. What the old teacher knew that his present-day counterpart seems to have forgotten is that "education worthy of the name is essentially education of character."[5]

The individual finds the courage to be, in Paul Tillich's formulation, in a resolute confrontation of nothingness or non-being; and he derives the courage to act from the examples of others who have acted in history.[6]

We turn to history, then, as an inexhaustible reservoir of "life styles," of models and examples, as a means of identification and completion. The man who participates in history even "incidentally and somewhat vicariously" overcomes his "impotence, guilt and worthlessness."[7] Paul Weiss echoes the words of Boris Pasternak when he writes: "Only by directly involving himself with other Actualities can a man really manage to survive. . . . When he enters history he is, by means of an effective life, able to continue in being long past the end of his natural span. He does this in the course of an effort, through the use of nature, to contribute to the work of mankind in time."[8] Selfhood, or identity, or authenticity is only achieved when larger dimensions are opened to the individual—the community, the nation, mankind, the transcendent, history. Solovyev tells the story of the huntsman lost in a dense forest. As he sits, filled with despair at his plight and eaten with feelings of futility, a bent and repulsive old woman touches him on the shoulder. She assures him that beyond the stream he faces lies her homeland, a paradise. If he will carry her over, she will lead him to this golden land. The young huntsman, skeptical though he is about her story, good-naturedly un-

---

[5] Ibid., p. 104.

[6] "The reenactments [of history] make us more vividly aware of the full nature of our being. . . . History, by bringing before us the memorable past, gives us material for desirable enactments today." Weiss: *History*, pp. 41–3.

[7] Paul Weiss: *History*, p. 136.

[8] Ibid., p. 136.

dertakes to carry the poor old woman. But when she mounts his back she is heavy as lead and he can hardly move. With a heroic effort he pushes out into the stream and with each step his burden grows lighter. When he reaches the other side, the ancient granny has turned into an enchanting maiden, who, true to her promise, guides him to her homeland.

The old crone, Solovyev tells us, "is the sacred antiquity of tradition"; the stream is history. Man, instead of being repulsed by the past, instead of "idly looking for phantomlike fairies beyond the clouds," should undertake the task of carrying this unappetizing burden "across the real stream of history." He dare not let the old woman perish in the forest because if she does he can never find his way out of the wilderness. "Those," Solovyev adds, "who do not believe in the future of the old and sacred, must at any rate remember its past," and in respect and gratitude for it, take it up. *"He who saves shall be saved,"* he tells us. "That is the secret of progress—there is not and there can be no other!"[9]

History is, of course, no panacea. I would not wish to leave the impression that I am attempting here to re-establish history as the source of all meaning, in some neo-Hegelian exercise, or as somehow a substitute for the Divine. (Such a view seems to me to require the belief that the salvation of man, however imagined, lies in the process, or dialectic, of history.)[1] Man lives in the light of some faith, even if it is only faith in himself, in his ability to live without a faith. Many men, the Marxists prominent among

---

[9] Vladimir Solovyev: *An Anthology*, edited by S. L. Frank, translated by Natalie Duddington (London: SCM Press; 1950), pp. 224–6.

[1] Karl Löwith makes this point very effectively in *Meaning in History: The Theological Implications of the Philosophy of History* (University of Chicago Press, 1949). History in this sense has no meaning *within* it. Paul Weiss, in *History as Written and Lived*, has pointed out also that ultimately it is the trans-historical which gives meaning and direction to history. See also Nathan Rotenstreich: *Between Past and Present: An Essay on History* (New Haven: Yale University Press; 1958).

them, have lived by a faith in the redemptive power of history, which in most such systems will ultimately annihilate history. My point is much less pretentious: to wit, that many of the ills which maim and distort the modern psyche have their source, in large part, in a faulty sense of history or of the historic.[2]

To the philosophical historians, the Utopians, and the idealists (who wish to appropriate history), we might add those who simply wish to escape from history through a form of modern stoicism that submits to it as a blind and brutal process. To live simply in the present, as so many have undertaken to do in this age, destroying systematically the links which bind them to preceding generations, is to leave oneself at the mercy of all those neuroses for which our society has proved so fertile a breeding ground. The modern odyssey—the search for identity—is doomed to shipwreck if it does not take unto itself the historic dimension of man's experience.

Historiography defined as the process of thinking and writing about the past in some orderly and systematic way has had a very short life; we might date its birth from the middle years of the eighteenth century. A sense of history as the unfolding of time pregnant with Divine, if only dimly perceived, potentiality has had a rather longer life. This concept has been associated, if we except the Greeks, with the notion of linear time moving to an anticipated end, however variously interpreted, in an inherently orderly universe. It is this older and profounder sense of history (which today we seem intent on destroying) that has provided the assumptions within whose scaffolding our world has taken

---

[2] "Nothing less than the whole panorama of history will tell us what man is as fully expressed in time. At every moment he reveals himself in a new way. By taking account of the totality of his manifestations, we can have a knowledge of him more detailed and better structured than we otherwise could get by speculation or introspection." Paul Weiss: *History Written and Lived*, p. 55.

shape. We may deplore the form; we may hate the world and ourselves, but it is a world made by countless generations of ancestors and if we lose faith in its potentialities we foreclose the future of mankind on this vastly shrunken planet.

Bibliography

A highly selective bibliography follows. Since the literature on the subject of history is so vast, I have chosen here only those works that seem to me to be of special interest.

I. Works on History by Practicing Historians

Abbott, Wilbur: *Adventures in Reputation*. Cambridge: Harvard University Press; 1935.

Acton, Lord: *Essays on Freedom and Power*, ed. Gertrude Himmelfarb. Boston: Beacon Press; 1948.

———: *Essays on Church and State*. New York: Viking Press; 1953.

Adams, Brooks: *The Law of Civilization and Decay*. New York: Alfred A. Knopf; 1943.

Adams, Henry: *The Degradation of the Democratic Dogma*. New York: Macmillan; 1919.

Ausubel, Herman: *Historians and Their Craft: A Study of the Presidential Addresses of the American Historical Association, 1884–1945*. New York: Columbia University Press; 1950.

Barnes, Harry Elmer: *A History of Historical Writing*. New York: Dover Press; 1962.

Barraclough, Geoffrey: *History in a Changing World*. New York: Oxford University Press; 1955.

Becker, Carl: *Everyman His Own Historian*. New York: Crofts; 1935.

Benson, Lee: *Turner and Beard: American Historical Writing Reconsidered*. Glencoe, Illinois: Free Press; 1960.

Berlin, Isaiah: *The Hedgehog and the Fox*. New York: Simon and Schuster; 1953.

——: *Historical Inevitability*. New York: Oxford University Press; 1954.

Bloch, Marc: *The Historian's Craft*, translated by Peter Putnam. New York: Alfred A. Knopf; 1953.

Brodie, Fawn: *Thaddeus Stevens: Scourge of the South*. New York: Alfred A. Knopf; 1959.

Burckhardt, Jacob: *Force and Freedom: Reflections on History*, ed. James Hastings Nichols. New York: Pantheon Books; 1953.

Bury, J. B.: *The Idea of Progress*. New York: Dover Press; 1955.

Butterfield, Herbert: *The Englishman and His History*. Cambridge: Cambridge University Press; 1944.

——: *History and Human Relations*. London: Collins; 1951.

——: *Man on His Past*. Cambridge: Cambridge University Press; 1955.

——: *Origins of Modern Science*. London: G. Bell & Sons; 1949.

——: *The Whig Interpretation of History*. London: G. Bell & Sons; 1950.

Carlyle, Thomas: *On Heroes and Hero-Worship and the Heroic in History*. London, 1840.

Carr, Edward Hallett: *What Is History?* New York: Alfred A. Knopf; 1962.

Cochrane, Charles Norris: *Christianity and Classical Culture*. New York: Oxford University Press; 1944.

——: *Thucydides and the Science of History*. London: Oxford University Press; 1929.

George, Alexander and Juliette L.: *Woodrow Wilson and Colonel House: A Personality Study*. New York: John Day; 1958.

Geyl, Pieter: *Encounters in History*. New York: Meridan Books; 1961.

———, Toynbee, Arnold J., and Sorokin, Pitirim: *The Pattern of the Past: Can We Determine It?* Boston: Beacon Press; 1949.

Gooch, G. P.: *History and Historians in the Nineteenth Century*. New York: Peter Smith; 1949.

Gottschalk, Louis, ed.: *Generalization in the Writing of History*. Chicago: University of Chicago Press; 1963.

Grene, David: *Man in His Pride: A Study in the Political Philosophy of Thucydides and Plato*. Chicago: University of Chicago Press; 1950.

Hexter, J. H.: *Reappraisals in History*. Evanston, Ill.: Northwestern University Press, 1961.

Higham, John, ed.: *The Reconstruction of American History*. New York: Harper Torchbooks; 1962.

———: "The Cult of American Consensus: Homogenizing Our History." *Commentary*, XXVII (1959), pp. 93–101.

———: "Beyond Consensus: The Historian as Moral Critic." *American Historical Review*, LXVII (1962), pp. 609–25.

Huizinga, Johan: "History's Changing Form." *Journal of the History of Ideas*, IV (1943), pp. 217–23.

———: *Homo Ludens*. London: Routledge & Kegan Paul; 1949.

———: *Men and Ideas*. New York: Meridian Books; 1959.

Jameson, J. Franklin: *The History of Historical Writing in America*. New York: Antiquarian Press; 1961.

Kraus, Michael: *The Writing of American History*. Norman, Okla.: University of Oklahoma; 1953.

Lee, Dwight, and Beck, Robert N.: "The Meaning of Historicism." *American Historical Review*, LIX (1954), pp. 568–78.

Lovejoy, Arthur O.: *Essays in the History of Ideas*. New York: Capricorn Books; 1960.

Mehta, Ved: "The Flight of the Crooked-Taloned Birds." The New Yorker, XXXVIII (December 8, 15, 22, 1962).

Oman, Sir Charles: *On the Writing of History*. New York: E. P. Dutton; 1939.

Palmer, R. R.: *The Age of Democratic Revolution*. Princeton: Princeton University Press; 1959.

Perkins, Dexter, and Snell, John: *The Education of Historians in the United States*. New York: McGraw-Hill; 1961.

Plekhanov, G. V.: *The Materialist Conception of History*. New York: International Publishers; 1940.

Renier, G. J.: *History: Its Purpose and Method*. London: Allen and Unwin; 1950.

Sée, Henri: *The Economic Interpretation of History*. New York: Adelphi; 1929.

Shotwell, James: *The History of History*. New York: Columbia University Press; 1939.

The Social Sciences in Historical Study: A Report of the Committee on Historiography. Social Science Research Council Bulletin 64, 1954.

Stern, Fritz, ed.: *Varieties of History*. New York: Meridian Books; 1956.

Strout, Cushing: *The Pragmatic Revolt in American History: Carl Becker and Charles Beard*. New Haven: Yale University Press; 1958.

Tawney, R. H.: *Religion and the Rise of Capitalism*. New York: Pelican Books; 1947.

Taylor, Henry O.: *A Historian's Creed*. Cambridge: Harvard University Press; 1939.

Teggart, Frederick J.: *Theory of History*. New Haven: Yale University Press; 1925.

Theory and Practice in Historical Study: A Report of the Committee on Historiography. Social Science Research Council Bulletin 54, 1946.

Thompson, J. W.: *A History of Historical Writing*, 2 vols. New York: Macmillan; 1942.

Trevelyan, George Macaulay: *Clio, a Muse and Other Essays, Literary and Pedestrian*. London: Longmans Green; 1913.

The Use of Personal Documents in History, Anthropology and Sociology, ed. Louis Gottschalk, Clyde Kluckholm, Robert Angell. Social Science Research Council *Bulletin* 53, 1945.

Van Tassel, David D.: *Recording America's Past . . . 1607–1884*. Chicago: University of Chicago Press; 1960.

Ware, Carolina, ed.: *The Cultural Approach to History*. New York: Columbia University Press; 1940.

Weber, Max: *The Protestant Ethic and the Spirit of Capitalism*. London: George Allen and Unwin; 1930.

Wilson, Edmund: *To the Finland Station: A Study in the Writing and Acting of History*. New York: Doubleday & Company; 1940.

Wish, Harvey: *The American Historians*. New York: Oxford University Press; 1960.

Wormald, B. H. G.: *Clarendon, Politics, History and Religion*. Cambridge: Cambridge University Press; 1951.

II. Religion and History

Augustine, Saint Aurelius: *The City of God*. New York: Modern Library; 1950.

Brunner, Emil: *Christianity and Civilization*, Parts I and II, Gifford Lectures. New York: Charles Scribner's; 1948.

Butterfield, Herbert: *Christianity and History*. New York: Charles Scribner's; 1950.

Cullman, Oscar: *Christ and Time: The Primitive Christian Conception of Time and History*, translated by Floyd V. Filson. Philadelphia: Westminster Press; 1950.

D'Arcy, Martin C.: *The Sense of History*. London: Faber; 1959.

———: *The Meaning and Matter of History: A Christian View*. New York: Farrar, Straus, and Cudahy; 1959.

Dawson, Christopher: *The Dynamics of World History*. New York: Mentor Books; 1962.

Löwith, Karl: *Meaning in History*. Chicago: University of Chicago; 1949.

Marcel, Gabriel: *The Mystery of Being: Reflection and History*, Gifford Lectures. London: Harvill; 1950.

Mehl, Roger: "Philosophy of History or Theology of History?" translated by Joseph Cunneen, *Cross Currents*, pp. 162–80.

Milburn, R. L. P.: *Early Christian Interpretations of History*. New York: Harper and Brothers; 1954.

Niebuhr, H. Richard: *Christ and Culture*. New York: Harper and Brothers; 1951.

Niebuhr, Reinhold: *Faith and History*. New York: Charles Scribner's; 1949.

———: *The Irony of American History*. New York: Charles Scribner's; 1952.

———: *The Nature and Destiny of Man*, Gifford Lectures. New York: Charles Scribner's; 1948.

———: *The Self and the Dramas of History*. New York: Charles Scribner's; 1955.

Niebuhr, Richard R.: *Resurrection and Historical Reason*. New York: Charles Scribner's; 1957.

Pieper, Josef: *The End of Time: A Mediation on the Philosophy of History*. London: Faber & Faber; 1954.

Rougement, Denis de: *Man's Western Quest: The Principles of Civilization*. New York: Harper and Brothers; 1957.

Schweitzer, Albert: *The Quest of the Historical Jesus*. New York: Macmillan; 1948.

Tillich, Paul: *The Interpretation of History*. New York: Scribner's; 1936.

———: *The Courage to Be*. New Haven: Yale University Press; 1953.

———: *The Protestant Era*. Chicago: University of Chicago Press; 1948.

Toynbee, Arnold: *An Historian's Approach to Religion*. New York: Oxford University Press; 1956.

III. *Philosophers on History*

Arendt, Hannah: *Between Past and Future.* New York: Viking Press; 1961.

———: *On Revolution.* New York: Viking Press; 1962.

Aron, Raymond: *Introduction to the Philosophy of History,* translated by George Irwin. Boston: Beacon Press; 1961.

Eliot, T. S.: *Notes Toward Definition of Culture.* New York: Harcourt, Brace; 1949.

Gardiner, Patrick: *The Nature of Historical Explanation.* New York: University of Oxford Press; 1955.

Heard, Gerald: *Is God in History?* New York: Harper and Brothers; 1950.

Hegel, G. W. F.: *Philosophy of History,* translated by J. Sibree. New York, 1902.

Heilbroner, Robert L.: *The Future as History.* New York: Harper and Brothers; 1960.

Hempel, C. G.: "The Function of General Laws in History." *Journal of Philosophy,* XXXIX (1942), pp. 35–48.

Herder, Johann G. von: *Outline of a Philosophy of the History of Man.* London, 1800.

Hocking, W. E.: "On the Law of History." *University of California Publications in Philosophy,* II (1909), pp. 45–65.

Hook, Sidney: *The Hero in History: A Study in Limitation and Possibility.* New York: John Day; 1943.

Jaspers, Karl: *Man in the Modern Age.* New York: Anchor Books; 1957.

———: *The Origin and Goal of History.* New Haven: Yale University Press; 1953.

Knowles, David: *The Historian and Character.* New York: Columbia University Press; 1955.

Machiavelli, Niccolò: *The Prince and the Discourses.* New York: Modern Library; 1940.

Mandelbaum, Maurice: "Historical Determinism and the

Gospel of Freedom." *Journal of General Education*, VI, (1951), pp. 7–16.

————: *The Problem of Historical Knowledge: An Answer to Relativism*. New York: Liveright; 1938.

Marcel, Gabriel: *Homo Viator: Introduction to a Metaphysic of Hope*. Chicago: Henry Regnery; 1951.

Maritain, Jacques: *On the Philosophy of History*. New York: Charles Scribner's; 1957.

Meyerhoff, Hans: *The Philosophy of History in Our Time: An Anthology Selected and Edited by Hans Meyerhoff*. New York: Anchor Books; 1959.

Montesquieu, Baron de: *The Spirit of the Laws*, 2 vols., translated by Mr. Nugent. London, 1752.

Mounier, Emmanuel: *Existentialist Philosophies*. New York: Macmillan; 1949.

————: *Personalism*. New York: Grove Press; 1952.

Nietzsche, Frederick: *The Use and Abuse of History*. New York: Liberal Arts Press; 1949.

Oakley, Hilda H.: "The World as Memory and as History." *Proceedings of the Aristotelian Society*, XXVII (1926–27), pp. 219–316.

————: "Perception and Historicity." *Proceedings of the Aristotelian Society*, XXXVIII (1937–38), pp. 21–46.

Ortega y Gasset, José: *Toward a Philosophy of History*. New York: W. W. Norton; 1941.

————: *Concord and Liberty*. New York: W. W. Norton; 1946.

Popper, Karl: *The Poverty of Historicism*. Boston: Beacon Press; 1957.

Rosenstock-Huessy, Eugen: *The Christian Future or the Modern Mind Outrun*. New York: Charles Scribner's; 1946.

————: *Europa und die Christenheit*. Munich: J. Kösel; 1919.

————: *Die Europäischen Revolutionen*. Jena, 1931.

————: *Die Hochzeit des Krieges und der Revolution*. Würzburg: Patmos-Verlag; 1920.

————: *Out of Revolution: The Autobiography of Western Man.* New York: William Morrow; 1938.

————: "The Predicament of History." *Journal of Philosophy,* XXXII (1935), pp. 93–100.

————: *Soziologie.* Berlin and Leipzig, 1925; reprinted 1956.

————: *Soziologie II: Die Vollzahl der Zeiten.* Stuttgart: K. Kohlhammer; 1958.

Rotenstreich, Nathan: *Between Past and Present: An Essay on History.* New Haven: Yale University Press; 1958.

Rule, John C.: *Bibliography of Works in the Philosophy of History, 1947–1957,* compiled for *History and Theory.* The Hague: Mouton & Company; 1961.

Schweitzer, Albert: *The Philosophy of Civilization,* 2 vols. London: Adams & Charles Black; 1947–49.

Van Zandt, Roland: *The Metaphysical Foundations of American History.* The Hague: Mouton and Company; 1959.

Vico, Giambattista: *The New Science,* translated by Thomas Goddard Bergin and Max Harold Fisch. Ithaca: Cornell University Press; 1948.

Voltaire, François de: *Essay on Universal History,* 4 vols. Dublin, 1759.

Walsh, W. H.: *An Introduction to the Philosophy of History.* London: Hutchinson's Universal Library; 1955.

Weiss, Paul: *History, Written and Lived.* Carbondale, Ill.: Southern Illinois University Press; 1962.

Whitehead, Alfred North: *Adventures of Ideas.* New York: Mentor Books, 1952.

Widgery, Alban: *Interpretations of History from Confucius to Toynbee.* London: George Allen & Unwin; 1961.

Wiener, P. P.: "On Methodology in the Philosophy of History." *Journal of Philosophy,* XXXVIII (1941), pp. 309–34.

Williams, Donald: "More on the Ordinariness of History." *Journal of Philosophy,* LII (1955), pp. 269–77.

Wollheim, R.: "Historicism Reconsidered." *Sociological Review* new series II (1954), pp. 76–97.

Zucker, Morris: *The Philosophy of American History*, 2 vols. New York: Arnold Harvard; 1945.

IV. History and the Social Sciences: Sociology

Berger, Peter L.: *Invitation to Sociology: A Humanistic Perspective*. New York: Anchor Books; 1963.

Kroeber, Arthur L.: *Style and Civilization*. Ithaca: Cornell University Press; 1957.

Mannheim, Karl: *Freedom, Power and Democratic Planning*. New York: Oxford University Press; 1950.

———: *Ideology and Utopia*. New York: Harcourt, Brace; 1949.

Mills, C. Wright: *The Sociological Imagination*. New York: Oxford University Press; 1959.

Pareto, Vilfredo: *Mind and Society*, 4 vols. New York: Harcourt, Brace; 1935.

Salvemini, Gaetano: *Historian and Scientist: An Essay on the Nature of History and the Social Sciences*. Cambridge: Harvard University Press; 1939.

Psychology

Brown, Norman O.: *Life Against Death*. New York: Vintage Books; 1961.

Erikson, Erik: "Ego Development and Historical Change." *Childhood and Society*. New York: W. W. Norton; 1952.

Lynd, Helen Merrell: "The Nature of Historical Objectivity." *Journal of Philosophy*, XLVII (1950).

———: *On Shame and the Search for Identity*. New York: Science Editions; 1961.

Marcuse, Herbert: *Eros and Civilization*. Boston: Beacon Press; 1955.

Mazlish, Bruce, ed.: *Psychoanalysis and History*. New Jersey: Prentice-Hall; 1963.

Roheim, Geza, ed.: *Psychoanalysis and the Social Sciences*, 3 vols. New York: International Universities Press; 1947–51.

V. *The Metahistorians*

Spengler, Oswald: *The Decline of the West,* 2 vols. New York: Alfred A. Knopf; 1944.

Toynbee, Arnold J.: *A Study of History,* 12 vols. New York: Oxford University Press; 1940–61.

Voegelin, Eric: *Order and History,* 6 vols. Baton Rouge: Louisiana State University Press, 1956–

Index

Abstracted Empiricists, 135
abstraction in Greek history, 10–11, 12
Acton, Lord, on French Revolution, 37
Adams, Herbert Baxter, 224
Adams, John, 27; on writing history of American Revolution, 37–8
Adams, Samuel, 188
Age of Louis XIV, The (Voltaire), 31
Age of Reason, *see* Enlightenment
Age of Revolution, 36, 46, 138
Albee, Edward, 233*n*
Amasis, king of Egypt, 8
American Historical Association, presidential addresses to, 113, 124
American Revolution, 36, 42, 44, 50, 111, 138, 154; Adams on writing history of, 37–8; Andrews on, 188–9; Bancroft on, 43, 177–80, 186, 190*n*, 193–8; Fisher on, 180–3, 190; Gipson on, 189–90; Morgans on, 191–3; Ramsay on, 166–76, 193–8, 205, 223; Schlesinger, Sr., on, 183–6, 192, 193; thesis that best interpretation of causes was made shortly after, 165, 197–9; Van Tyne on, 186–8
Andrews, Charles McLean, on causes of American Revolution, 188–9

Annual Register, 38, 166, 196–7
Antinomian Controversy, 127
Arendt, Hannah, 209
Ariès, Philippe, 122, 123
Aristotle, 33
Arnheim, Rudolf, 122*n*
Artabanus, 8
Augustine, *see* Saint Augustine
"Axial Period," 90
Aztecs, Prescott on, 46–7

Bagby, Philip, 105
Bancroft, George: on causes of American Revolution, 43, 177–80, 186, 190*n*, 193; Hegel and, 42–3; on history as "social science," 48
Barth, Karl, 79
Battis, Emery, psychoanalytic study of Anne Hutchinson by, 126–7, 128
Beale, Howard K., on causes of Civil War, 116–18
Beard, Charles, 111; on Constitution, 147, 150–1; views on history of, 112–14
Becker, Carl, views on history of, 111–12
behavioristic psychology, 120
Bell, Daniel, 235
Berdyaev, Nikolay, views on history of, 73–4
Berger, Peter L., 135*n*
Bolingbroke, Lord, 35
Boorstein, Daniel, 133
Brinton, Crane, 106
Brodie, Bernard, 125

A NOTE ABOUT THE AUTHOR

PAGE SMITH, Provost at the University of California, Santa Cruz, was born in Baltimore, Maryland, on September 6, 1917. He received his B.A. from Dartmouth College in 1940, his M.A. from Harvard in 1948, and his Ph.D. from the same university in 1951. From 1951 to 1953 he was a research associate at the Institute of Early American History and Culture, Williamsburg, Virginia, and he has been at UCLA since 1953. His great biography, *John Adams*, received the Kenneth Roberts Memorial Award in 1962, and earned its author a Bancroft Award from Columbia University.

VINTAGE HISTORY—AMERICAN

A free catalogue of VINTAGE BOOKS *will be sent at your request. Write to* Vintage Books, 457 Madison Avenue, New York, New York 10022.